Jeffrey's Criticism

Francis Jeffrey
Portrait by an anonymous artist, reproduced by courtesy of Mr. Alan Bell.

Jeffrey's Criticism

A Selection
Edited, with an Introduction, by
Peter F. Morgan

Edinburgh
Scottish Academic Press

Published by
Scottish Academic Press Ltd.
33 Montgomery Street, Edinburgh EH7 5JX

ISBN 0 7073 0300 1

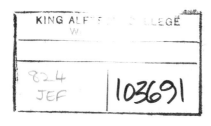
Printed in Northern Ireland at The Universities Press (Belfast) Ltd.

Dedicated
to Kathleen Tillotson
as a token of esteem for her consummate
scholarship and critical tact, and of
gratitude for her help over many years

Contents

Preface

Jeffrey wrote most of his criticism in the form of articles which appeared in the *Edinburgh Review* between 1802 and 1829. He produced an anthology from these in the *Contributions* of 1844. Jeffrey was the editor of the *Edinburgh Review* in the years when his articles appeared; its other contributors included Sydney Smith and later Carlyle and Macaulay. In collecting his work Jeffrey was following the example of their volumes of 1838, 1839 and 1843. In his own anthology, Jeffrey's divisions indicate the wide range of his interests. They extend from philosophy over poetry, fiction, history and politics. Since Jeffrey's own time, attention has been focussed on him as a literary critic. The last representative selections were made from this aspect of his work and were published as long ago as 1894 and 1910, by Lewis Gates and David Nichol Smith. The intention in the present collection is to continue the emphasis on Jeffrey the critic, indicating the range of his work and its theoretical base. The aim is to present examples which he himself considered important, which are characteristic of him, but which are also representative of the spirit of his time, as well as relevant to the trend of modern interests.

I am most grateful for financial help towards this publication received from the University of Toronto Research Board. I am also very grateful to Professor Philip Flynn for his comments on a draft of my Introduction. I wish to thank Mr Douglas Grant, Managing Director of the Scottish Academic Press, for his kind consideration, and Heather Finch for her patient editorial assistance.

Note on the Text

All of the material collected here is taken from Jeffrey's articles in the *Edinburgh Review*. When he reprinted these, slightly modified, in his *Contributions* (1844), I have followed this, his own final version. Otherwise, I have gone back to the *Edinburgh*. Only printer's errors have been corrected. When material has been omitted from a continuous passage, this is indicated by a note in the text in brackets.

PETER F. MORGAN

Introduction

General View

I

Criticism in English from the time of Sidney can be seen as made up of a series of discrete contributions without pretensions to exercising literary authority over the reading public. A change came about through the sensitive, thoughtful and urbane essays of Addison in *The Spectator* and the sustained critical and biographical effort of Johnson in the *Lives of the Poets*. Also influential in the eighteenth century was the elaborate aesthetic, moral, psychological and sociological theorizing of the Scottish school of philosophers, from Hutcheson to Alison. These, with Johnson, insisted on what Walter Jackson Bate calls 'the premise of general nature.'[1]

These writers had a great impact on the critical sensibility of their age, Johnson in particular speaking with assurance and authority of the writer and his work. Francis Jeffrey (1773–1850) can be seen as standing at a culminating point of this eighteenth-century tradition. He sought something of the authority of Johnson. He spoke, not only with the assurance of the Scottish philosophers, but also with their sense of the importance of feeling and with their appreciation of historical change and of the relationship between literature and social circumstances. He relished the malice of Pope's attacks on literary vanity and folly, but he also inherited the gentler touch of the Pope of the 'Essay on Criticism,' of Addison, and of the Scottish man of feeling, Henry Mackenzie. As a periodical critic Jeffrey was the heir to the tradition of the eighteenth-century essayists.[2] He shared the moral certainty and concern of all these writers.[3]

II

Jeffrey addressed a large audience through his articles in the *Edinburgh Review,* which he edited from its inception in 1802 until 1829. He spoke there, not only as a sampler and publicizer of literary works, but also as their judge with ample views and well-established criteria. However, at the beginning of the nineteenth century, with the burgeoning of the romantic movement, some poets were unwilling to accept the authority of the critic. In the critical writings of Wordsworth and Coleridge themselves we see formal analysis of poetry given less emphasis, as in the Preface to *Lyrical Ballads* (1800), or given less fully articulated expression, as in *Biographia Literaria* (1817). Significantly, the highly suggestive criticism of Keats is to be found in the informal comments of his private letters; and the views of Shelley in the *Defence of Poetry,* not published during his lifetime, take a broadly philosophical form.

For Jeffrey as for Wordsworth the poet was a man speaking to men. However, for Wordsworth the relationship was a direct one, whereas for Jeffrey it took place in the context of a highly structured, civilized society whose decorum was accepted. Indeed, the preservation of this decorum at a time of revolutionary change at home and abroad, in every aspect of the culture, was a primary goal for him. Thus Jeffrey saw the poet as standing at the bar of public opinion, both as artist and as moral being, with the critic, however temperate and sensitive, as his judge.

The great romantic poets as critics themselves—Wordsworth, Coleridge, Keats and Shelley—were more interested in examining anew the psychology of the poet, in identifying the nature of the poetic process, and in asserting the importance of the poetic experience for the welfare of man and of society at large. They believed that poetry had roots in common humanity and that it possessed an essential human significance. Poetry was so important to them that mediation between the poet-critic's insights and the sensibility of the individual reader was hardly thinkable, least of all through the established notions of critic and reading public to which Jeffrey appealed.

Unlike that of the poets, Jeffrey's critical voice was a public one; that is, what he said was immediately available to the large readership of the *Edinburgh Review.* It is ironical that the voices most loudly heard by his contemporaries were those of Jeffrey and his fellow periodical critics, not those which we today think of as expressive of the period: the voices of Wordsworth, Coleridge, Byron, Shelley, Keats, and the essayists Lamb, Hazlitt and De Quincey. It is true that Byron and Scott were popular, but Wordsworth and Coleridge had to struggle over the years in order to achieve a hearing. Wordsworth's own early critical writings produced a public impression feebler than that created by Jeffrey's vigorous reviews. Coleridge's *Biographia Literaria,* lambasted by Hazlitt in the *Edinburgh Review,* was difficult enough in itself on account of its fragmented presentation of a variegated subject-matter. The *Edinburgh* opened up the periodical field in which

Lamb, Hazlitt and De Quincey worked prolifically but without much immediate recognition and success: the *London Magazine* (1820–29) provided one framework for their endeavours. Shelley blamed the *Edinburgh*'s rival the *Quarterly Review* for the death of Keats, and his own work met a hostile reception from the more influential journals. His *Defence of Poetry,* though written in 1821, was not published until 1840; and the brilliant criticism in Keats's letters only began to become available with the selection in Milnes's biography of 1848.

III

Thus Jeffrey held an important position as leader and moulder of public taste in the crucial first third of the nineteenth century. What were his views? He was not a nationalist in the modern sense, but he was a Scottish patriot. He based his outlook as a critic on the aesthetic theory of his contemporary Alison (see no. 25). In doing so, he recognized the legitimacy and the variety of national taste, for example, in writing on Mme. de Staël and Goethe (nos. 23 and 24), though he was not always as sympathetic towards the foreign as he might have been. Moreover, as the heir of the Scottish historical social thinking of the eighteenth century, Jeffrey saw the connection between literature and the state of society, expressing this in European terms in his review of Mme. de Staël, and in English terms in his article on Ford's *Dramatic Works* (no. 16). Educated more deeply in philosophy and law than in the classics, Jeffrey had little to say about Rome and Greece, except Greek poetry and drama, on which he expatiated in his review of Mme. de Staël. However, he was alert to developments in the literature of modern Europe, particularly the aristocratic memoirs of late eighteenth-century France and the contemporary, wide-ranging speculations of Mme. de Staël. He praised Alfieri, and he treated Ugo Foscolo with hospitality as an émigré contributor to the *Edinburgh Review.* However, his tolerance towards the German was low, as witnessed by his treatment of Goethe's *Wilhelm Meister's Apprenticeship* (no. 24). Jeffrey saw the growing importance of the new literature of America, and he particularly admired the very different contributions of Franklin and Washington Irving.

Surveying European literature, Jeffrey contrasted the artistically polished technique of continental, particularly French, literature and drama with the freshness and truth to life of the English, pre-eminently Shakespeare (no. 15).

As part of his historical perspective on English literature, Jeffrey's review of Campbell's *Specimens of the British Poets* (no. 2) indicated the catholicity of his taste. He appreciated the traditional poetic line of Chaucer, Spenser and Milton. However, his greatest admiration was for Shakespeare, towering above the other Elizabethans (nos. 16 and 17). Of the poetry of their age, to use the words of Lewis E. Gates, he 'delights in its passion, celebrates its imaginative beauty, its figurative richness, its fervor and wayward splendor.'[4]

Jeffrey's attitude towards the literature of the period since the Restoration was ambivalent. At first an admirer of the wit, elegance and skill of Dryden and Pope, he later tended to adopt the view that a breakdown had occurred in English literature with the Restoration. This opinion was shared by the Poet Laureate Southey, a stalwart of the rival *Quarterly Review,* though other contributors to the *Quarterly,* particularly Scott and Croker, continued to regard the past century and a half more leniently. Jeffrey's own later opinion was strongly and elaborately expressed in his reviews of Ford's *Dramatic Works* (no. 16) and of Scott's edition of Swift (no. 20).[5]

Jeffrey looked back with some awe to the drama and poetry of Shakespeare and the Elizabethans. He took pleasure in the sociable literature of the age preceding his own, for example, the memoirs of Lucy Hutchinson, the diary of Pepys (no. 19), the letters of Lady Mary Wortley Montagu, and the novels of Richardson (no. 21). He admired the poetry of Cowper and Burns in the recent past (nos. 3 and 4) and that of his conservative contemporaries Scott and Crabbe (nos. 9 and 5). He admired particularly the Scottish contribution of Burns and Scott. He was attracted to the original sensibility of Cowper and the restrained moral realism of Crabbe.

As a leading Whig, Jeffrey shared with many of his contemporaries a deep apprehension of social breakdown, with the awful example of the French Revolution before them. The powerful impact of this phenomenon was fully recorded by Wordsworth in *The Prelude,* published in 1850. Like Scott, Jeffrey feared a revolution nurtured by disaffected intellectuals. This is probably the main reason why he reacted so strongly against the early publications of Southey, Wordsworth and Coleridge (no. 6). Their work was avowedly innovative. Jeffrey recognized the power of poetry and poets, and he feared the misuse of this power. Moreover, as he feared the innovation as potentially political, so his outlook was too limited to appreciate its metaphysical dimension. Furthermore, he never acknowledged the conservative developments in Wordsworth's poetry and thought. Anyway, the later Tory stance of Wordsworth, Southey and Coleridge was anathema to him on sheer political grounds.

With many other contemporary critics Jeffrey fully recognized the artistic power of the second generation of romantic poets, though like Southey he feared what he held to be the dangerously irreligious, immoral and anti-social tendencies of Byron (no. 18). As an older man, he relaxed to enjoy the freshness, sensuousness and vitality of Keats (no. 12). At a more personal level, he later strove to convert the irascible young Carlyle to his own values of sociability, and, as with Keats, though more self-indulgently, he was at ease with the emotionalism of Dickens.

Finally, Jeffrey's inheritance from the eighteenth-century Scottish speculators on cultural history created a dilemma for him which he shared with contemporaries like Peacock, Shelley and Macaulay. The cultural historians valued poetry, but they associated its pre-eminence with an earlier, less sophisticated stage of society. The modern problem was not only the vast accumulation of knowledge, including the awesome masterpieces of the past, but also the shift in spirit from the poetic to the philosophical. Genius dwindled, as taste broadened. Jeffrey in his later years saw the romantic poetry of his age in the light of this view, as a revival of the greatness of Elizabethan literature, but only as a revival, without independent strength of its own.

In general rather than historical terms, Jeffrey admired in literature vivacity of thought and expression, above all, of feeling. He appreciated the realization in art of the human, and of the affinity between the human and the natural world. He acknowledged detailed fidelity to nature in the presentation of character and behaviour: truth in the concrete and in its relation to the universal. He judged what was new by its conformity to the organic tradition. At the same time, his moral standards were defensively conventional. Political affiliation strongly coloured his judgment. He recognized private as he recognized national taste. However, more important to him than individual enjoyment was the cultivation of the national taste. This demanded common standards amongst readers, critics and writers. These standards he hastened to erect, to repair and to defend.

IV

For Wordsworth being a poet was the outcome of a life-time's wholehearted dedication. For Jeffrey being a critic was only incidental to editing the *Edinburgh Review* and to an active life as lawyer and politician. In fact, when Jeffrey gave up the review, he was elected to Parliament and became Lord Advocate, responsible for steering the Scottish Reform Bill through the House of Commons. He was made a Judge in 1834. Jeffrey was thus a public critic, in the sense that his criticism constituted only part of his activity as a man of affairs. In this respect his work is closer to that of his protégé Macaulay than to that of the romantics.

Jeffrey was also a public critic, as opposed to Wordsworth, Coleridge, and the others, because his voice was loudly heard through the wide circulation of the *Edinburgh Review.* This reached over 12,000 by 1813, and four years before that Jeffrey claimed that the review was read by 50,000 people within a month of its appearance. As Gates puts it, the *Edinburgh* became 'an organ of thought, a busy intellectual center, from which the newest ideas were sent out in a perpetual stream through the minds of sympathetic readers.'[6] It was read not only in the British Isles, but throughout Europe and in North America.

Jeffrey's Whig review was so successful that it provoked a Tory reaction with the publication of the *Quarterly Review,* begun in 1809. This journal perhaps never quite achieved so much in persuasion and power, though under the editorship of Gifford and Lockhart it was the vehicle of conservative politics and criticism, sometimes expressed trenchantly and sometimes with savage ridicule, as, for example, at the expense of Keats and Tennyson. So successful was the *Edinburgh Review* under the editorship of Jeffrey that it brought about a second reaction with the publication of the utilitarian *Westminster Review,* begun in 1824. Here John Stuart Mill spoke in mild, rational terms, very different from the enthusiastic rhetoric of Jeffrey's most remarkable successors in the *Edinburgh,* Carlyle and Macaulay.

The influence of Jeffrey was felt not only immediately in the quarterlies, but also indirectly amongst the monthly periodicals, with *Blackwood's Magazine,* a vigorous Tory organ, appearing in 1817, and *Fraser's Magazine,* of the same political complexion, in 1830. Their format made possible the expression of a wider variety of responses to literature than those which Jeffrey's criticism in the *Edinburgh Review* exemplifies. This variety is illustrated in the colourful outpourings of John Wilson in *Blackwood's.* The monthly magazine also came to provide an appropriate medium not only for criticism, but also for essayists like Lamb and Hazlitt and for such writers of serial fiction as Thackeray, Dickens, George Eliot and Trollope.

It has been argued that Jeffrey through his editorship and many contributions to the *Edinburgh Review* fathered the influential nineteenth-century periodical. Certainly, his inherited principles led him to see the importance of intellectual leadership in a growing society, but they also made him to a degree tolerant of change, as well as an instigator of it. They underlay his successful work as editor of the *Edinburgh,* as contributor to it, and as the deviser, inasmuch as it originated with one man, of the form of the review article which remained dominant throughout the rest of the century. This form, as moulded by Jeffrey, was usually based on a recently published book. The work was summarized and freely quoted, in order to give an impression of its contents. It was considered judicially, defects weighed against qualities, as well as put into the context of general considerations. Often too, these general considerations, frequently political, took over the foreground, and a recently published pamphlet would form the pretext for the article. Gradually, as in Macaulay's *Edinburgh Review* essay on Milton and Carlyle's 'Signs of the Times,' the reviewing purpose of a particular contribution was lost from sight, in favour of broad and full treatment of the topic in hand. This was the mode taken over by the *Quarterly Review* and the *Westminster Review* in the first half of the century, and later by, for example, the *Contemporary Review* and the *Fortnightly Review,* with such diverse contributors as Arnold, Bagehot, Froude, Gladstone, Gosse, Morley, Saintsbury, Stephen and Swinburne.[7]

V

Perhaps what most struck Jeffrey's ungrateful successors later in the nineteenth century was his lack of depth and his partisanship. Bagehot, Arnold, Stephen and Swinburne dismissed him on these grounds. Arnold appealed urgently for a disinterested, classically based criticism, though he shared with Jeffrey a belief that a broad, enlightened critical view was important. Also he made use of the kind of forum that Jeffrey had established. The same was true of Bagehot, Stephen and Swinburne. A later writer in the same medium, Saintsbury, strove to give Jeffrey his due. But the tradition collapsed with the era itself. The *Edinburgh Review* ceased publication in 1929, though the *Quarterly* continued until 1967. It is noteworthy that T. S. Eliot, concerned with the primacy of the poet, but active critically because of his hope to preserve a social context and a sense of tradition for poetry, emulated the old quarterlies in editing *The Criterion* (1922–39). Its rival, F. R. Leavis's *Scrutiny* (1932–53), despite the discomfort of its editor, belonged to the academic world. Leavis plangently lamented 'the absence of any educated public large and coherent enough to support an intelligent literary review'[8]—such as Jeffrey's *Edinburgh.*

Jeffrey can be seen as standing at the end of a period of intense critical thought, the eighteenth century, particularly in the Lowlands of Scotland. At the same time, he stood at the beginning of a period of critical discussion at a high level, presented at length, to a large and influential audience, throughout the British Isles and abroad.

He thus also belonged at the source of a literary development which provided a framework for much of the important prose writing of the nineteenth century, not only in literary criticism, but also in general polemics and in fiction.

Unfortunately, the structure of criticism and expression which the periodicals provided was not highly congenial to the poets, though the fame of Wordsworth, for example, grew in spite of it, and Keats, Tennyson and Browning achieved popularity and status despite early critical neglect. Although Jeffrey can be seen as initiating a development which had a negative impact on English poetry, this cannot take away from the fact that he communicated his warm appreciation of essential elements in the English literary tradition, making his many readers consider the importance in literature of intellectuality and morality, as well as of emotion.

Perhaps most importantly, Jeffrey dramatically illustrates one phase of the necessary relationship between artist and society. He knew that the two did not exist in isolation from one another. Indeed, there was an integral relationship between them. He sought to define this relationship as one in which the artist recognized the authority of the critic as a judge of his work, as a spokesman for his readers, and as a mediator between the artist and society. Appropriate alternatives to this pattern as asserted by Jeffrey are still urgently needed in the wide global context of the present day.

Life and Criticism

I

Jeffrey was born in Edinburgh in 1773 in the golden age of the culture of the Scottish capital. He was the son of a Tory law-court official who was able to send him to the High School. There he studied the classics in the same setting as Scott and Brougham. Following the Scottish tradition of precocity, he attended Glasgow University from 1787 to 1789, studying Greek, Logic and Moral Philosophy. His father forbade him to attend the classes of the Whig John Millar, but this did not hinder Jeffrey's admiration for that lively philosopher of history and society. Indeed, Jeffrey later described him in terms which could in large part be used for himself: his intellectual character 'corresponded pretty nearly with the abstract idea that the learned of England entertain of a *Scottish philosopher;* a personage, that is, with little or no deference to the authority of great names, and not very apt to be startled at conclusions that seem to run counter to received opinions or existing institutions; acute, sagacious, and systematical; irreverent towards classical literature; rather indefatigable in argument, than patient in investigation; vigilant in the observation of facts, but not so strong in their number, as skilful in their application'.[9]

Back in Edinburgh, Jeffrey studied law, before spending a year at Oxford, 1791 to 1792, where his experience was less happy than that of Scott's son-in-law Lockhart. In Edinburgh again, he continued the study of law and history, though it is surprising, as with Millar in Glasgow, that there is no evidence that he attended the classes of Dugald Stewart. As with Millar, this did not hinder his admiration for the professor's genial philosophical and aesthetic views.

Jeffrey thus took advantage of the broad, humane training of the Scottish universities which later proved so unhelpful to the mystically minded Carlyle. Jeffrey certainly preferred the Scottish approach to the narrow classicism of the English system. James McCosh appropriately called him 'the genuine product of the lecture-hearing, essay-writing, debating-society privileges of the Scottish colleges.'[10]

Leaving university, Jeffrey became a member of the Speculative Society of Edinburgh. Like Mill later, he found the opportunity to debate with superior intellectual companions educational in itself. He was admitted to the bar in 1794, but as a 'philosophical Whig' he was able to find little employment in law-courts dominated by the Tories. Jeffrey's Whiggism is important in his criticism as well as in his life. It shows him to be a moderate reformer, but at the same time, as Gates points out, he 'desires in both spheres the supremacy of a chosen aristocracy.'[11]

Jeffrey married in 1801, but a son died in the following year, and his wife four years later. He married again in 1813, adventurously travelling to America in the midst of war in order to gain his bride. They had one cherished daughter. All this while, Jeffrey enjoyed the intellectual social life of Edinburgh, but in 1815 he bought Craigcrook, just outside the city, where he could retire from its bustle. He loved his wife and child, and he also enjoyed the companionship of lawyers, politicians and men of the world, as well as of attractive women like Jane Welsh Carlyle. He threw himself into the activity of the city, in the law-court, the drawing-room and the club, but he also liked to retreat to the quiet of his own home and of the Scottish countryside.[12]

In 1802 perhaps the most important public event of Jeffrey's life took place. Together with Sydney Smith, Brougham, Horner and others, he founded the *Edinburgh Review*. Smith suggested the appropriate motto, *Tenui musam meditamur avena* (We cultivate literature upon a little oatmeal), but the more pretentious and foreboding *Judex damnatur, cum nocens absolvitur* (The judge is damned when the guilty is absolved) was chosen.[13] Jeffrey at once became editor. His strong independent editorial policy, pertinacity and energetic contributions were to a large degree responsible for making the review a success. It achieved a wide circulation and an undisputed eminence in the eyes of contemporaries, as well as of modern historians. Jeffrey himself wrote that the review had two legs to stand on, one politics and the other literature. It provided the influential medium through which his critical views were expressed over more than a quarter of a century.

Jeffrey gave up both editing and regularly contributing to the *Edinburgh Review* in 1829, though he remained associated with it in an advisory capacity until his death. Throughout these years he continued to build up his practice at the bar. In fact, legal advancement caused his withdrawal from the review when he was elected Dean of the Faculty of Advocates at Edinburgh. Jeffrey also continued political work, and when the Whigs at last came into power in 1830, he entered Parliament and then the Government as Lord Advocate, charged with Scottish affairs, especially the Scottish Reform Bill.[14] Jeffrey did not enjoy his new political career, taken up so late in life, but he did relish London society. The society of the capital, like that of Edinburgh, was not only a source of personal enjoyment to him; he regarded it as the heart of the cultural life of the country. Thus he believed that participation in it was necessary for the man of letters, in order for him to contribute more effectively to his country's cultural health.

Jeffrey's legal career influenced his criticism through the fluency, ability to argue a case, and the willingness to decide and judge which were necessary to it. As Gates laconically writes, 'Jeffrey's mastery of his subject is like the successful barrister's knowledge of his brief.'[15] The legal career reached a climax when he was appointed Judge in 1834. He occupied this post until his death sixteen years later.

II

A personal perspective on Jeffrey the critic may be gained if we consider the character of the man so active throughout these years. The tributes paid to him are remarkable. There is no reason to doubt their validity if we take into account the different points of view from which they were paid and the different circumstances of their expression. Brougham considered Jeffrey in every way the best man to edit the *Edinburgh Review*. Hazlitt and Carlyle, poles apart temperamentally, agreed in considering him 'the prince of critics and the king of men.'[16] And the enthusiastic Macaulay considered him 'more nearly an universal genius than any man of our time.'[17]

The tributes of Jeffrey's friends are impressive. Yet it must be admitted that his character was complex, almost to the point of paradox. Though sensitive, generous and affectionate, he callously wounded the reputation of a great poet. Doing what he could to bring about gradual political advancement, he lived in fear of war and violent revolution. Sceptical of the rewards of ambition, he rose to become Lord Advocate, Judge and eminent man of letters. This duality is strikingly represented in Jeffrey's attitude towards nature and the city, particularly if seen from the point of view of a student of his criticism in the context of romantic literature.

As a young man Jeffrey was attuned to the side of eighteenth-century British philosophy and literature which stressed the affections and sympathy. Consequently, he felt the call of poetry, of nature and of solitude, as well as the charm of social life. As a practical Scot, still with philosophical justification, he plunged into metropolitan law and politics. Throughout his life, however, Jeffrey continued to enjoy the escape from the city to the peace and beauty of nature, for example, at Craigcrook or along the shores of Loch Lomond. This shows an attractively ambivalent personal attitude which is not always evident in his best-known criticism. Since it has not been commented on it deserves to be illustrated at some length.[18]

In 1794 Jeffrey wrote that with his romantic temper he preferred the country to the city. Two years later he exclaimed, 'All great passions are born in solitude,' yet he was soon 'far advanced ... upon that dirty highway called the way of the world.'[19] In 1806 he declared that he trusted to 'the quietness of the heart, and the activity of the imagination.' He preferred 'pacing alone on the lovely sands' to life in London; yet the next year he admitted that he was afraid of solitude and that he was 'driven by a cruel instinct into the company of strangers.'[20]

Nevertheless, in the following busy, gregarious years Jeffrey still turned to nature for refreshment in a way that echoes the familiar yearning of Wordsworth, both more romantic and more spiritual. In 1822 he wrote, 'The roaring of the mountain torrents in a calm morning after a raining night has something quite delicious to my ears.'[21] These words suggest the opening lines of Wordsworth's 'Resolution and Independence.' Two years later Jeffrey described how 'in the most magnificent sunset,' he 'met two of the most beautiful girls in the Highlands gathering nuts in the woods; and the splendid light reflected back from their bright eyes and teeth and shining curls, as they sat on a tuft of heath, with the dark oak coppice behind them, made the loveliest and most romantic picture

I ever looked on.'[22] These picturesque lines suggest Wordsworth's delight in viewing the 'Solitary Reaper.' In 1831 Jeffrey, during the turmoil of the Reform discussions in the House of Commons, wrote again:

> It was a beautiful, rosy, dead calm, morning when we broke up a little before five to-day; and I took three pensive turns along the solitude of Westminster Bridge; admiring the sharp clearness of St. Paul's, and all the city spires soaring up in a cloudless sky, the orange red light that was beginning to play on the trees of the Abbey, and the old windows of the speaker's house, and the flat, green mist of the river floating under a few lazy hulks on the tide, and moving low under the arches. It was a curious contrast with the long previous imprisonment in the stifling roaring House, amidst dying candles, and every sort of exhalation.[23]

Here Jeffrey vividly depicts and admires a scene, enjoyed in a different way by Wordsworth, as shown in his sonnet 'Composed upon Westminster Bridge.'

Jeffrey's word-pictures speak for themselves, but they are supported by his later comments. In 1833 he wrote, 'If it were not for my love of beautiful nature and poetry, my heart would have died within me long ago;' and over a decade later, 'My affections and my enjoyment of beautiful nature, I thank heaven, are as fresh and lively, as in the first poetical days of my youth.'[24]

Thus, in the midst of a busy public life Jeffrey turned eagerly for refreshment to nature. His feelings were nourished by his sensations of its beauty. This shows that, despite critical differences, there was yet some common ground in personal experience between Jeffrey and his romantic contemporaries.

Moreover, Jeffrey cherished the feelings in themselves. He wrote in 1804, 'there is no happiness but in good affections,' and a quarter of a century later to Carlyle, 'true affection sustains me.'[25] He seems to have felt this especially strongly in the last decade of his long life. He wrote in 1847 that the world was 'a world to be loved and only to be enjoyed by those who find objects of love in it;' and to Dickens, just before his death, 'I love all that is loveable, or can respond to love as intensely as in youth, and hope to die before that capacity forsakes me.'[26]

This trust in his own good nature, and its reflection in the nature of his friends, his society and the world around him bore Jeffrey on. It was partly the legacy of the milder side of eighteenth-century English literature. It was also the legacy of eighteenth-century psychological theory, handed down through the Scottish universities and the intellectual life of the capital Edinburgh, together with a colder inheritance of argument and debate. It was passed on by Jeffrey and many others in the Romantic age to the Victorians, notably Dickens.

The expression of Jeffrey's personal sensibilities was muted in the *Edinburgh Review,* because he felt that his function there was to praise the quieter contemporary literature which bore witness to his own values, and also to defend them by stronger criticism of more self-willed and powerful spirits, like Wordsworth and Byron. He felt that in his own life and in the society around him a delicate balance had been achieved, at the same time as urgent currents were moving the society forwards in an unknown direction. It was his task as a literary critic to try to maintain this balance as eloquently as he could.[27]

Conclusion

In this final section of the Introduction it might be profitable to tie up the comments which have been made on Jeffrey's personality and its relationship with his criticism. This can be done through considering his association with three great writers of his age, very different in character as well as in achievement. These are Wordsworth, Carlyle and Dickens. Jeffrey was closely involved with all three in different critical ways: with Wordsworth as hostile reviewer, from 1802 to 1822; with Carlyle as editor, mentor and friend from 1824; and with Dickens as friend from 1841 until his death. Emphasis on these relationships illuminates Jeffrey's critical contribution. A study of them should also throw light incidentally on the general changes which took place in the literary culture between the Romantic and the Victorian periods.

I. Jeffrey and Wordsworth[28]

It has been shown above that though Jeffrey descended to ridicule of Wordsworth there was some philosophical background and depth to his attack. The onslaught certainly affected the poet himself and produced a strong response, particularly in the 'Essay, supplementary to the Preface' of 1815, as well as in revisions of the poetry. Coleridge also leaped to his friend's defence in the *Biographia Literaria,* 1817. However, Wordsworth's poetic statement, most relevantly in *The Excursion,* 1814, remained basically unaffected either by Jeffrey's attacks or by the poet's own tinkerings and modifications of style.

In the essay of 1815 Wordsworth refutes Jeffrey's position by asserting impressively that the original poet must create the taste by which he is to be admired. He cannot rely, as Jeffrey and his school would, on 'immediate and universal' effects, since language is 'subject to endless fluctuations and arbitrary associations. The genius of the poet melts these down for his purpose.'[29] The interaction between poet and reader, here as in the Preface to *Lyrical Ballads,* leaves small space for the mere critic. Wordsworth, like Coleridge later in *Biographia Literaria,* paints a portrait of the ideal critic, in order to show by implication how far such reviewers as Jeffrey are removed from it, but he adds that even the ideal critic is untrustworthy. He turns away towards the sensitive individual reader who, with those like him, comes to make up, not the unreliable 'public,' but the 'people' whose sanction is won only through the course of long centuries. Thus Wordsworth rejects Jeffrey, the critic—and the public—in favour of the inspired poet and the sensitive reader.[30] The conflict, here adumbrated in the relationship between Wordsworth and Jeffrey, has remained unresolved until the present day.

Wordsworth's doughty defence of himself is supported by the judicious arguments of Coleridge in *Biographia Literaria.* In chapter XXI of that work his friend objects to the criticism of Jeffrey and the *Edinburgh Review* on five comprehensive grounds: as unphilosophical, personal, political, trivial and uncritical. Yet, in spite of Coleridge's onslaught on Jeffrey, one can still discover general points of contact between their critiques. The editor's argument lacks Coleridge's profundity, subtlety and judicial sympathy. He cannot appreciate the vital contribution of idealism towards creating the poetic whole. Nevertheless, for both journalist and theorist, poetry and criticism are general in concern. Both criticize Wordsworth's theory of poetic language and subject matter on social and aesthetic grounds. Similarly, Coleridge's view of Shakespearian imagery is parallel to that set forth by Jeffrey in his articles on Alison and Hazlitt (nos. 25 and 17).

Wordsworth himself was unyielding in theory to Jeffrey's attacks, but there is evidence of responsive changes in his poetic style. As he gave ground, his fame grew, until he became a central figure in the Victorian pantheon. A basic, permanent difference between Wordsworth and Jeffrey is illustrated when the poet affirms the nobility of the life of the poor peasant in Book IV of *The Excursion.* He does this as part of his attack on the spiritual shortcomings of modern society. But this onslaught was absolutely unacceptable to Jeffrey who occupied a position of literary, judicial and political authority in the society to whose values he is committed. Wordsworth's poetry has an irreducible quality of radical greatness and originality which can be diminished and obscured neither by the afterthoughts and the revisions of the poet himself, nor by the cavillings of the critic. On the other hand, the scholar must sympathize with Jeffrey, the harassed man of affairs, yearning, on behalf of himself and of the public, for spiritual refreshment. He must also appreciate the impact which Jeffrey made not only on the poet, but also on the climate of public opinion in which Wordsworth's poetry was ultimately accepted.

II. Jeffrey and Carlyle[31]

As a relatively young man Jeffrey had been harsh to his contemporary Wordsworth. He did not recant when he collected some of his contributions to the *Edinburgh Review* in 1844. On the other hand, as a man of over fifty Jeffrey lent an encouraging hand to his compatriot Carlyle, a youth of humble origin, an ungrateful graduate of Edinburgh University, without a professional career, and anxious to make his way and find a message to communicate in literature. Jeffrey soon recognized Carlyle's genius—a feeling which was to a degree reciprocated—even though his unorthodox style and opinions often enraged him.

Though Jeffrey obtusely attacked Goethe's *Wilhelm Meister's Apprenticeship,* translated by Carlyle (no. 24), he later welcomed the young Germanophile as a contributor to the *Edinburgh Review,* where his articles appeared between 1827 and 1832. Carlyle seized the opportunity offered by its editor to achieve some reputation by presenting a critical appreciation of modern German literature, by re-evaluating Burns, and, later, by diagnosing the ills of contemporary English society. Carlyle's views sometimes directly opposed and contradicted those which Jeffrey himself had expressed. For example, he rejected the accusation against the Germans both of mysticism and of bad taste. His view of Burns, like that of Jeffrey (no. 4), was appreciative of the poetry, but critical of the man. However, Carlyle judged not by the conventional, but by his own nascent morality of the hero. Finally, like Jeffrey, Carlyle saw his own times as turbulent, but he did not fearfully withdraw from the prospect into a defence of the gentle amelioration of the status quo by parliamentary means. On the contrary, he relished the depiction of disorder, the diagnosis of social debility, including the threadbare nature of English institutions, and the prognosis of radical remedies, both political and spiritual.

In spite of these indications of serious differences in outlook, Jeffrey's early attempts at editorial control over Carlyle were relatively mild. However, his contributor was indignant over the mutilations inflicted on the Burns article in the name of the same objections which Jeffrey had raised against Wordsworth: mysticism, exaggeration, jargon and verbosity. Jeffrey tried a milder method than that which he had employed upon Wordsworth, in order to win over Carlyle as both writer and fellow human being to what Carlyle himself called 'the joys of sociality.'[32] This method took the form of social intercourse, including long friendly discussions and a frequent correspondence. However, though Carlyle enjoyed the debates and appreciated Jeffrey's generosity of spirit, he remained untempted. Early in the relationship, he stubbornly withdrew from Edinburgh to the isolation of Craigenputtock, where he penned the independent article on Burns and began to write *Sartor Resartus*.

It is ironical that, having scorned Jeffrey's urbane advances, Carlyle later settled in London. He himself came to judge Jeffrey as a *'Scotch* Voltaire.'[33] Jeffrey for his part was disappointed by the younger man as he manifested himself in a later contribution to the *Edinburgh Review,* 'Characteristics':

I fear Carlyle will not do . . . . The misfortune is, that he is very obstinate and . . . conceited, and unluckily in a place like [London], he finds people enough to abet and applaud him, to intercept the operation of the otherwise infallible remedy of general avoidance and neglect. It is a great pity, for he is a man of genius and industry, and with the capacity of being an elegant and impressive writer.[34]

Elegance certainly was not one of Carlyle's goals. Both men continued to recognize a bond of affection between them, but when Jeffrey tried to insist upon it he went too far. His comparison of Jane Welsh to Titania and Carlyle to Bottom (himself by inference Oberon!) led to the breaking-off of the intimacy.

Carlyle himself finally summed up his view of Jeffrey, many years after his death, in 1867: 'He was not deep enough, pious or reverent enough, to have been great in Literature; but he was a man intrinsically of veracity; said nothing without meaning it in some considerable degree; had the quickest perceptions, excellent practical discernment of what lay before him; was in earnest, too, though not "dreadfully in earnest";—in short was well fitted to set forth that *Edinburgh Review* . . . and become *Coryphaeus* of his generation.'[35]

Jeffrey, as man, editor and critic, offered Carlyle a great deal, in fact more than that individualist was willing to accept. What he did take advantage of was the platform which the *Edinburgh Review* and its editor's friendship provided for him in beginning to achieve a literary reputation. What Jeffrey offered and Carlyle did not want to accept on any terms was advice. He felt that he did not need the advice which Jeffrey proffered concerning how to manage his wife, where to live, how to get on with other people, what to write and how to think. Similarly with Jane Welsh. The advice which Jeffrey offered her, playfully and condescendingly, she rejected. The break came, never to be entirely healed. The warm friendship between the two men was never resumed.

Jeffrey's critical theorizing and political and philosophical speculations were spurned as shallow and outdated by the metaphysical Carlyle. On the other hand, Carlyle in retrospect and in a few moments of social intercourse delighted in Jeffrey's vivacity, even though he recognized all too well the limitations of its intellectual base. For Carlyle life was a struggle. In spite of this and because of the breadth of his sympathy he knew Jeffrey as a 'bright island' in the midst of the stormy ocean of experience. Memories of him rose, with others more poignant, 'benignantly luminous from the bosom of the grim dead night!'[36] Thus Carlyle provides the reader with his characteristically emotional personal perspective from which to view Jeffrey the man and critic.

III. Jeffrey and Dickens

There was little trace of Jeffrey's failure in his relationships with Wordsworth and Carlyle in his friendship with Dickens. Now he was an even older man, still looking down upon the world from the eminence of the judge's bench, but no longer the public critic or the manager of men. He was instead the self-indulgent reader, though his feelings still retained the freshness of youth, influenced by the thought and sensibility of that time. Lockhart commented scornfully and unfairly: 'He who had bragged of "crushing" Skiddaw, has learned to gaze with awe upon Brixton Rise.'[37] The element of sentimentality had always been present in Jeffrey. After all, this is another term for the cultivation of the feelings. Part of Dickens's early Victorian work appealed to the tender spot in Jeffrey's heart, and Jeffrey only lamented that he could not shed still more tears as he commented on the young writer's novels and Christmas stories as they appeared. Furthermore, he was pleased and impressed by the combination of emotional expression with material and social success in Dickens's achievement.

In his relationship with Dickens, Jeffrey was friendly and concerned. He advised him concerning financial matters. He rejoiced in the popularity of his works, and he urged him to write in such a way as to extend that popularity still further. His views of the novels are characteristic of the critic in retirement, at his ease, indulging the harmless emotions in the carefully guarded precincts of Dickens's early fiction. He expressed his immediate emotional reaction to the appearance of the characters as they struck him in the convenient form of Christmas book or monthly part. At the same time, Jeffrey's views are representative of the feelings of a large number of Dickens's contemporaries.

Jeffrey took pleasure in Dickens's portrayal of the innocent, whether comic or serious. Especially, he luxuriated in the feeling of grief over the loss of this innocence; it may be in a boy, for example, Paul Dombey. More strongly felt, the innocence is embodied in a girl who loses either by death, as Little Nell does, or by unbearable social and sexual pressures, as do Lilian in *The Chimes* and Edith Dombey. For Jeffrey such figures as Nell, Lilian and Edith were symbols of a victimization prevalent in contemporary society. He was moved by them, as he was affected by Dickens generally as a social moralist.

At the same time, Jeffrey, now the self-indulgent sentimentalist, was loath to allow the moralist his prerogative of satire. Though he accepted the comic-moral combination in Tom Pinch in *Chuzzlewit,* he criticized Dickens's caricatures at both decoratively comic and seriously thematic levels. He objected to the minor figures of the first kind in *Dombey and Son* and *David Copperfield.* He disliked the moral caricature exemplified in such variously large-scale figures as Uriah Heep, Pecksniff and Dombey. He refused the social satire, directed against the city and utilitarianism in *The Chimes,* and against American culture in *American Notes* and *Martin Chuzzlewit.*

The following paragraph on Dickens's presentation of Edith in *Dombey and Son* is typical. Jeffrey is discussing the July 1847 number of the novel:

> It is the most finished, perhaps, in diction; and in the delicacy and fineness of its touches, both of pleasantry and pathos, of any you have ever given us; while it rises to higher and deeper passions; not resting, like most of the former, in sweet thoughtfulness, and thrilling attractive tenderness, but boldly wielding all the lofty and terrible elements of tragedy, and bringing before us the appalling struggles of a proud, scornful, and repentant spirit. I am proud that you should thus shew us new views of your genius—but I shall always love its gentler magic the most; and never leave Nelly and Paul and Florence for Edith, with whatever potent spells you may invest her; though I am prepared for great things from her.[38]

For his part, Dickens took pleasure in Jeffrey's esteem and friendship, showing his gratitude by naming his son after the critic and by dedicating *The Chimes* and *The Cricket on the Hearth* to him. What Jeffrey praised remained a strong element in Dickens's work throughout these years. Perhaps his warning concerning the anti-American element in *Martin Chuzzlewit* was heeded. More probably, his suggestion concerning a mollified fate for Edith Dombey was taken. At the same time, the caricature to which Jeffrey objected remained an integral part of Dickens's writing.

Towards the end Jeffrey's reaction to Dickens and his fiction was marked by an exaggeration of the feeling which he displayed personally towards Carlyle and which had led him to urge his angry compatriot to come over into the camp of sociable humanity, and had even led him to make the same attempt critically with the uncongenial Wordsworth. Jeffrey's attitude towards Dickens was patronizing and comfortable. He warmed his aged heart at the fires of Dickens's youthful sentimentalism. At the same time, he applauded the novelist's success, sought to direct it to a certain extent, and gave him sensible advice concerning the management of his affairs. Here there was none of the critical animosity which marked the relationship with Wordsworth, and none of the philosophical and personal tension which characterized that with Carlyle.

This survey of personal relationships with great writers should illuminate the view of Jeffrey's critical opinions as expressed directly through his articles in the *Edinburgh Review* and indirectly through editorial policy there. For Jeffrey literature was important both personally and socially. His views are limited, but nevertheless to be respected, as often cogently argued, eloquently expressed, and to a degree representative of his time, as well as highly influential. In particular, Jeffrey enjoyed the warm humanity of Dickens, but he could not appreciate the mysticism of Wordsworth or Carlyle. Both of these reactions stemmed from his late eighteenth-century Anglo-Scottish upbringing. At the same time, and because of the same cultural heritage, Jeffrey deplored the self-imposed isolation which accompanies the mysticism of Wordsworth and Carlyle. As thinker and critic, reviewer, editor and man of affairs, as well as human being, Jeffrey resisted the notion of the isolation of the artist. He asserted a form of relationship between artist and public which won assent from Dickens and his readers, though not from Wordsworth and Carlyle, nor from posterity. Nevertheless, alternative patterns still remain to be found.

English Literature—Poetry

Jeffrey, the follower of the eighteenth-century Scottish cultural historians, associated poetry at its most flourishing with a more unsophisticated culture than his own, and he considered it to be very influential there. This is illustrated by his comments on Mrs. Grant's *Essays on the Highlanders* (no. 1). Nevertheless, Jeffrey appreciated the aesthetic and moral importance of the whole range of English poetry: witness his review of Campbell's *Specimens* (no. 2). He considered that English poetry reached its peak with the achievement of Shakespeare in the Elizabethan age. Most of his attention focussed on what he considered to be the revival of English poetry amongst the moderns, from Cowper (no. 3) and Burns (no. 4). Jeffrey appreciated the un-innovative style of Crabbe (no. 5), used in presenting an honest, moral picture of social life. He recognized, with the reading public at large, the energy of Byron (nos. 10 and 11) and Scott (no. 9), though his enthusiasm for the latter was tempered, probably for political reasons, and he shared Southey's apprehension of a diabolical element in Byron. In earlier years Jeffrey was shocked by the unyielding eccentricity of Southey (no. 6) and Wordsworth (nos. 7 and 8), and he did not recognize any softening in them as the years went by. His attitude was not moderated by the rigid Toryism which they chose to adopt. Later, Jeffrey welcomed the 'pure poetry' of Keats (no. 12), though he preferred to relax over the less taxing achievements of Campbell and Mrs. Hemans (no. 14).

1. Poetry and the social life of the Highlands of Scotland,
from a review of Anne Grant's *Essays on the Highlanders*

Edinburgh Review, 18, August 1811

This extract shows how Jeffrey appreciated the place of poetry in an unpolished society very different from his own.

The most powerful . . . of all the causes that contributed to give an air of dignity and refinement to the whole highland population, is no doubt the great abundance and the lofty character of their popular poetry. We would not, upon any account, take such an occasion as the present to enter into the controversy as to the authenticity of some celebrated works, purporting to be translations from their poetry;—but, that poetry has existed in great quantities, from a very remote antiquity, in those regions, and possessing the same general tone that characterizes these translations, is a fact perfectly notorious to all who have conversed with the natives, and which might indeed have been anticipated from a well known part of their institution. We allude now to the regular establishment, not only of Senachies or genealogists, but of Bards or poets, in all considerable families,—an establishment suggested naturally by their pride of ancestry, and their delight in the praises of their illustrious progenitors. These circumstances, too, would naturally determine the character of the poetry that was produced. Being intended primarily to celebrate the virtues and exploits of departed chiefs and warriors, it would treat principally, and with the customary exaggerations, of feats of arms and generosity; and be prolonged into eloquent lamentations for departed heroes, invocations to their ghosts, and exhortations to their descendants. It would assume, therefore, an heroic, and enthusiastic, and melancholy tone: and, without allowing any thing for the ardent temperament of the people, or the inspiration of their adventurous way of life, and the sublime aspects of the regions they inhabited, it is impossible to doubt that, in the course of ages, these national epics must have accumulated and been diffused in very extraordinary abundance.

Consider now the prodigious effects that must have been produced on the character of a people so circumstanced, by the prevalence of such a body of poetry. In the first place, it is to be observed, that it was almost all preserved by oral tradition, and published and diffused among the descendants of those whom it celebrated, by those extraordinary recitations which are still known to form the favourite entertainment of a Highland winter evening. Among a people fond of society, and abounding in leisure, it was diffused, therefore, much more universally than any written poetry can ever be, even in the most improved and cultivated societies. In these, there must always be many who cannot read, and many who will not; and of those who both can and will, a great proportion will be found to dedicate themselves to other branches of study, and to have neither taste nor leisure for the perusal of poetry. Every man, however, can listen; and where the whole stock of literature consists in poetry, the chance is, that every man has listened to a great deal of it.

But, in the second place, and this is of still greater importance, it should be remembered, that their poetry was accommodated, in a most singular degree, to the character and capacity, to the prejudices and affections, of those for whose use it was produced. It did not treat, like most of the written poetry of Europe, of remote regions and nations long ago extinguished; of gods that are known to have had no existence, or men whose existence is known only to the learned and studious: It spoke of the exploits of their own progenitors;—of the very mountains and the valleys, to the echoes of which it was recited;—of the fields of battle, where they still saw the mouldering bones and the rusted arms of their kindred;—of the feats and the fall of chiefs, whose gathered heaps still met their eyes in the desert. It painted no manners, but those with which their own experience was familiar;—it recounted no prodigies that were not still current in their belief, and reported no language but that which was ever resounding in their ears. It is impossible that such poetry as this should not be listened to with eagerness, and treasured up in the memory with avidity: And it is equally impossible that it should not produce a great and conspicuous effect upon the character and manners of those to whom its study not only stood in the place of all literature, but constituted an occupation and a duty of the first magnitude. Every step they took after their enemies, their game, or their cattle, presented to their eyes the scene of some lofty description, or some daring exploit. Every valley and every cliff,—every river, and cavern, and defile, reminded them of some feat of their ancestors; and every such feat was clothed, in their conception of it, in the brightness of poetical description, and rose to their recollection with all the splendid accompaniments of sublime imagery or passionate expression, with which the genius of the poet had invested it. Their poetry was not written, indeed, in books, which might be illegible or neglected; but it was written on the rocks and the mountains, the cairns and the caverns of their country, and in the hearts, and lives, and daily occupations of its inhabitants. Even if such poetry had existed in the low country, it would not have produced the same effects,—for it would not have existed alone: and there would have been neither leisure nor disposition in the body of the people to attend to it. But, in reality, it never did exist in the low country. The gods and heroes of our dignified poetry are beings quite incomprehensible and uninteresting to the uninstructed; and the few humble ballads that have been indited upon subjects accommodated to their condition, are calculated to do any thing but to expand the heart, or elevate the imagination. In the Highlands, however, there is no one so poor as not to reckon chieftains and celebrated warriors in his genealogy; and, the humblest peasant being early fed with legends of his ancestors' glory, finds no poetry so congenial to his taste, as that which is devoted to their praise.

Without going further, then, into this curious subject, we think it may be asserted, without any great extravagance, that this universal pride of family, with its cherished domestic chronicles, added to their early and continual familiarity with such a species of poetry as has been described, must have communicated to the Highland tribes a degree both of polish and of elevation, which we would look for in vain among the more luxurious commonalty of the South; and that this 'traditionary and poetical education,' as Mrs Grant has happily termed it, in which every one is unintentionally trained, may have done as much for the illiterate natives of the Grampians, as could have been accomplished by a more systematic course of instruction.

2. Campbell's *Specimens of the British Poets*

Edinburgh Review, 31, March 1819; *Contributions*, 2

This ground-breaking anthology gave Jeffrey an opportunity to show his own appreciation of the range and richness of English poetry.

The character of our poetry depends not a little on the taste of our poetical readers;—and though some bards have always been before their age, and some behind it, the greater part must be pretty nearly on its level. Present popularity, whatever disappointed writers may say, is, after all, the only safe presage of future glory;—and it is really as unlikely that good poetry should be produced in any quantity where it is not relished, as that cloth should be manufac-tured and thrust into the market, of a pattern and fashion for which there was no demand. A shallow and uninstructed taste is indeed the most flexible and inconstant—and is tossed about by every breath of doctrine, and every wind of authority; so as neither to derive any permanent delight from the same works, nor to assure any permanent fame to their authors;—while a taste that is formed upon a wide and large survey of enduring models, not only affords a secure basis for all future judgments, but must compel, whenever it is general in any society, a salutary conformity to its great principles from all who depend on its suffrage.—To accomplish such an object, the general study of a work like this certainly is not enough:—But it would form an excellent preparation for more extensive reading—and would, of itself, do much to open the eyes of many self-satisfied persons, and startle them into a sense of their own ignorance, and the poverty and paltriness of many of their ephemeral favourites. Considered as a nation, we are yet but very imperfectly recovered from that strange and ungrateful forgetfulness of our older poets, which began with the Restoration, and continued almost unbroken till after the middle of the last century.—Nor can the works which have chiefly tended to dispel it among the instructed orders, be ranked in a higher class than this which is before us.—Percy's Relics of Antient Poetry produced, we believe, the first revulsion—and this was followed up by Wharton's History of Poetry.—Johnson's Lives of the Poets did something;—and the great effect has been produced by the modern commentators on Shakespeare. Those various works recommended the older writers, and reinstated them in some of their honours;—but still the works themselves were not placed before the eyes of ordinary readers. This was done in part, perhaps overdone, by the entire republication of some of our older dramatists—and with better effect by Mr. Ellis's Specimens. If the former, however, was rather too copious a supply for the returning appetite of the public, the latter was too scanty; and both were confined to too narrow a period of time to enable the reader to enjoy the variety, and to draw the comparisons, by which he might be most pleased and instructed.—Southey's continuation of Ellis did harm rather than good; for though there is some cleverness in the introduction, the work itself is executed in a crude, petulant, and superficial manner,—and bears all the marks of being a mere bookseller's speculation.—As we have heard nothing of it from the time of its first publication, we suppose it has had the success it deserved.

There was great room therefore,—and, we will even say, great occasion, for such a work as this of Mr. Campbell's, in the present state of our literature;—and we are persuaded, that all who care about poetry, and are not already acquainted with the authors of whom it treats—and even all who are—cannot possibly do better than read it fairly through, from the first page to the last—without skipping the extracts which they know, or those which may not at first seem very attractive. There is no reader, we will venture to say, who will rise from the perusal even of these partial and scanty fragments, without a fresh and deep sense of the matchless richness, variety, and originality of English Poetry: while the juxtaposition and arrangements of the pieces not only gives room for endless comparisons and contrasts,—but displays, as it were in miniature, the whole of its wonderful progress; and sets before us, as in a great gallery of pictures, the whole course and history of the art, from its first rude and infant beginnings, to its maturity, and perhaps its decline. While it has all the grandeur and instruction that belongs to such a gallery, it is free from the perplexity and distraction which is generally complained of in such exhibitions; as each piece is necessarily considered separately and in succession, and the mind cannot wander, like the eye, through the splendid labyrinth in which it is enchanted. Nothing, we think, can be more delightful, than thus at our ease to trace, through all its periods, vicissitudes, and aspects, the progress of this highest and most intellectual of all the arts—coloured as it is in every age by the manners of the times which produce it, and embodying, besides those flights of fancy and touches of pathos that constitute its more immediate essence, much of the wisdom and much of the morality that was then current among the people; and thus presenting us, not merely with almost all that genius has ever created for delight, but with a brief chronicle and abstract of all that was once interesting to the generations which have gone by.

The steps of the progress of such an art, and the circumstances by which they have been effected, would form, of themselves, a large and interesting theme of speculation. Conversant as poetry necessarily is with all that touches human feelings, concerns, and occupations, its character must have been impressed by every change in the moral and political condition of society, and must even retain the lighter traces of their successive follies, amusements, and pursuits; while, in the course of ages, the very multiplication and increasing business of the people have forced it through a progress not wholly dissimilar to that which the same causes have produced on the agriculture and landscape of the country;—where at first we had rude and dreary wastes, thinly sprinkled with sunny spots of simple cultivation—then vast forests and chases, stretching far around feudal castles and pinnacled abbeys—then woodland hamlets, and goodly mansions, and gorgeous gardens, and parks rich with waste fertility, and lax habitations—and, finally, crowded cities, and road-side villas, and brick-walled gardens, and turnip fields, and canals, and artificial ruins, and ornamented farms, and cottages trellised over with exotic plants! . . .

Next to the impression of the vast fertility, compass, and beauty of our English poetry, the reflection that recurs most frequently and forcibly to us, in accompanying Mr. C. through his wide survey, is that of the perishable nature of poetical fame, and the speedy oblivion that has overtaken so many of the promised heirs of immortality! Of near two hundred and fifty authors, whose works are cited in these volumes, by far the greater part of whom were celebrated in their generation, there are not thirty who now enjoy any thing that can be called popularity—whose works are to be found in the hands of ordinary readers—in the shops of ordinary booksellers—or in the press for republication. About fifty more may be tolerably familiar to men of taste or literature:—the rest slumber on the shelves of collectors, and are partially known to a few antiquaries and scholars. Now, the fame of a Poet is popular, or nothing. He does not address himself, like the man of science, to the learned, or those who desire to learn, but to all mankind; and his purpose being to delight and be praised, necessarily extends to all who can receive pleasure, or join in applause. It is strange, then, and somewhat humiliating, to see how great a proportion of those who had once fought their way successfully to distinction, and surmounted the rivalry of contemporary envy, have again sunk into neglect. We have great deference for public opinion; and readily admit, that nothing but what is good can be permanently popular. But though its *vivat* be generally oracular, its *pereat* appears to us to be often sufficiently capricious; and while we would foster all that it bids to live, we would willingly revive much that it leaves to die. The very multiplication of works of amusement, necessarily withdraws many from notice that deserve to be kept in remembrance; for we should soon find it labour, and not amusement, if we were obliged to make use of them all, or even to take all upon trial. As the materials of enjoyment and instruction accumulate around us, more and more, we fear, must thus be daily rejected, and left to waste: For while our tasks lengthen, our lives remain as short as ever; and the calls on our time multiply, while our time itself is flying swiftly away. This superfluity and abundance of our treasures, therefore, necessarily renders much of them worthless; and the veriest accidents may, in such a case, determine what part shall be preserved, and what thrown away and neglected. When an army is *decimated,* the very bravest may fall; and many poets, worthy of eternal remembrance, have probably been forgotten, merely because there was not room in our memories for all.

By such a work as the present, however, this injustice of fortune may be partly redressed—some small fragments of an immortal strain may still be rescued from oblivion—and a wreck of a name preserved, which time appeared to have swallowed up for ever. There is something pious we think, and endearing, in the office of thus gathering up the ashes of renown that has passed away; or rather, of calling back the departed life for a transitory glow, and enabling those great spirits which seemed to be *laid* for ever, still to draw a tear of pity, or a throb of admiration, from the hearts of a forgetful generation. The body of their poetry, probably, can never be revived; but some sparks of its spirit may yet be preserved, in a narrower and feebler frame.

When we look back upon the havoc which two hundred years have thus made in the ranks of our immortals—and, above all, when we refer their rapid disappearance to the quick succession of new competitors, and the accumulation of more good works than there is time to peruse,—we cannot help being dismayed at the prospect which lies before the writers of the present day. There never was an age so prolific of popular poetry as that in which we now live;—and as wealth, population, and education extend, the produce is likely to go on increasing. The last ten years have produced, we think, an annual supply of about ten thousand lines of good staple poetry— poetry from the very first hands that we can boast of—that runs quickly to three or four large editions—and is as likely to be permanent as present success can make it. Now, if this goes on for a hundred years longer, what a task will await the poetical readers of 1919! Our living poets will then be nearly as old as Pope and Swift are at present—but there will stand between them and that genera- tion nearly ten times as much fresh and fashionable poetry as is now interposed between us and those writers:—and if Scott and Byron and Campbell have already cast Pope and Swift a good deal into the shade, in what form and dimensions are they themselves likely to be presented to the eyes of our great grandchildren? The thought, we own, is a little appalling;—and we confess we see nothing better to imagine than that they may find a comfortable place in some new collection of specimens—the centenary of the present publication. There—if the future editor have any thing like the indulgence and veneration for antiquity of his predecessor—there shall posterity still hang with rapture on the half of Campbell—and the fourth part of Byron—and the sixth of Scott—and the scattered tythes of Crab- be—and the three *per cent* of Southey,—while some good-natured critic shall sit in our mouldering chair, and more than half prefer them to those by whom they have been superseded!—It is an hyperbole of good nature, however, we fear, to ascribe to them even those dimensions at the end of a century. After a lapse of 250 years, we are afraid to think of the space they may have shrunk into. We have no Shakespeare, alas! to shed a never-setting light on his contemporaries:—and if we continue to write and rhyme at the present rate for 200 years longer, there must be some new art of *short-hand reading* invented—or all reading will be given up in despair.

3. Hayley's *Life and Posthumous Writings of William Cowper*

Edinburgh Review, 2, April 1803; *Contributions*, 1

Jeffrey declares characteristically that the time has come for a public judgment of Cowper. He not only possesses Shakespearian qual- ities, but is particularly important as (according to a running title in the *Contributions*) 'the modern liberator of our poetry.'

The personal character of Cowper is easily estimated, from the writings he has left, and the anecdotes contained in this publication. He seems to have been chiefly remarkable for a certain feminine gentleness, and delicacy of nature, that shrunk back from all that was boisterous, presumptuous, or rude. His secluded life, and awful impressions of religion, concurred in fixing upon his manners, something of a saintly purity and decorum, and in cherishing that pensive and contemplative turn of mind, by which he was so much distinguished. His temper appears to have been yielding and benevolent; and though sufficiently steady and confident in the opinions he had adopted, he was very little inclined, in general, to force them upon the conviction of others. The warmth of his religious zeal made an occasional exception: but the habitual temper of his mind was toleration and indulgence; and it would be difficult, perhaps, to name a satirical and popular author so entirely free from jealousy and fastidiousness, or so much disposed to make the most liberal and impartial estimate of the merit of others, in literature, in politics, and in the virtues and accomplishments of social life. No angry or uneasy passions, indeed, seem at any time to have found a place in his bosom; and, being incapable of malevolence himself, he probably passed through life, without having once excited that feeling in the breast of another.

As the whole of Cowper's works are now before the public, and as death has finally closed the account of his defects and excellencies, the public voice may soon be expected to proclaim the balance; and to pronounce that impartial and irrevocable sentence which is to assign him his just rank and station in the poetical commonwealth, and to ascertain the value and extent of his future reputation. As the success of his works has, in a great measure, anticipated this sentence, it is the less presumptuous in us to offer our opinion of them.

The great merit of this writer appears to us to consist in the boldness and originality of his composition, and in the fortunate audacity with which he has carried the dominion of poetry into regions that had been considered as inaccessible to her ambition. The gradual refinement of taste had, for nearly a century, been weakening the force of original genius. Our poets had become timid and fastidious, and circumscribed themselves both in the choice and the management of their subjects, by the observance of a limited number of models, who were thought to have exhausted all the legitimate resources of the art. Cowper was one of the first who crossed this enchanted circle; who reclaimed the natural liberty of invention, and walked abroad in the open field of observation as freely as those by whom it was originally trodden. He passed from the imitation of poets, to the imitation of nature, and ventured boldly upon the representation of objects that had not been sanctified by the description of any of his predecessors. In the ordinary occupations and duties of domestic life, and the consequences of modern manners, in the common scenery of a rustic situation, and the obvious contemplation of our public institutions, he has found a multitude of subjects for ridicule and reflection, for pathetic and picturesque description, for moral declamation, and devotional rapture, that would have been looked upon with disdain, or with despair, by most of our poetical adventurers. He took as wide a range in language too, as in matter; and, shaking off the tawdry incumbrance of that poetical diction which had nearly reduced the art to the skilful collocation of a set of conventional phrases, he made no scruple to set down in verse every expression that would have been admitted in prose, and to take advantage of all the varieties with which our language could supply him.

But while, by the use of this double licence, he extended the sphere of poetical composition, and communicated a singular character of freedom, force, and originality to his own performances, it must not be dissembled, that the presumption which belongs to most innovators, has betrayed him into many defects. In disdaining to follow the footsteps of others, he has frequently mistaken the way, and has been exasperated, by their blunders, to rush into opposite extremes. In his contempt for their scrupulous selection of topics, he has introduced some that are unquestionably low and uninteresting; and in his zeal to strip off the tinsel and embroidery of their language, he has sometimes torn it (like Jack's coat in the Tale of a Tub) into terrible rents and beggarly tatters. He is a great master of English, and evidently values himself upon his skill and facility in the application of its rich and diversified idioms: but he has indulged himself in this exercise a little too fondly, and has degraded some grave and animated passages by the unlucky introduction of expressions unquestionably too colloquial and familiar. His impatience of control, and his desire to have a great scope and variety in his compositions, have led him not only to disregard all order and method so entirely in their construction, as to have made each of his larger poems professedly a complete miscellany, but also to introduce into them a number of subjects, that prove not to be very susceptible of poetical discussion. There are specimens of argument, and dialogue, and declamation, in his works, that partake very little of the poetical character, and make rather an awkward appearance in a metrical production, though they might have had a lively and brilliant effect in an essay or a sermon. The structure of his sentences, in like manner, has frequently much more of the copiousness and looseness of oratory, than the brilliant compactness of poetry; and he heaps up phrases and circumstances upon each other, with a profusion that is frequently dazzling, but which reminds us as often of the exuberance of a practised speaker, as of the holy inspiration of a poet.

Mr. Hayley has pronounced a warm eulogium on the satirical talents of his friend: but it does not appear to us, either that this was the style in which he was qualified to excel, or that he has made a judicious selection of subjects upon which to exercise it. There is something too keen and vehement in his invective, and an excess of austerity in his doctrines, that is not atoned for by the truth or the beauty of his descriptions. Foppery and affectation are not such hateful and gigantic vices, as to deserve all the anathemas that are bestowed upon them; nor can we believe that soldiership, or Sunday music, have produced all the terrible effects which he ascribes to them: There is something very undignified, too, to say no worse of them, in the protracted parodies and mock-heroic passages with which he seeks to enliven some of his gravest productions. The *Sofa* (for instance, in the *Task*) is but a feeble imitation of 'The Splendid Shilling;' the *Monitor* is a copy of something still lower; and the tedius directions for *raising cucumbers,* which begin with calling a hotbed 'a *stercorarious* heap,' seem to have been intended as a counterpart to the tragedy of Tom Thumb. All his serious pieces contain some fine devotional passages: but they are not without a taint of that enthusiastic intolerance which religious zeal seems but too often to produce.

It is impossible to say any thing of the defects of Cowper's writings, without taking notice of the occasional harshness and inelegance of his versification. From his correspondence, however, it appears that this was not with him the effect of negligence merely, but that he really imagined that a rough and incorrect line now and then had a very agreeable effect in a composition of any length. This prejudice, we believe, is as old as Cowley among English writers; but we do not know that it has of late received the sanction of any one poet of eminence. In truth, it does not appear to us to be at all capable of defence. The very essence of versification is uniformity; and while any thing like versification is preserved, it must be evident that uniformity continues to be aimed at. What pleasure is to be derived from an occasional failure in this aim, we cannot exactly understand. It must afford the same gratification, we should imagine, to have one of the buttons on a coat a little larger than the rest, or one or two of the pillars in a colonnade a little out of the perpendicular. If variety is wanted, let it be variety of excellence, and not a relief of imperfection: let the writer alter the measure of his piece, if he thinks its uniformity disagreeable; or let him interchange it every now and then, if he thinks proper, with passages of plain and professed prose; but do not let him torture an intractable scrap of prose into the appearance of verse, nor slip in an illegitimate line or two among the genuine currency of his poem.

There is another view of the matter, no doubt, that has a little more reason in it. A smooth and harmonious verse is not so easily written, as a harsh and clumsy one; and, in order to make it smooth and elegant, the strength and force of the expression must often be sacrificed. This seems to have been Cowper's view of the subject, at least in one passage. 'Give me,' says he, in a letter to his publisher, 'a manly rough line, with a deal of meaning in it, rather than a whole poem full of musical periods, that have nothing but their smoothness to recommend them.' It is obvious, however, that this is not a defence of harsh versification, but a confession of inability to write smoothly. Why should not harmony and meaning go together? It is difficult, to be sure; and so it is, to make meaning and verse of any kind go together: But it is the business of a poet to overcome these difficulties, and if he do not overcome them both, he is plainly deficient in an accomplishment that others have attained. To those who find it impossible to pay due attention both to the sound and the sense, we would not only address the preceding exhortation of Cowper, but should have no scruple to exclaim, 'Give us a sentence of plain prose, full of spirit and meaning, rather than a poem of any kind that has nothing but its versification to recommend it.'

Though it be impossible, therefore, to read the productions of Cowper, without being delighted with his force, his originality, and his variety; and although the enchantment of his moral enthusiasm frequently carries us insensibly through all the mazes of his digressions, it is equally true, that we can scarcely read a single page with attention, without being offended at some coarseness or lowness of expression, or disappointed by some 'most lame and impotent conclusion.' The dignity of his rhetorical periods is often violated by the intrusion of some vulgar and colloquial idiom, and the full and transparent stream of his diction broken upon some obstreperous verse, or lost in the dull stagnation of a piece of absolute prose. The effect of his ridicule is sometimes impaired by the acrimony with which it is attended; and the exquisite beauty of his moral painting and religious views, is injured in a still greater degree by the darkness of the shades which his enthusiasm and austerity have occasionally thrown upon the canvas. With all these defects, however, Cowper will probably very long retain his popularity with the readers of English poetry. The great variety and truth of his descriptions; the minute and correct painting of those home scenes, and private feelings with which every one is internally familiar; the sterling weight and sense of most of his observations, and, above all, the great appearance of facility with which every thing is executed, and the happy use he has so often made of the most common and ordinary language; all concur to stamp upon his poems the character of original genius, and remind us of the merits that have secured immortality to Shakespeare.

4. *Reliques of Robert Burns*, collected by R. H. Cromek

Edinburgh Review, 13, January 1809; *Contributions*, 2

This generous yet judicial appraisal probably settled Burns's position among the reading public, until the appearance of Carlyle's article in the *Edinburgh* in 1828.

Burns is certainly by far the greatest of our poetical prodigies—from Stephen Duck down to Thomas Dermody. *They* are forgotten already; or only remembered for derision. But the name of Burns, if we are not mistaken, has not yet 'gathered all its fame;' and will endure long after those circumstances are forgotten which contributed to its first notoriety. So much indeed are we impressed with a sense of his merits, that we cannot help thinking it a derogation from them to consider him as a prodigy at all; and are convinced that he will never be rightly estimated as a poet, till that vulgar wonder be entirely repressed which was raised on his having been a ploughman. It is true, no doubt, that he was born in an humble station; and that much of his early life was devoted to severe labour, and to the society of his fellow-labourers. But he was not himself either uneducated or illiterate; and was placed in a situation more favourable, perhaps, to the development of great poetical talents, than any other which could have been assigned him. He was taught, at a very early age, to read and write; and soon after acquired a competent knowledge of French, together with the elements of Latin and Geometry. His taste for reading was encouraged by his parents and many of his associates; and, before he had ever composed a single stanza, he was not only familiar with many prose writers, but far more intimately acquainted with Pope, Shakespeare, and Thomson than nine tenths of the youth that now leave our schools for the university. Those authors, indeed, with some old collections of songs, and the lives of Hannibal and of Sir William Wallace, were his habitual study from the first days of his childhood; and, co-operating with the solitude of his rural occupations, were sufficient to rouse his ardent and ambitious mind to the love and the practice of poetry. He had about as much scholarship, in short, we imagine, as Shakespeare; and far better models to form his ear to harmony, and train his fancy to graceful invention.

We ventured, on a former occasion, to say something of the effects of regular education, and of the general diffusion of literature, in repressing the vigour and originality of all kinds of mental exertion. That speculation was perhaps carried somewhat too far; but if the paradox have proof any where, it is in its application to poetry. Among well educated people, the standard writers of this description are at once so venerated and so familiar, that it is thought equally impossible to rival them, as to write verses without attempting it. If there be one degree of fame which excites emulation, there is another which leads to despair: Nor can we conceive any one less likely to be added to the short list of original poets, than a young man of fine fancy and delicate taste, who has acquired a high relish for poetry, by perusing the most celebrated writers, and conversing with the most intelligent judges. The head of such a person is filled, of course, with all the splendid passages of ancient and modern authors, and with the fine and fastidious remarks which have been made even on those passages. When he turns his eyes, therefore, on his own conceptions or designs, they can scarcely fail to appear rude and contemptible. He is perpetually haunted and depressed by the ideal presence of those great masters, and their exacting critics. He is aware to what comparisons his productions will be subjected among his own friends and associates; and recollects the derision with which so many rash adventurers have been chased back to their obscurity. Thus, the merit of his great predecessors chills, instead of encouraging his ardour; and the illustrious names which have already reached to the summit of excellence, act like the tall and spreading trees of the forest, which overshadow and strangle the saplings which may have struck root in the soil below— and afford efficient shelter to nothing but creepers and parasites.

There is, no doubt, in some few individuals, 'that strong divinity of soul'—that decided and irresistible vocation to glory, which, in spite of all these obstructions, calls out, perhaps once or twice in a century, a bold and original poet from the herd of scholars and academical literati. But the natural tendency of their studies, and by far their most common effect, is to repress originality, and discourage enterprize; and either to change those whom nature meant for poets, into mere readers of poetry, or to bring them out in the form of witty parodists, or ingenious imitators. Independent of the reasons which have been already suggested, it will perhaps be found, too, that necessity is the mother of invention, in this as well as in the more vulgar arts; or, at least, that inventive genius will frequently slumber in inaction, where the preceding ingenuity has in part supplied the wants of the owner. A solitary and uninstructed man, with lively feelings and an inflammable imagination, will often be irresistibly led to exercise those gifts, and to occupy and relieve his mind in poetical composition: But if his education, his reading, and his society supply him with an abundant store of images and emotions, he will probably think but little of those internal resources, and feed his mind contentedly with what has been provided by the industry of others.

To say nothing, therefore, of the distractions and the dissipation of mind that belong to the commerce of the world, nor of the cares of minute accuracy and high finishing which are imposed on the professed scholar, there seem to be deeper reasons for the separation of originality and accomplishment; and for the partiality which has led poetry to choose almost all her prime favourites among the recluse and uninstructed. A youth of quick parts, in short, and creative fancy—with just so much reading as to guide his ambition, and rough-hew his notions of excellence—if his lot be thrown in humble retirement, where he has no reputation to lose, and where he can easily hope to excel all that he sees around him, is much more likely, we think, to give himself up to poetry, and to train himself to habits of invention, than if he had been encumbered by the pretended helps of extended study and literary society.

If these observations should fail to strike of themselves, they may perhaps derive additional weight from considering the very remarkable fact, that almost all the great poets of every country have appeared in an early stage of their history, and in a period comparatively rude and unlettered. Homer went forth, like the morning star, before the dawn of literature in Greece and almost all the great and sublime poets of modern Europe are already between two and three hundred years old. Since that time, although books and readers, and opportunities of reading, are multiplied a thousand fold, we have improved chiefly in point and terseness of expression, in the art of raillery, and in clearness and simplicity of thought. Force, richness, and variety of invention, are now at least as rare as ever. But the literature and refinement of the age does not exist at all for a rustic and illiterate individual; and, consequently, the present time is to him what the rude times of old were to the vigorous writers which adorned them.

But though, for these and for other reasons, we can see no propriety in regarding the poetry of Burns chiefly as the wonderful work of a peasant, and thus admiring it much in the same way as if it had been written with his toes; yet there are peculiarities in his works which remind us of the lowness of his origin, and faults for which the defects of his education afford an obvious cause, if not a legitimate apology. In forming a correct estimate of these works, it is necessary to take into account those peculiarities.

The first is, the undisciplined harshness and acrimony of his invective. The great boast of polished life is the delicacy, and even the generosity of its hostility—that quality which is still the characteristic, as it furnishes the denomination, of a gentleman—that principle which forbids us to attack the defenceless, to strike the fallen, or to mangle the slain—and enjoins us, in forging the shafts of satire, to increase the polish exactly as we add to their keenness or their weight. For this, as well as for other things, we are indebted to chivalry; and of this Burns had none. His ingenious and amiable biographer has spoken repeatedly in praise of his talents for satire—we think, with a most unhappy partiality. His epigrams and lampoons appear to us, one and all, unworthy of him;—offensive from their extreme coarseness and violence—and contemptible from their want of wit or brilliancy. They seem to have been written, not out of playful malice or virtuous indignation, but out of fierce and ungovernable anger. His whole raillery consists in railing; and his satirical vein displays itself chiefly in calling names and in swearing. We say this mainly with a reference to his personalities. In many of his more general representations of life and manners, there is no doubt much that may be called satirical, mixed up with admirable humour, and description of inimitable vivacity.

There is a similar want of polish, or at least of respectfulness, in the general tone of his gallantry. He has written with more passion, perhaps, and more variety of natural feeling, on the subject of love, than any other poet whatever—but with a fervour that is sometimes indelicate, and seldom accommodated to the timidity and 'sweet austere composure' of women of refinement. He has expressed admirably the feelings of an enamoured peasant, who, however refined or eloquent he may be, always approaches his mistress on a footing of equality; but has never caught that tone of chivalrous gallantry which uniformly abases itself in the presence of the object of its devotion. Accordingly, instead of suing for a smile, or melting in a tear, his muse deals in nothing but locked embraces and midnight rencontres; and, even in his complimentary effusions to ladies of the highest rank, is for straining them to the bosom of her impetuous votary. It is easy, accordingly, to see from his correspondence, that many of his female patronesses shrunk from the vehement familiarity of his admiration; and there are even some traits in the volumes before us, from which we can gather, that he resented the shyness and estrangement to which those feelings gave rise, with at least as little chivalry as he had shown in producing them.

But the leading vice in Burns's character, and the cardinal deformity, indeed, of all his productions, was his contempt, or affectation of contempt, for prudence, decency and regularity; and his

admiration of thoughtlessness, oddity, and vehement sensibility;—
his belief, in short, in *the dispensing power* of genius and social
feeling, in all matters of morality and common sense. This is the
very slang of the worst German plays, and the lowest of our
town-made novels; nor can any thing be more lamentable, than that
it should have found a patron in such a man as Burns, and
communicated to many of his productions a character of immorality,
at once contemptible and hateful. It is but too true, that men of the
highest genius have frequently been hurried by their passions into a
violation of prudence and duty; and there is something generous, at
least, in the apology which their admirers may make for them, on
the score of their keener feelings and habitual want of reflection.
But this apology, which is quite unsatisfactory in the mouth of
another, becomes an insult and an absurdity whenever it proceeds
from their own. A man may say of his friend, that he is a noble-
hearted fellow—too generous to be just, and with too much spirit to
be always prudent and regular. But he cannot be allowed to say
even this of himself; and still less to represent himself as a hair-
brained sentimental soul, constantly carried away by fine fancies and
visions of love and philanthropy, and born to confound and despise
the cold-blooded sons of prudence and sobriety. This apology,
indeed, evidently destroys itself: For it shows that conduct to be the
result of deliberate system, which it affects at the same time to
justify as the fruit of mere thoughtlessness and casual impulse. Such
protestations, therefore, will always be treated, as they deserve, not
only with contempt, but with incredulity; and their magnanimous
authors set down as determined profligates, who seek to disguise
their selfishness under a name somewhat less revolting. That
profligacy is almost always selfishness, and that the excuse of
impetuous feeling can hardly ever be justly pleaded for those who
neglect the ordinary duties of life, must be apparent, we think, even
to the least reflecting of those sons of fancy and song. It requires no
habit of deep thinking, nor any thing more, indeed, than the
information of an honest heart, to perceive that it is cruel and base
to spend, in vain superfluities, that money which belongs of right to
the pale industrious tradesman and his famishing infants; or that it is
a vile prostitution of language, to talk of that man's generosity or
goodness of heart, who sits raving about friendship and philanthropy in a tavern, while his wife's heart is breaking at her cheerless
fireside, and his children pining in solitary poverty.

This pitiful cant of careless feeling and eccentric genius, accordingly, has never found much favour in the eyes of English sense
and morality. The most signal effect which it ever produced, was on
the muddy brains of some German youth, who are said to have left
college in a body to rob on the highway! because Schiller had

represented the captain of a gang as so very noble a creature.—But in this country, we believe, a predilection for that honourable profession must have preceded this admiration of the character. The style we have been speaking of, accordingly, is now the heroics only of the hulks and the house of correction; and has no chance, we suppose, of being greatly admired, except in the farewell speech of a young gentleman preparing for Botany Bay.

It is humiliating to think how deeply Burns has fallen into this debasing error. He is perpetually making a parade of his thoughtlessness, inflammability, and imprudence, and talking with much complacency and exultation of the offence he has occasioned to the sober and correct part of mankind. This odious slang infects almost all his prose, and a very great proportion of his poetry; and is, we are persuaded, the chief, if not the only source of the disgust with which, in spite of his genius, we know that he is regarded by many very competent and liberal judges. His apology, too, we are willing to believe, is to be found in the original lowness of his situation, and the slightness of his acquaintance with the world. With his talents and powers of observation, he could not have seen *much* of the beings who echoed this raving, without feeling for them that distrust and contempt which would have made him blush to think he had ever stretched over them the protecting shield of his genius.

Akin to this most lamentable trait of vulgarity, and indeed in some measure arising out of it, is that perpetual boast of his own independence, which is obtruded upon the readers of Burns in almost every page of his writings. The sentiment itself is noble, and it is often finely expressed;—but a gentleman would only have expressed it when he was insulted or provoked; and would never have made it a spontaneous theme to those friends in whose estimation he felt that his honour stood clear. It is mixed up, too, in Burns with too fierce a tone of defiance; and indicates rather the pride of a sturdy peasant, than the calm and natural elevation of a generous mind.

The last of the symptoms of rusticity which we think it necessary to notice in the works of this extraordinary man, is that frequent mistake of mere exaggeration and violence, for force and sublimity, which has defaced so much of his prose composition, and given an air of heaviness and labour to a good deal of his serious poetry. The truth is, that his *forte* was in humour and in pathos—or rather in tenderness of feeling; and that he has very seldom succeeded, either where mere wit and sprightliness, or where great energy and weight of sentiment were requisite. He had evidently a very false and crude notion of what constituted *strength* of writing; and instead of that simple and brief directness which stamps the character of vigour upon every syllable, has generally had recourse to a mere accumulation of hyperbolical expressions, which encumber the diction instead of exalting it, and show the determination to be impressive, without the power of executing it. This error also we are inclined to ascribe entirely to the defects of his education. The value of simplicity in the expression of passion, is a lesson, we believe, of nature and of genius;—but its importance in mere grave and impressive writing, is one of the latest discoveries of rhetorical experience.

With the allowances and exceptions we have now stated, we think Burns entitled to the rank of a great and original genius. He has in all his compositions great force of conception; and great spirit and animation in its expression. He has taken a large range through the region of Fancy, and naturalized himself in almost all her climates. He has great humour—great powers of description—great pathos—and great discrimination of character. Almost every thing that he says has spirit and originality; and every thing that he says well, is characterized by a charming facility, which gives a grace even to occasional rudeness, and communicates to the reader a delightful sympathy with the spontaneous soaring and conscious inspiration of the poet.

Considering the reception which these works have met with from the public, and the long period during which the greater part of them have been in their possession, it may appear superfluous to say any thing as to their characteristic or peculiar merit. Though the ultimate judgment of the public, however, be always sound, or at least decisive as to its general result, it is not always very apparent upon what grounds it has proceeded; nor in consequence of what, or in spite of what, it has been obtained. In Burns's works there is much to censure, as well as much to praise; and as time has not yet separated his ore from its dross, it may be worth while to state, in a very general way, what we presume to anticipate as the result of this separation. Without pretending to enter at all into the comparative merit of particular passages, we may venture to lay it down as our opinion—that his poetry is far superior to his prose; that his Scottish compositions are greatly to be preferred to his English ones; and that his Songs will probably outlive all his other productions.

5. Crabbe's *Poems*

Edinburgh Review, 12, April 1808; *Contributions*, 3

Jeffrey has been considered 'the most reliable of Crabbe's contemporary critics.'[39] He reviewed his work four times. He admires here

the secure traditionalism of Crabbe, as contrasted with the innova-
tions of Wordsworth. In later reviews Jeffrey considers how the poet
tackles the problems of humble life as subject-matter and of achiev-
ing a balance between 'satire and sympathy.'[40]

We receive the proofs of Mr. Crabbe's poetical existence, which are
contained in this volume, with the same sort of feeling that would be
excited by tidings of an ancient friend, whom we no longer expected
to hear of in this world. We rejoice in his resurrection, both for his
sake and for our own: But we feel also a certain movement of
self-condemnation, for having been remiss in our inquiries after
him, and somewhat too negligent of the honours which ought, at
any rate, to have been paid to his memory.

It is now, we are afraid, upwards of twenty years since we were
first struck with the vigour, originality, and truth of description of
'The Village;' and since we regretted that an author, who could
write so well, should have written so little. From that time to the
present, we have heard little of Mr. Crabbe; and fear that he has
been in a great measure lost sight of by the public, as well as by us.
With a singular, and scarcely pardonable indifference to fame, he
has remained, during this long interval, in patient or indolent
repose; and, without making a single movement to maintain or
advance the reputation he had acquired, has permitted others to
usurp the attention which he was sure of commanding, and allowed
himself to be nearly forgotten by a public, which reckons upon
being reminded of all the claims which the living have on its favour.
His former publications, though of distinguished merit, were
perhaps too small in volume to remain long the objects of general
attention, and seem, by some accident, to have been jostled aside in
the crowd of more clamorous competitors.

Yet, though the name of Crabbe has not hitherto been very
common in the mouths of our poetical critics, we believe there are
few real lovers of poetry to whom some of his sentiments and
descriptions are not secretly familiar. There is a truth and a force in
many of his delineations of rustic life, which is calculated to sink
deep into the memory; and, being confirmed by daily observation,
they are recalled upon innumerable occasions—when the ideal
pictures of more fanciful authors have lost all their interest. For
ourselves at least, we profess to be indebted to Mr. Crabbe for
many of these strong impressions; and have known more than one
of our unpoetical acquaintances, who declared they could never pass
by a parish workhouse, without thinking of the description of it they
had read at school in the Poetical Extracts. The volume before us
will renew, we trust, and extend many such impressions. It contains

all the former productions of the author, with about double their bulk of new matter; most of it in the same taste and manner of composition with the former; and some of a kind, of which we have had no previous example in this author. The whole, however, is of no ordinary merit, and will be found, we have little doubt, a sufficient warrant for Mr. Crabbe to take his place as one of the most original, nervous, and pathetic poets of the present century.

His characteristic, certainly, is force, and truth of description, joined for the most part to great selection and condensation of expression;—that kind of strength and originality which we meet with in Cowper, and that sort of diction and versification which we admire in 'The Deserted Village' of Goldsmith, or 'The Vanity of Human Wishes' of Johnson. If he can be said to have imitated the manner of any author, it is Goldsmith, indeed, who has been the object of his imitation; and yet his general train of thinking, and his views of society, are so extremely opposite, that, when 'The Village' was first published, it was commonly considered as an antidote or an answer to the more captivating representations of 'The Deserted Village.' Compared with this celebrated author, he will be found, we think, to have more vigour and less delicacy; and while he must be admitted to be inferior in the fine finish and uniform beauty of his composition, we cannot help considering him as superior, both in the variety and the truth of his pictures. Instead of that uniform tint of pensive tenderness which overspreads the whole poetry of Goldsmith, we find in Mr. Crabbe many gleams of gaiety and humour. Though his habitual views of life are more gloomy than those of his rival, his poetical temperament seems far more cheerful; and when the occasions of sorrow and rebuke are gone by, he can collect himself for sarcastic pleasantry, or unbend in innocent playfulness. His diction, though generally pure and powerful, is sometimes harsh, and sometimes quaint; and he has occasionally admitted a couplet or two in a state so unfinished, as to give a character of inelegance to the passages in which they occur. With a taste less disciplined and less fastidious than that of Goldsmith, he has, in our apprehension, a keener eye for observation, and a readier hand for the delineation of what he has observed. There is less poetical keeping in his whole performance; but the groups of which it consists are conceived, we think, with equal genius, and drawn with greater spirit as well as far greater fidelity.

It is not quite fair, perhaps, thus to draw a detailed parallel between a living poet, and one whose reputation has been sealed by death, and by the immutable sentence of a surviving generation. Yet there are so few of his contemporaries to whom Mr. Crabbe bears any resemblance, that we can scarcely explain our opinion of his merit, without comparing him to some of his predecessors. There is one set of writers, indeed, from whose works those of Mr. Crabbe might receive all that elucidation which results from contrast, and from an entire opposition in all points of taste and opinion. We allude now to the Wordsworths, and the Southeys, and Coleridges, and all that ambitious fraternity, that, with good intentions and extraordinary talents, are labouring to bring back our poetry to the fantastical oddity and puling childishness of Withers, Quarles or Marvel [*sic*]. These gentlemen write a great deal about rustic life, as well as Mr. Crabbe; and they even agree with him in dwelling much on its discomforts; but nothing can be more opposite than the views they take of the subject, or the manner in which they execute their representation of them.

Mr. Crabbe exhibits the common people of England pretty much as they are, and as they must appear to every one who will take the trouble of examining into their condition; at the same time that he renders his sketches in a very high degree interesting and beautiful—by selecting what is most fit for description—by grouping them into such forms as must catch the attention or awake the memory—and by scattering over the whole such traits of moral sensibility, of sarcasm, and of deep reflection, as every one must feel to be natural, and own to be powerful. The gentlemen of the new school, on the other hand, scarcely ever condescend to take their subjects from any description of persons at all known to the common inhabitants of the world; but invent for themselves certain whimsical and unheard-of beings, to whom they impute some fantastical combination of feelings, and then labour to excite our sympathy for them, either by placing them in incredible situations, or by some strained and exaggerated moralisation of a vague and tragical description. Mr. Crabbe, in short, shows us something which we have all seen, or may see, in real life; and draws from it such feelings and such reflections as every human being must acknowledge that it is calculated to excite. He delights us by the truth, and vivid and picturesque beauty of his representations, and by the force and pathos of the sensations with which we feel that they are connected. Mr. Wordsworth and his associates, on the other hand, introduce us to beings whose existence was not previously suspected by the acutest observers of nature; and excite an interest for them—where they do excite any interest—more by an eloquent and refined analysis of their own capricious feelings, than by any obvious or intelligible ground of sympathy in their situation.

Those who are acquainted with the Lyrical Ballads, or the more recent publications of Mr. Wordsworth, will scarcely deny the justice of this representation; but in order to vindicate it to such as do not enjoy that advantage we must beg leave to make a few hasty references to the former, and by far the least exceptionable of those productions.

A village schoolmaster, for instance, is a pretty common poetical character. Goldsmith has drawn him inimitably; so has Shenstone, with the slight change of sex; and Mr. Crabbe, in two passages, has followed their footsteps. Now, Mr. Wordsworth has a village schoolmaster also—a personage who makes no small figure in three or four of his poems. But by what traits is this worthy old gentleman delineated by the new poet? No pedantry—no innocent vanity of learning—no mixture of indulgence with the pride of power, and of poverty with the consciousness of rare acquirements. Every feature which belongs to the situation, or marks the character in common apprehension, is scornfully discarded by Mr. Wordsworth; who represents his grey-haired rustic pedagogue as a sort of half crazy, sentimental person, overrun with fine feelings, constitutional merriment, and a most humorous melancholy . . . .

A frail damsel again is a character common enough in all poems; and one upon which many fine and pathetic lines have been expended. Mr. Wordsworth has written more than three hundred on the subject: but, instead of new images of tenderness, or delicate representation of intelligible feelings, he has contrived to tell us nothing whatever of the unfortunate fair one, but that her name is Martha Ray; and that she goes up to the top of a hill, in a red cloak, and cries 'O misery!' All the rest of the poem is filled with a description of an old thorn and a pond, and of the silly stories which the neighbouring old women told about them.

The sports of childhood, and the untimely death of promising youth, is also a common topic of poetry. Mr. Wordsworth has made some blank verse about it; but, instead of the delightful and picturesque sketches with which so many authors of moderate talents have presented us on this inviting subject, all that he is pleased to communicate of *his* rustic child, is, that he used to amuse himself with shouting to the owls, and hearing them answer. To make amends for this brevity, the process of his mimicry is most accurately described.

> —'With fingers interwoven, both hands
> Press'd closely palm to palm, and to his mouth
> Uplifted, he, as through an instrument,
> Blew mimic hootings to the silent owls,
> That they might answer him.'—

This is all we hear of him; and for the sake of this one accomplishment, we are told, that the author has frequently stood mute, and gazed on his grave for half an hour together!

Love, and the fantasies of lovers, have afforded an ample theme to poets of all ages. Mr. Wordsworth, however, has thought fit to compose a piece, illustrating this copious subject by one single thought. A lover trots away to see his mistress one fine evening, gazing all the way on the moon; when he comes to her door,

> 'O mercy! to myself I cried,
> If Lucy should be dead!'

And there the poem ends!

Now, we leave it to any reader of common candour and discernment to say, whether these representations of character and sentiment are drawn from that eternal and universal standard of truth and nature, which every one is knowing enough to recognise, and no one great enough to depart from with impunity; or whether they are not formed, as we have ventured to allege, upon certain fantastic and affected peculiarities in the mind or fancy of the author, into which it is most improbable that many of his readers will enter, and which cannot, in some cases, be comprehended without much effort and explanation. Instead of multiplying instances of these wide and wilful aberrations from ordinary nature, it may be more satisfactory to produce the author's own admission of the narrowness of the plan upon which he writes and of the very extraordinary circumstances which he himself sometimes thinks it necessary for his readers to keep in view, if they would wish to understand the beauty or propriety of his delineations.

A pathetic tale of guilt or superstition may be told, we are apt to fancy, by the poet himself, in his general character of poet, with full as much effect as by any other person. An old nurse, at any rate, or a monk or parish clerk, is always at hand to give grace to such a narration. None of these, however, would satisfy Mr. Wordsworth. He has written a long poem of this sort, in which he thinks it indispensably necessary to apprise the reader, that he has endeavoured to represent the language and sentiments of a particular character—of which character, he adds, 'the reader will have a general notion, if he has ever known a man, *a captain of a small trading vessel,* for example, who being *past the middle age of life,* has retired upon *an annuity, or small independent income,* to some *village* or country town, of which he was *not a native,* or in which he had not been accustomed to live!'

Now, we must be permitted to doubt, whether, among all the readers of Mr. Wordsworth (few or many), there is a single individual who has had the happiness of knowing a person of this very peculiar description; or who is capable of forming any sort of conjecture of the particular disposition and turn of thinking which such a combination of attributes would be apt to produce. To us, we will confess, the *annonce* appears as ludicrous and absurd as it would be in the author of an ode or an epic to say, 'Of this piece the reader will necessarily form a very erroneous judgment, unless he is apprised, that it was written by a pale man in a green coat—sitting cross-legged on an oaken stool—with a scratch on his nose, and a spelling dictionary on the table.'

From these childish and absurd affectations, we turn with plea-sure to the manly sense and correct picturing of Mr. Crabbe; and, after being dazzled and made giddy with the elaborate raptures and obscure originalities of these new artists, it is refreshing to meet again with the spirit and nature of our old masters, in the nervous pages of the author now before us.

6. Southey's *Thalaba*

Edinburgh Review, 1, October 1802

In this article in the first number of the *Review* Jeffrey begins dogmatically, and he proceeds to set out his view of the sectarian movement in modern poetry. Note that he did not reprint this piece.

Poetry has this much, at least, in common with religion, that its standards were fixed long ago, by certain inspired writers, whose authority it is no longer lawful to call in question; and that many profess to be entirely devoted to it, who have no *good works* to produce in support of their pretensions. The catholic poetical church, too, has worked but few miracles since the first ages of its establishment; and has been more prolific, for a long time, of Doctors, than of Saints: it has had its corruptions and reformation also, and has given birth to an infinite variety of heresies and errors, the followers of which have hated and persecuted each other as cordially as other bigots.

The author who is now before us, belongs to a *sect* of poets, that has established itself in this country within these ten or twelve years, and is looked upon, we believe, as one of its chief champions and apostles. The peculiar doctrines of this sect, it would not, perhaps, be very easy to explain; but, that they are *dissenters* from the established systems in poetry and criticism, is admitted, and proved indeed, by the whole tenor of their compositions. Though they lay claim, we believe, to a creed and a revelation of their own, there can be little doubt, that their doctrines are of *German* origin, and have been derived from some of the great modern reformers in that country. Some of their leading principles, indeed, are probably of an earlier date, and seem to have been borrowed from the great apostle of Geneva. As Mr. Southey is the first author, of this persuasion, that has yet been brought before us for judgment, we cannot discharge our inquisitorial office conscientiously, without premising a few words upon the nature and tendency of the tenets he has helped to promulgate.

The disciples of this school boast much of its originality, and seem to value themselves very highly, for having broken loose from the bondage of ancient authority, and re-asserted the independence of genius. Originality, however, we are persuaded, is rarer than mere alteration; and a man may change a good master for a bad one, without finding himself at all nearer to independence. That our new poets have abandoned the old models, may certainly be admitted; but we have not been able to discover that they have yet created any models of their own; and are very much inclined to call in question the worthiness of those to which they have transferred their admiration. The productions of this school, we conceive, are so far from being entitled to the praise of originality, that they cannot be better characterised, than by an enumeration of the sources from which their materials have been derived. The greater part of them, we apprehend, will be found to be composed of the following elements: 1. The antisocial principles, and distempered sensibility of Rousseau—his discontent with the present constitution of society—his paradoxical morality, and his perpetual hankerings after some unattainable state of voluptuous virtue and perfection. 2. The simplicity and energy (*horresco referens*[41]) of Kotzebue and Schiller. 3. The homeliness and harshness of some of Cowper's language and versification, interchanged occasionally with the *innocence* of Ambrose Philips, or the quaintness of Quarles and Dr. Donne. From the diligent study of these few originals, we have no doubt that an entire art of poetry may be collected, by the assistance of which, the very *gentlest* of our readers may soon be qualified to compose a poem as correctly versified as Thalaba, and to deal out sentiment and description, with all the sweetness of Lambe [*sic*], and all the magnificence of Coleridge.

The authors, of whom we are now speaking, have, among them, unquestionably, a very considerable portion of poetical talent, and have, consequently, been enabled to seduce many into an admiration of the false taste (as it appears to us) in which most of their productions are composed. They constitute, at present, the most formidable conspiracy that has lately been formed against sound judgement in matters poetical; and are entitled to a larger share of our censorial notice, than could be spared for an individual delinquent. We shall hope for the indulgence of our readers, therefore, in taking this opportunity to inquire a little more particularly into their merits, and to make a few remarks upon those pecularities which seem to be regarded by their admirers as the surest proofs of their excellence.

Their most distinguishing symbol, is undoubtedly an affectation of great simplicity and familiarity of language. They disdain to make use of the common poetical phraseology, or to ennoble their diction by a selection of fine or dignified expressions. There would be too much *art* in this, for that great love of nature with which they are all of them inspired; and their sentiments, they are determined shall be indebted, for their effect, to nothing but their intrinsic tenderness or elevation. There is something very noble and conscientious, we will confess, in this plea of composition; but the misfortune is, that there are passages in all poems, that can neither be pathetic nor sublime; and that, on these occasions, a neglect of the embellishments of language is very apt to produce absolute meanness and insipidity. The language of passion, indeed, can scarcely be deficient in elevation; and when an author is wanting in that particular, he may commonly be presumed to have failed in the truth, as well as in the dignity of his expression. The case, however, is extremely different with the subordinate parts of a composition; with the narrative and description, that are necessary to preserve its connexion; and the explanation, that must frequently prepare us for the great scenes and splendid passages. In these, all the requisite ideas may be conveyed, with sufficient clearness, by the meanest and most negligent expressions; and, if magnificence or beauty is ever to be observed in them, it must have been introduced from some other motive than that of adapting the style to the subject. It is in such passages, accordingly, that we are most frequently offended with low and inelegant expressions; and that the language, which was intended to be simple and natural, is found oftenest to degenerate into mere slovenliness and vulgarity. It is in vain, too, to expect that the meanness of those parts may be redeemed by the excellence of others. A poet, who aims at all at sublimity or pathos, is like an actor in a high tragic character, and must sustain his dignity throughout, or become altogether ridiculous. We are apt enough to laugh at the mock-majesty of those whom we know to be but common mortals in private; and cannot permit Hamlet to make use of a single provincial intonation, although it should only be in his conversation with the grave-diggers.

The followers of simplicity are, therefore, at all times in danger of occasional degradation; but the simplicity of this new school seems intended to ensure it. *Their* simplicity does not consist, by any means, in the rejection of glaring or superfluous ornament,—in the substitution of elegance to splendour, or in that refinement of art which seeks concealment in its own perfection. It consists, on the contrary, in a very great degree, in the positive and *bona fide* rejection of art altogether, and in the bold use of those rude and negligent expressions, which would be banished by a little discrimination. One of their own authors, indeed, has very ingenuously set forth, (in a kind of manifesto that preceded one of their most flagrant acts of hostility), that it was their capital object 'to adapt to the uses of poetry, the ordinary language of conversation among the middling and lower orders of the people.' What advantages are to be gained by the success of this project, we confess ourselves unable to conjecture. The language of the higher and more cultivated orders may fairly be presumed to be better than that of their inferiors: at any rate, it has all those associations in its favour, by means of which, a style can ever appear beautiful or exalted, and is adapted to the purposes of poetry, by having been long consecrated to its use. The language of the vulgar, on the other hand, has all the opposite associations to contend with; and must seem unfit for poetry, (if there were no other reason), merely because it has scarcely ever been employed in it. A great genius may indeed overcome these disadvantages; but we can scarcely conceive that he should court them. We may excuse a certain homeliness of language in the productions of a ploughman or a milkwoman; but we cannot bring ourselves to admire it in an author, who has had occasion to indite odes to his college bell, and inscribe hymns to the Penates.

But the mischief of this new system, is not confined to the depravation of language only; it extends to the sentiments and emotions, and leads to the debasement of all those feelings which poetry is designed to communicate. It is absurd to suppose, that an author should make use of the language of the vulgar, to express the sentiments of the refined. His professed object, in employing that language, is to bring his compositions nearer to the true standard of nature; and his intention to copy the sentiments of the lower orders, is implied in his resolution to make use of their style. Now, the different classes of society have each of them a distinct character, as well as a separate idiom; and the names of the various passions to which they are subject respectively, have a signification that varies essentially, according to the condition of the persons to whom they are applied. The love, or grief, or indignation of an enlightened and refined character, is not only expressed in a different language, but is in itself a different emotion from the love, or grief, or anger of a clown, a tradesman, or a market-wench. The things themselves are radically and obviously distinct; and the representation of them is calculated to convey a very different train of sympathies and sensations to the mind. The question, therefore, comes simply to be—

which of them is the most proper object for poetical imitation? It is needless for us to answer a question, which the practice of all the world has long ago decided irrevocably. The poor and vulgar may interest us, in poetry, by the *situation;* but never, we apprehend, by any sentiments that are peculiar to their condition, and still less by any language that is characteristic of it. The truth is, that it is impossible to copy their diction or their sentiments correctly, in a serious composition; and this, not merely because poverty makes men ridiculous, but because just taste and refined sentiment are rarely to be met with among the uncultivated part of mankind; and a language, fitted for their expression, can still more rarely form any part of their 'ordinary conversation.'

The low-bred heroes, and interesting rustics of poetry, have no sort of affinity to the real vulgar of this world; they are imaginary beings, whose characters and language are in contrast with their situation; and please those who can be pleased with them, by the marvellous, and not by the nature of such a combination. In serious poetry, a man of the middling or lower order *must necessarily* lay aside a great deal of his ordinary language; he must avoid errors in grammar and orthography; and steer clear of the cant of particular professions, and of every impropriety that is ludicrous or disgusting: nay, he must speak in good verse, and observe all the graces in prosody and collocation. After all this, it may not be very easy to say how we are to find him out to be a low man, or what marks can remain of the ordinary language of conversation in the inferior orders of society. If there be any phrases that are not used in good society, they will appear as blemishes in the composition, no less palpably, than errors in syntax or quantity; and, if there be no such phrases, the style cannot be characteristic of that condition of life, the language of which it professes to have adopted. All approximation to that language, in the same manner, implies a deviation from that purity and precision, which no one, we believe, ever violated spontaneously.

It has been argued, indeed, (for men will argue in support of what they do not venture to practise), that as the middling and lower order of society constitute by far the greater part of mankind, so, their feelings and expressions should interest more extensively, and may be taken, more fairly than any other, for the standards of what is natural and true. To this, it seems obvious to answer, that the arts that aim at exciting admiration and delight, do not take their models from what is ordinary, but from what is excellent; and that our interest in the representation of any event, does not depend upon our familiarity with the original, but on its intrinsic importance, and the celebrity of the parties it concerns. The sculptor employs his art in delineating the graces of Antinous or Apollo, and not in the representation of those ordinary forms that belong the the crowd of his admirers. When a chieftain perishes in battle, his followers mourn more for him, than for thousands of their equals that may have fallen around him.

After all, it must be admitted, that there is a class of persons (we are afraid they cannot be called *readers*), to whom the representation of vulgar manners, in vulgar language, will afford much entertainment. We are afraid, however, that the ingenious writers who supply the hawkers and ballad-singers, have very nearly monopolized that department, and are probably better qualified to hit the taste of their customers, than Mr. Southey, or any of his brethren, can yet pretend to be. To fit them for the higher task of original composition, it would not be amiss if they were to undertake a translation of Pope or Milton into the vulgar tongue, for the benefit of those children of nature.

There is another disagreeable effect of this affected simplicity, which, though of less importance than those which have been already noticed, it may yet be worth while to mention: This is, the extreme difficulty of supporting the same low tone of expression throughout, and the inequality that is consequently introduced into the texture of the composition. To an author of reading and education, it is a style that must always be assumed and unnatural, and one from which he will be perpetually tempted to deviate. He will rise, therefore, every now and then, above the level to which he has professedly degraded himself; and make amends for that transgression, by a fresh effort of descension. His composition, in short, will be like that of a person who is attempting to speak in an obsolete or provincial dialect; he will betray himself by expressions of occasional purity and elegance, and exert himself to efface that impression, by passages of unnatural meanness or absurdity.

In making these strictures on the perverted taste for simplicity, that seems to distinguish our modern school of poetry, we have no particular allusion to Mr. Southey, or the production now before us: On the contrary, he appears to us, to be less addicted to this fault than most of his fraternity; and if we were in want of examples to illustrate the preceding observations, we should certainly look for them in the effusions of that poet who commemorates, with so much effect, the chattering of Harry Gill's teeth, tells the tale of the one-eyed huntsman 'who had a cheek like a cherry,' and beautifully warns his studious friend of the risk he ran of 'growing double.'

[Jeffrey includes Southey in this blame by quoting a passage from *Thalaba,* then he continues:]

The *style* of our modern poets, is that, no doubt, by which they are most easily distinguished: but their genius has also an internal character; 'and the peculiarities of their taste may be discovered, without the assistance of their diction. Next after great familiarity of language, there is nothing that appears to them so meritorious as perpetual exaggeration of thought. There must be nothing moderate, natural, or easy, about their sentiments. There must be a 'qu'il mourut,' and a 'let there be light,' in every line; and all their characters must be in agonies and ecstasies, from their entrance to their exit. To those who are acquainted with their productions, it is needless to speak of the fatigue that is produced by this unceasing summons to admiration, or of the compassion which is excited by the spectacle of these eternal strainings and distortions. Those authors appear to forget, that a whole poem cannot be made up of striking passages; and that the sensations produced by sublimity, are never so powerful and entire, as when they are allowed to subside and revive, in a slow and spontaneous succession. It is delightful, now and then, to meet with a rugged mountain, or a roaring stream; but where there is no sunny slope, nor shaded plain, to relieve them—where all is beetling cliff and yawning abyss, and the landscape presents nothing on every side but prodigies and terrors—the head is apt to grow giddy, and the heart to languish for the repose and security of a less elevated region.

The effect even of genuine sublimity, therefore, is impaired by the injudicious frequency of its exhibition, and the omission of those intervals and breathing-places, at which the mind should be permitted to recover from its perturbation or astonishment: but, where it has been summoned upon a false alarm, and disturbed in the orderly course of its attention, by an impotent attempt at elevation, the consequences are still more disastrous. There is nothing so ridiculous (at least for a poet) as to fail in great attempts. If the reader foresaw the failure, he may receive some degree of mischievous satisfaction from its punctual occurrence; if he did not, he will be vexed and disappointed; and, in both cases, he will very speedily be disgusted and fatigued. It would be going too far, certainly, to maintain, that our modern poets have never succeeded in their persevering endeavours at elevation and emphasis; but it is a melancholy fact, that their successes bear but a small proportion to their miscarriages; and that the reader who has been promised an energetic sentiment, or sublime allusion, must often be contented with a very miserable substitute. Of the many contrivances they employ to give the appearance of uncommon force and animation to a very ordinary conception, the most usual is, to wrap it up in a veil of mysterious and unintelligible language, which flows past with so much solemnity, that it is difficult to believe it conveys nothing of any value. Another device for improving the effect of a cold idea, is, to embody it in a verse of unusual harshness and asperity. Compound words, too, of a portentous sound and conformation, are very useful in giving an air of energy and originality; and a few lines of scripture, written out into verse from the original prose, have been found to have a very happy effect upon those readers to whom they have the recommendation of novelty.

The qualities of style and imagery, however, form but a small part of the characteristics by which a literary faction is to be distinguished. The subject and object of their compositions, and the principles and opinions they are calculated to support, constitute a far more important criterion, and one to which it is usually altogether as easy to refer. Some poets are sufficiently described as the flatterers of greatness and power, and others as the champions of independence. One set of writers is known by its antipathy to decency and religion; another, by its methodistical cant and intolerance. Our new school of poetry has a moral character also; though it may not be possible, perhaps, to delineate it quite so concisely.

A splenetic and idle discontent with the existing institutions of society, seems to be at the bottom of all their serious and peculiar sentiments. Instead of contemplating the wonders and the pleasures which civilization has created for mankind, they are perpetually brooding over the disorders by which its progress has been attended. They are filled with horror and compassion at the sight of poor men spending their blood in the quarrels of princes, and brutifying their sublime capabilities in the drudgery of unremitting labour. For all sorts of vice and profligacy in the lower orders of society, they have the same virtuous horror, and the same tender compassion. While the existence of these offences overpowers them with grief and confusion, they never permit themselves to feel the smallest indignation or dislike towards the offenders. The present vicious constitution of society alone is responsible for all these enormities: the poor sinners are but the helpless victims or instruments of its disorders, and could not possibly have avoided the errors into which they have been betrayed. Though they can bear with crimes, therefore, they cannot reconcile themselves to punishments; and have unconquerable antipathy to prisons, gibbets, and houses of correction, as engines of oppression, and instruments of atrocious injustice. While the plea of moral necessity is thus artfully brought forward to convert all the excesses of the poor into innocent misfortunes, no sort of indulgence is shown to the offences of the powerful and rich. Their oppressions, and seductions, and debaucheries, are the theme of many an angry verse; and the indignation and abhorrence of the reader is relentlessly conjured up against those perturbators of society, and scourges of mankind.

[After examining *Thalaba* more closely, Jeffrey concludes:]

All the productions of this author, it appears to us, bear very distinctly the impression of an amiable mind, a cultivated fancy, and a perverted taste. His genius seems naturally to delight in the representation of domestic virtues and pleasures, and the brilliant delineation of external nature. In both these departments, he is frequently very successful; but he seems to want vigour for the loftier flights of poetry. He is often puerile, diffuse, and artificial, and seems to have but little acquaintance with those chaster and severer graces, by whom the epic muse would be most suitably attended. His faults are always aggravated, and often created, by his partiality for the peculiar manner of that new school of poetry, of which he is a faithful disciple, and to the glory of which, he has sacrificed greater talents and acquisitions, than can be boasted of by any of his associates.

7. Wordsworth's *Poems*

Edinburgh Review, 11, October 1807

This is Jeffrey's first direct review of Wordsworth, part of a generally hostile reception, marking the beginning of the depression of the poet's fame which lasted for some twenty years. Jeffrey's general observations are thoughtful, but they give way to comments on particular poems which are often merely abusive. He unfairly omits from the quotations from 'Song at the Feast of Brougham Castle' the one stanza which epitomizes Wordsworth's views:

> Love had he found in huts where poor men lie;
> His daily teachers had been woods and rills,
> The silence that is in the starry sky,
> The sleep that is among the lonely hills.

(11. 161-4)

However, when Jeffrey fears that Wordsworth's defects may proceed 'from the self-illusion of a mind of extraordinary sensibility, habituated to solitary meditation,' he is echoing the poet's own admission of 'diseased impulses' in himself.[42] Jeffrey did not reprint the article.

This author is known to belong to a certain brotherhood of poets, who have haunted for some years about the Lakes of Cumberland;

and is generally looked upon, we believe, as the purest model of the excellences and peculiarities of the school which they have been labouring to establish. Of the general merits of that school, we have had occasion to express our opinion pretty fully, in more places than one, and even to make some allusion to the former publications of the writer now before us. We are glad, however, to have found an opportunity of attending somewhat more particularly to his pretensions.

The Lyrical Ballads were unquestionably popular; and, we have no hesitation in saying, deservedly popular; for in spite of their occasional vulgarity, affectation, and silliness, they were undoubtedly characterised by a strong spirit of originality, of pathos, and natural feeling; and recommended to all good minds by the clear impression which they bore of the amiable dispositions and virtuous principles of the author. By the help of these qualities, they were enabled, not only to recommend themselves to the indulgence of many judicious readers, but even to beget among a pretty numerous class of persons, a sort of admiration of the very defects by which they were attended. It was upon this account chiefly, that we thought it necessary to set ourselves against this alarming innovation. Childishness, conceit, and affectation, are not of themselves very popular or attractive; and though mere novelty has sometimes been found sufficient to give them a temporary currency, we should have had no fear of their prevailing to any dangerous extent, if they had been graced with no more seductive accompaniments. It was precisely because the perverseness and bad taste of this new school was combined with a great deal of genius and of laudable feeling, that we were afraid of their spreading and gaining ground among us, and that we entered into the discussion with a degree of zeal and animosity which some might think unreasonable towards authors, to whom so much merit had been conceded. There were times and moods indeed, in which we were led to suspect ourselves of unjustifiable severity, and to doubt, whether a sense of public duty had not carried us rather too far in reprobation of errors, that seemed to be atoned for, by excellences of no vulgar description. At other times, the magnitude of these errors—the disgusting absurdities into which they led their feebler admirers, and the derision and contempt which they drew from the more fastidious, even upon the merits with which they were associated, made us wonder more than ever at the perversity by which they were retained, and regret that we had not declared ourselves against them with still more formidable and decided hostility.

In this temper of mind, we read the *annonce* of Mr. Wordsworth's publication with a good deal of interest and expectation, and opened his volumes with greater anxiety, than he or his admirers will probably give us credit for. We have been greatly disappointed certainly as to the quality of the poetry; but we doubt whether the publication has afforded so much satisfaction to any other of his readers:—it has freed us from all doubt or hesitation as to the justice of our former censures, and has brought the matter to a test, which we cannot help hoping may be convincing to the author himself.

Mr. Wordsworth, we think, has now brought the question, as to the merit of his new school of poetry, to a very fair and decisive issue. The volumes before us are much more strongly marked by all its peculiarities than any former publication of the fraternity. In our apprehension, they are, on this very account, infinitely less interesting or meritorious; but it belongs to the public, and not to us, to decide upon their merit, and we will confess, that so strong is our conviction of their obvious inferiority, and the grounds of it, that we are willing for once to wave our right of appealing to posterity, and to take the judgment of the present generation of readers, and even of Mr. Wordsworth's former admirers, as conclusive on this occasion. If these volumes, which have all the benefit of the author's former popularity, turn out to be nearly as popular as the lyrical ballads—if they sell nearly to the same extent—or are quoted and imitated among half as many individuals, we shall admit that Mr. Wordsworth has come much nearer the truth in his judgment of what constitutes the charm of poetry, than we had previously imagined—and shall institute a more serious and respectful inquiry into his principles of composition than we have yet thought necessary. On the other hand,—if this little work, selected from the compositions of five maturer years, and written avowedly for the purpose of exalting a system, which has already excited a good deal of attention, should be generally rejected by those whose prepossessions were in its favour, there is room to hope, not only that the system itself will meet with no more encouragement, but even that the author will be persuaded to abandon a plan of writing, which defrauds his industry and talents of their natural reward.

Putting ourselves thus upon our country, we certainly look for a verdict against this publication; and have little doubt indeed of the result, upon a fair consideration of the evidence contained in these volumes.—To accelerate that result, and to give a general view of the evidence, to those into whose hands the record may not have already fallen, we must now make a few observations and extracts.

We shall not resume any of the particular discussions by which we formerly attempted to ascertain the value of the improvements which this new school has effected in poetry; but shall lay the grounds of our opposition, for this time, a little more broadly. The end of poetry, we take it, is to please—and the name, we think, is strictly applicable to every metrical composition from which we receive pleasure, without any laborious exercise of the understanding. This pleasure, may, in general, by analyzed into three parts—that which we receive from the excitement of Passion or emotion—that which is derived from the play of Imagination, or the easy exercise of Reason—and that which depends on the character and qualities of the Diction. The two first are the vital and primary springs of poetical delight, and can scarcely require explanation to any one. The last has been alternately overrated and undervalued by the professors of the poetical art, and is in such low estimation with the author now before us and his associates, that it is necessary to say a few words in explanation of it.

One great beauty of diction exists only for those who have some degree of scholarship or critical skill. This is what depends on the exquisite *propriety* of the words employed, and the delicacy with which they are adapted to the meaning which is to be expressed. Many of the finest passages in Virgil and Pope derive their principal charm from the fine propriety of their diction. Another source of beauty, which extends only to the more instructed class of readers, is that which consists in the judicious or happy application of expressions which have been sanctified by the use of famous writers, or which bear the stamp of a simple or venerable antiquity. There are other beauties of diction, however, which are perceptible by all—the beauties of sweet sound and pleasant associations. The melody of words and verses is indifferent to no reader of poetry; but the chief recommendation of poetical language is certainly derived from those general associations, which give it a character of dignity or elegance, sublimity or tenderness. Every one known that there are low and mean expressions, as well as lofty and grave ones; and that some words bear the impression of coarseness and vulgarity, as clearly as others do of refinement and affection. We do not mean, of course, to say any thing in defence of the hackneyed common-places of ordinary versemen. Whatever might have been the original character of these unlucky phrases, they are now associated with nothing but ideas of schoolboy imbecility and vulgar affectation. But what we do maintain is, that much of the most popular poetry in the world owes its celebrity chiefly to the beauty of its diction; and that no poetry can be long or generally acceptable, the language of which is coarse, inelegant or infantine.

From this great source of pleasure, we think the readers of Mr. Wordsworth are in a great measure cut off. His diction has no where any pretensions to elegance or dignity; and he has scarcely ever condescended to give the grace of correctness or melody to his versification. If it were merely slovenly and neglected, however, all this might be endured. Strong sense and powerful feeling will ennoble any expressions; or, at least, no one who is capable of estimating those higher merits, will be disposed to mark these little defects. But, in good truth, no man, now-a-days, composes verses for publication with a slovenly neglect of their language. It is a fine and laborious manufacture, which can scarcely ever be made in a hurry; and the faults which it has, may, for the most part, be set down to bad taste or incapacity, rather than to carelessness or oversight. With Mr. Wordsworth and his friends, it is plain that their peculiarities of diction are things of choice, and not of acci-dent. They write as they do, upon principle and system; and it evidently costs them much pains to keep *down* to the standard which they have proposed to themselves. They are, to the full, as much mannerists, too, as the poetasters who ring changes on the common-places of magazine versification; and all the difference between them is, that they borrow their phrases from a different and a scantier *gradus ad Parnassum.* If they were, indeed, to discard all imitation and set phraseology, and to bring in no words merely for show or for metre,—as much, perhaps, might be gained in freedom and originality, as would infallibly be lost in allusion and authority; but, in point of fact, the new poets are just as great borrowers as the old; only that, instead of borrowing from the more popular passages of their illustrious predecessors, they have prefer-red furnishing themselves from vulgar ballads and plebeian nurseries.

Their peculiarities of diction alone, are enough, perhaps, to render them ridiculous; but the author before us really seems anxious to court this literary martydom by a device still more infallible,—we mean, that of connecting his most lofty, tender, or impassioned conceptions, with objects and incidents, which the greater part of his readers will probably persist in thinking low, silly, or uninteresting. Whether this is done from affectation and conceit alone, or whether it may not arise, in some measure, from the self-illusion of a mind of extraordinary sensibility, habituated to solitary meditation, we cannot undertake to determine. It is possible enough, we allow, that the sight of a friend's garden-spade, or a sparrow's nest, or a man gathering leeches, might really have suggested to such a mind a train of powerful impressions and interesting reflections; but it is certain, that, to most minds, such associations will always appear forced, strained, and unnatural; and that the composition in which it is attempted to exhibit them, will always have the air of parody, or ludicrous and affected singularity.

All the world laughs at Elegiac stanzas to a sucking-pig—a Hymn on Washing-day—Sonnets to one's grandmother—or Pindarics on gooseberry-pye; and yet, we are afraid, it will not be quite easy to convince Mr. Wordsworth, that the same ridicule must infallibly attach to most of the pathetic pieces in these volumes.

[After giving many excerpts to illustrate Wordsworth's folly, Jeffrey quotes appreciatively from 'Song at the Feast of Brougham Castle' and from the sonnets. He concludes:]

When we look at these, and many still finer passages, in the writings of this author, it is impossible not to feel a mixture of indignation and compassion, at that strange infatuation which has bound him up from the fair exercise of his talents, and withheld from the public the many excellent productions that would otherwise have taken the place of the trash now before us. Even in the worst of these productions, there are, no doubt, occasional little traits of delicate feeling and original fancy; but these are quite lost and obscured in the mass of childishness and insipidity with which they are incorporated; nor can any thing give us a more melancholy view of the debasing effects of this miserable theory, than that it has given ordinary men a right to wonder at the folly and presumption of a man gifted like Mr. Wordsworth, and made him appear, in his second avowed publication, like a bad imitator of the worst of his former productions.

We venture to hope, that there is now an end of this folly; and that, like other follies, it will be found to have cured itself by the extravagances resulting from its unbridled indulgence. In this point of view, the publication of the volumes before us may ultimately be of service to the good cause of literature. Many a generous rebel, it is said, has been reclaimed to his allegiance by the spectacle of lawless outrage and excess presented in the conduct of the insurgents; and we think there is every reason to hope, that the lamentable consequences which have resulted from Mr. Wordsworth's open violation of the established laws of poetry, will operate as a wholesome warning to those who might otherwise have been seduced by his example, and be the means of restoring to that ancient and venerable code its due honour and authority.

8. Wordsworth's *The Excursion*

Edinburgh Review, 24, November 1814; *Contributions*, 3

Jeffrey is notorious for the hostility epitomized in his first sentence, but it should also be remembered that his strictures bear some similarity to those of Coleridge, particularly in the *Biographia Literaria*. Coleridge admits that Jeffrey cites 'a large number' of passages which he acknowledges to possess 'eminent and original beauty.'[43] In spite of his objections, Jeffrey is determined to try 'to be thankful for the occasional gleams of tenderness and beauty which the natural force of [Wordsworth's] imagination and affections must still shed over all his productions.'

Though the review gave *The Excursion* some publicity, J. S. Lyon comments that it 'permanently injured the fortunes' of the poem.[44]

This will never do! It bears no doubt the stamp of the author's heart and fancy: But unfortunately not half so visibly as that of his peculiar system. His former poems were intended to recommend that system, and to bespeak favour for it by the individual merit;—but this, we suspect, must be recommended by the system—and can only expect to succeed where it has been previously established. It is longer, weaker, and tamer, than any of Mr. Wordsworth's other productions; with less boldness of originality, and less even of that extreme simplicity and lowliness of tone which wavered so prettily, in the Lyrical Ballads, between silliness and pathos. We have imitations of Cowper, and even of Milton here; engrafted on the natural drawl of the Lakers—and all diluted into harmony by that profuse and irrepressible wordiness which deluges all the blank verse of this school of poetry, and lubricates and weakens the whole structure of their style.

Though it fairly fills four hundred and twenty good quarto pages, without note, vignette, or any sort of extraneous assistance, it is stated in the title—with something of an imprudent candour—to be but 'a portion' of a larger work; and in the preface, where an attempt is rather unsuccessfully made to explain the whole design, it is still more rashly disclosed, that it is but *'a part of the second part,* of a *long* and laborious work'—which is to consist of three parts!

What Mr. Wordsworth's ideas of length are, we have no means of accurately judging: But we cannot help suspecting that they are liberal, to a degree that will alarm the weakness of most modern readers. As far as we can gather from the preface, the entire poem—or one of them, (for we really are not sure whether there is to be one or two,) is of a biographical nature; and is to contain the history of the author's mind, and of the origin and progress of his poetical powers, up to the period when they were sufficiently matured to qualify him for the great work on which he has been so long employed. Now, the quarto before us contains an account of one of his youthful rambles in the vales of Cumberland, and occupies precisely the period of three days! So that, by the use of a

very powerful *calculus,* some estimate may be formed of the probable extent of the entire biography.

This small specimen, however, and the statements with which it is
prefaced, have been sufficient to set our minds at rest in one
particular. The case of Mr. Wordsworth, we perceive, is now
manifestly hopeless; and we give him up as altogether incurable,
and beyond the power of criticism. We cannot indeed altogether
omit taking precautions now and then against the spreading of the
malady;—but for himself, though we shall watch the progress of his
symptoms as a matter of professional curiosity and instruction, we
really think it right not to harass him any longer with nauseous
remedies,—but rather to throw in cordials and lenitives, and wait in
patience for the natural termination of the disorder. In order to
justify this desertion of our patient, however, it is proper to state
why we despair of the success of a more active practice.

A man who has been for twenty years at work on such matter as is
now before us, and who comes complacently forward with a whole
quarto of it, after all the admonitions he has received, cannot
reasonably be expected to 'change his hand, or check his pride,'
upon the suggestion of far weightier monitors than we can pretend
to be. Inveterate habit must now have given a kind of sanctity to
the errors of early taste; and the very powers of which we lament
the perversion, have probably become incapable of any other application. The very quantity, too, that he has written, and is at this
moment working up for publication upon the old pattern, makes it
amost hopeless to look for any change of it. All this is so much
capital already sunk in the concern; which must be sacrificed if that
be abandoned: and no man likes to give up for lost the time and
talent and labour which he has embodied in any permanent production. We were not previously aware of these obstacles to Mr.
Wordsworth's conversion; and, considering the peculiarities of his
former writings merely as the result of certain wanton and capricious experiments on public taste and indulgence, conceived it to be
our duty to discourage their repetition by all the means in our
power. We now see clearly, however, how the case stands;—and,
making up our minds, though with the most sincere pain and
reluctance, to consider him as finally lost to the good cause of
poetry, shall endeavour to be thankful for the occasional gleams of
tenderness and beauty which the natural force of his imagination
and affections must still shed over all his productions,—and to
which we shall ever turn with delight, in spite of the affectation and
mysticism and prolixity, with which they are so abundantly contrasted.

Long habits of seclusion, and an excessive ambition of originality, can alone account for the disproportion which seems to exist between this author's taste and his genius; or for the devotion with which he has sacrificed so many precious gifts at the shrine of those paltry idols which he has set up for himself among his lakes and his mountains. Solitary musings, amidst such scenes, might no doubt be expected to nurse up the mind to the majesty of poetical conception,—(though it is remarkable, that all the greater poets lived, or had lived, in the full current of society):—But the collision of equal minds,—the admonition of prevailing impressions—seems necessary to reduce its redundancies, and repress that tendency to extravagance or puerility, into which the self-indulgence and self-admiration of genius is so apt to be betrayed, when it is allowed to wanton, without awe or restraint, in the triumph and delight of its own intoxication. That its flights should be graceful and glorious in the eyes of men, it seems almost to be necessary that they should be made in the consciousness that men's eyes are to behold them,—and that the inward transport and vigour by which they are inspired, should be tempered by an occasional reference to what will be thought of them by those ultimate dispensers of glory. An habitual and general knowledge of the few settled and permanent maxims, which form the canon of general taste in all large and polished societies—a certain tact, which informs us at once that many things, which we still love and are moved by in secret, must necessarily be despised as childish, or derided as absurd, in all such societies— though it will not stand in the place of genius, seems necessary to the success of its exertions; and though it will never enable any one to produce the higher beauties of art, can alone secure the talent which does produce them from errors that must render it useless. Those who have most of the talent, however, commonly acquire this knowledge with the greatest facility;—and if Mr. Wordsworth, instead of confining himself almost entirely to the society of the dalesmen and cottagers, and little children, who form the subjects of his book, had condescended to mingle a little more with the people that were to read and judge of it, we cannot help thinking that its texture might have been considerably improved: At least it appears to us to be absolutely impossible, that any one who had lived or mixed familiarly with men of literature and ordinary judgment in poetry, (of course we exclude the coadjutors and disciples of his own school,) could ever have fallen into such gross faults, or so long mistaken them for beauties. His first essays we looked upon in a good degree as poetical paradoxes,—maintained experimentally, in order to display talent, and court notoriety;—and so maintained, with no more serious belief in their truth, than is usually generated by an ingenious and animated defence of other paradoxes. But

when we find that he has been for twenty years exclusively employed upon articles of this very fabric, and that he has still enough
of raw material on hand to keep him so employed for twenty years
to come, we cannot refuse him the justice of believing that he is a
sincere convert to his own system, and must ascribe the peculiarities
of his composition, not to any transient affectation, or accidental
caprice of imagination, but to a settled perversity of taste or
understanding, which has been fostered, if not altogether created,
by the circumstances to which we have alluded.

The volume before us, if we were to describe it very shortly, we
should characterise as a tissue of moral and devotional ravings, in
which innumerable changes are rung upon a few very simple and
familiar ideas:—But with such an accompaniment of long words,
long sentences, and unwieldy phrases—and such a hubbub of
strained raptures and fantastical sublimities, that it is often difficult
for the most skilful and attentive student to obtain a glimpse of the
author's meaning—and altogether impossible for an ordinary reader
to conjecture what he is about. Moral and religious enthusiasm,
though undoubtedly poetical emotions, are at the same time but
dangerous inspirers of poetry; nothing being so apt to run into
interminable dulness or mellifluous extravagance, without giving the
unfortunate author the slightest intimation of his danger. His laudable zeal for the efficacy of his preachments, he very naturally
mistakes for the ardour of poetical inspiration;—and, while dealing
out the high words and glowing phrases which are so readily supplied by themes of this description, can scarcely avoid believing that
he is eminently original and impressive:—All sorts of commonplace
notions and expressions are sanctified in his eyes, by the sublime
ends for which they are employed; and the mystical verbiage of the
Methodist pulpit is repeated, till the speaker entertains no doubt
that he is the chosen organ of divine truth and persuasion. But if
such be the common hazards of seeking inspiration from those
potent fountains, it may easily be conceived what chance Mr.
Wordsworth had of escaping their enchantment,—with his natural
propensities to wordiness, and his unlucky habit of debasing pathos
with vulgarity. The fact accordingly is, that in this production he is
more obscure that a Pindaric poet of the seventeenth century; and
more verbose 'than even himself of yore;' while the wilfulness with
which he persists in choosing his examples of intellectual dignity and
tenderness exclusively from the lowest ranks of society, will be
sufficiently apparent, from the circumstance of his having thought fit
to make his chief prolocutor in this poetical dialogue, and chief
advocate of Providence and Virtue, *an old Scotch Pedlar*—retired
indeed from business—but still rambling about in his former haunts,

and gossiping among his old customers, without his pack on his shoulders. The other persons of the drama are, a retired military chaplain, who has grown half an atheist and half a misanthrope—the wife of an unprosperous weaver—a servant girl with her natural child—a parish pauper, and one or two other personages of equal rank and dignity.

The character of the work is decidedly didactic; and more than nine tenths of it are occupied with a species of dialogue, or rather a series of long sermons or harangues which pass between the pedlar, the author, the old chaplain, and a worthy vicar, who entertains the whole party at dinner on the last day of their excursion. The incidents which occur in the course of it are as few and trifling as can well be imagined;—and those which the different speakers narrate in the course of their discourses, are introduced rather to illustrate their arguments or opinions, than for any interest they are supposed to possess of their own.—The doctrine which the work is intended to enforce, we are by no means certain that we have discovered. In so far as we can collect, however, it seems to be neither more nor less than the old familiar one, that a firm belief in the providence of a wise and beneficent Being must be our great stay and support under all afflictions and perplexities upon earth—and that there are indications of his power and goodness in all the aspects of the visible universe, whether living or inanimate—every part of which should therefore be regarded with love and reverence, as exponents of those great attributes. We can testify, at least, that these salutary and important truths are inculcated at far greater length, and with more repetitions, than in any ten volumes of sermons that we ever perused. It is also maintained, with equal conciseness and original- ity, that there is frequently much good sense, as well as much enjoyment, in the humbler conditions of life; and that, in spite of great vices and abuses, there is a reasonable allowance both of happiness and goodness in society at large. If there be any deeper or more recondite doctrines in Mr. Wordsworth's book, we must confess that they have escaped us;—and, convinced as we are of the truth and soundness of those to which we have alluded, we cannot help thinking that they might have been better enforced with less parade and prolixity. His effusions on what may be called the physiognomy of external nature, or its moral and theological ex- pression, are eminently fantastic, obscure, and affected.

[Jeffrey proceeds to summarize the poem, with comments on what he considers intolerable in it. Extracts, largely uncomprehended, follow. The critic continues:]

These examples, we perceive, are not very well chosen—but we have not leisure to improve the selection; and, such as they are, they may serve to give the reader a notion of the sort of merit which we meant to illustrate by their citation. When we look back to them, indeed, and to the other passages which we have now extracted, we feel half inclined to rescind the severe sentence which we passed on the work at the beginning:—But when we look into the work itself, we perceive that it cannot be rescinded. Nobody can be more disposed to do justice to the great powers of Mr. Wordsworth than we are; and, from the first time that he came before us, down to the present moment, we have uniformly testified in their favour, and assigned indeed our high sense of their value as the chief ground of the bitterness with which we resented their perversion. That perversion, however, is now far more visible than their original dignity; and while we collect the fragments, it is impossible not to mourn over the ruins from which we are condemned to pick them. If any one should doubt of the existence of such a perversion, or be disposed to dispute about the instances we have hastily brought forward, we would just beg leave to refer him to the general plan and character of the poem now before us. Why should Mr. Wordsworth have made his hero a superannuated Pedlar? What but the most wretched affectation, or provoking perversity of taste, could induce any one to place his chosen advocate of wisdom and virtue in so absurd and fantastic a condition? Did Mr. Wordsworth really imagine, that his favourite doctrines were likely to gain any thing in point of effect or authority by being put into the mouth of a person accustomed to higgle about tape, or brass sleeve-buttons? Or is it not plain that, independent of the ridicule and disgust which such a personification must excite in many of his readers, its adoption exposes his work throughout to the charge of revolting incongruity, and utter disregard of probability or nature? For, after he has thus wilfully debased his moral teacher by a low occupation, is there one word that he puts into his mouth, or one sentiment of which he makes him the organ, that has the most remote reference to that occupation? Is there any thing in his learned, abstract, and logical harangues, that savours of the calling that is ascribed to him? Are any of their materials such as a pedlar could possibly have dealt in? Are the manners, the diction, the sentiments, in any, the very smallest degree, accommodated to a person in that condition? or are they not eminently and conspicuously such as could not by possibility belong to it? A man who went about selling flannel and pocket-handkerchiefs in this lofty diction, would soon frighten away all his customers; and would infallibly pass either for a madman, or for some learned and affected gentleman, who, in a frolic, had taken up a character which he was peculiarly ill qualified for supporting.

The absurdity in this case, we think, is palpable and glaring: but it is exactly of the same nature with that which infects the whole substance of the work—a puerile ambition of singularity engrafted on an unlucky predilection for truisms; and an affected passion for simplicity and humble life, most awkwardly combined with a taste for mystical refinements, and all the gorgeousness of obscure phraseology. His taste for simplicity is evinced by sprinkling up and down his interminable declamations a few descriptions of baby-houses, and of old hats with wet brims; and his amiable partiality for humble life, by assuring us that a wordy rhetorician, who talks about Thebes, and allegorizes all the heathen mythology, was once a pedlar—and making him break in upon his magnificent orations with two or three awkward notices of something that he had seen when selling winter raiment about the country—or of the changes in the state of society, which had almost annihilated his former calling.

9. Scott's *The Lady of the Lake*

Edinburgh Review, 16, August 1810; *Contributions,* 2

A full discussion of historical developments in the language of poetry leads to a judicial appraisal of this particular poet.

Mr. Scott, though living in an age unusually prolific of original poetry, has manifestly outstripped all his competitors in the race of popularity; and stands already upon a height to which no other writer has attained in the memory of any one now alive. We doubt, indeed, whether any English poet *ever* had so many of his books sold, or so many of his verses read and admired by such a multitude of persons in so short a time. We are credibly informed that nearly thirty thousand copies of 'The Lay' have been already disposed of in this country; and that the demand for Marmion, and the poem now before us, has been still more considerable,—a circulation we believe, altogether without example, in the case of a bulky work, not addressed to the bigotry of the mere mob, either religious or political.

A popularity so universal is a pretty sure proof of extraordinary merit,—a far surer one, we readily admit, than would be afforded by any praises of ours: and, therefore, though we pretend to be privileged, in ordinary cases, to foretell the ultimate reception of all claims on public admiration, our function may be thought to cease, where the event is already so certain and conspicuous. As it is a sure thing, however, to be deprived of our privileges on so important an occasion, we hope to be pardoned for insinuating, that, even in such a case, the office of the critic may not be altogether superfluous. Though the success of the author be decisive, and even likely to be permanent, it still may not be without its use to point out, in consequence of what, and in spite of what, he has succeeded; nor altogether uninstructive to trace the precise limits of the connection which, even in this dull world, indisputably subsists between success and desert, and to ascertain how far unexampled popularity does really imply unrivalled talent.

As it is the object of poetry to give pleasure, it would seem to be a pretty safe conclusion, that that poetry must be the best which gives the greatest pleasure to the greatest number of persons. Yet we must pause a little, before we give our assent to so plausible a proposition. It would not be quite correct, we fear, to say that those are invariably the best judges who are most easily pleased. The great multitude, even of the reading world, must necessarily be uninstructed and injudicious; and will frequently be found, not only to derive pleasure from what is worthless in finer eyes, but to be quite insensible to those beauties which afford the most exquisite delight to more cultivated understandings. True pathos and sublimity will indeed charm every one: but, out of this lofty sphere, we are pretty well convinced, that the poetry which appears most perfect to a very refined taste, will not often turn out to be very popular poetry.

This, indeed, is saying nothing more, than that the ordinary readers of poetry have not a very refined taste; and that they are often insensible to many of its highest beauties, while they still more frequently mistake its imperfections for excellence. The fact, when stated in this simple way, commonly excites neither opposition nor surprise: and yet, if it be asked, why the taste of a few individuals, who do not perceive beauty where many others perceive it, should be exclusively dignified with the name of a good taste; or why poetry, which gives pleasure to a very great number of readers, should be thought inferior to that which pleases a much smaller number,—the answer, perhaps, may not be quite so ready as might have been expected from the alacrity of our assent to the first proposition. That there is a good answer to be given, however, we entertain no doubt: and if that which we are about to offer should not appear very clear or satisfactory, we must submit to have it thought, that the fault is not altogether in the subject.

In the first place, then, it should be remembered, that though the taste of very good judges is necessarily the taste of a few, it is implied, in their description, that they are persons eminently qualified, by natural sensibility, and long experience and reflection, to perceive all beauties that really exist, as well as to settle the relative value and importance of all the different sorts of beauty;—they are in that very state, in short, to which all who are in any degree capable of tasting those refined pleasures would certainly arrive, if their sensibility were increased, and their experience and reflection enlarged. It is difficult, therefore, in following out the ordinary analogies of language, to avoid considering them as in the right, and calling their taste the true and the just one; when it appears that it is such as is uniformly produced by the cultivation of those faculties upon which all our perceptions of taste so obviously depend.

It is to be considered also, that though it be the end of poetry to please, one of the parties whose pleasure, and whose notions of excellence, will always be primarily consulted in its composition, is the poet himself; and as he must necessarily be more cultivated than the great body of his readers, the presumption is, that he will always belong, comparatively speaking, to the class of good judges, and endeavour, consequently, to produce that sort of excellence which is likely to meet with *their* approbation. When authors, therefore, and those of whose suffrages authors are most ambitious, thus conspire to fix upon the same standard of what is good in taste and composition, it is easy to see how it should come to bear this name in society, in preference to what might afford more pleasure to individuals of less influence. Besides all this, it is obvious that it must be infinitely more *difficult* to produce any thing conformable to this exalted standard, than merely to fall in with the current of popular taste. To attain the former object, it is necessary, for the most part, to understand thoroughly all the feelings and associations that are modified or created by cultivation:—To accomplish the latter, it will often be sufficient merely to have observed the course of familiar preferences. Success, however, is rare, in proportion as it is difficult; and it is needless to say, what a vast addition rarity makes to value,—or how exactly our admiration at success is proportioned to our sense of the difficulty of the undertaking.

Such seem to be the most general and immediate causes of the apparent paradox, of reckoning that which pleases the greatest number as inferior to that which pleases the few; and such the leading grounds for fixing the standard of excellence, in a question of mere feeling and gratification, by a different rule than that of the quantity of gratification produced. With regard to some of the fine arts—for the distinction between popular and actual merit obtains in them all—there are no other reasons, perhaps, to be assigned; and, in Music for example, when we have said that it is the *authority* of those who are best qualified by nature and study, and the *difficulty* and *rarity* of the attainment, that entitles certain exquisite performances to rank higher than others that give far more general delight, we have probably said all that can be said in explanation of this mode of speaking and judging. In poetry, however, and in some other departments, this familiar, though somewhat extraordinary rule of estimation, is justified by other considerations.

As it is the cultivation of natural and perhaps universal capacities, that produces that refined taste which takes away our pleasure in vulgar excellence, so, it is to be considered, that there is an universal tendency to the propagation of such a taste; and that, in times tolerably favourable to human happiness, there is a continual progress and improvement in this, as in the other faculties of nations and large assemblages of men. The number of intelligent judges may therefore be regarded as perpetually on the increase. The inner circle, to which the poet delights chiefly to pitch his voice, is perpetually enlarging; and, looking to that great futurity to which his ambition is constantly directed, it may be found, that the most refined style of composition to which he can attain, will be, at the last, the most extensively and permanently popular. This holds true, we think, with regard to all the productions of art that are open to the inspection of any considerable part of the community; but, with regard to poetry in particular, there is one circumstance to be attended to, that renders this conclusion peculiarly safe, and goes far indeed to reconcile the taste of the multitude with that of more cultivated judges.

As it seems difficult to conceive that mere cultivation should either absolutely create or utterly destroy any natural capacity of enjoyment, it is not easy to suppose, that the qualities which delight the uninstructed should be *substantially* different from those which give pleasure to the enlightened. They may be arranged according to a different scale,—and certain shades and accompaniments may be more or less indispensable; but the qualities in a poem that give most pleasure to the refined and fastidious critic, are in substance, we believe, the very same that delight the most injudicious of its admirers:—and the very wide difference which exists between their usual estimates, may be in a great degree accounted for, by considering, that the one judges absolutely, and the other relatively— that the one attends only to the intrinsic qualities of the *work,* while the other refers more immediately to the merit of the *author.* The most popular passages in popular poetry, are in fact, for the most part, very beautiful and striking; yet they are very often such passages as could never be ventured on by any writer who aimed at the praise of the judicious; and this, for the obvious reason, that they are trite and hackneyed,—that they have been repeated till they have lost all grace and propriety,—and, instead of exalting the imagination by the impression of original genius or creative fancy, only nauseate and offend, by the association of paltry plagiarism and impudent inanity. It is only, however, on those who have read and remembered the original passages, and their better imitations, that this effect is produced. To the ignorant and the careless, the twentieth imitation has all the charm of an original; and that which oppresses the more experienced reader with weariness and disgust, rouses them with all the force and vivacity of novelty. It is not then, because the ornaments of popular poetry are deficient in intrinsic worth and beauty, that they are slighted by the critical reader, but because he at once recognises them to be stolen, and perceives that they are arranged without taste or congruity. In his indignation at the dishonesty, and his contempt for the poverty of the collector, he overlooks altogether the value of what he has collected, or remembers it only as an aggravation of his offence,—as converting larceny into sacrilege, and adding the guilt of profanation to the folly of unsuitable finery. There are other features, no doubt, that distinguish the idols of vulgar admiration from the beautiful exemplars of pure taste; but this is so much the most characteristic and remarkable, that we know no way in which we could so shortly describe the poetry that pleases the multitude, and displeases the select few, as by saying that it consisted of all the most known and most brilliant parts of the most celebrated authors,—of a splendid and unmeaning accumulation of those images and phrases which had long charmed every reader in the works of their original inventors.

The justice of these remarks will probably be at once admitted by all who have attended to the history and effects of what may be called *Poetical diction* in general, or even of such particular phrases and epithets as have been indebted to their beauty for too great a notoriety. Our associations with all this class of expressions, which have become trite only in consequence of their intrinsic excellence, now suggest to us no ideas but those of schoolboy imbecility and childish affectation. We look upon them merely as the common, hired, and tawdry trappings of all who wish to put on, for the hour, the masquerade habit of poetry; and, instead of receiving from them any kind of delight or emotion, do not even distinguish or attend to the signification of the words of which they consist. The ear is so palled with their repetition, and so accustomed to meet with them as the habitual expletives of the lowest class of versifiers, that they come at last to pass over it without exciting any sort of conception whatever, and are not even so much attended to as to expose their most gross incoherence or inconsistency to detection. It is of this quality that Swift has availed himself in so remarkable a manner, in his famous 'Song by a person of quality,' which consists entirely in a selection of some of the most trite and well-sounding phrases and epithets in the poetical lexicon of the time, strung together without any kind of meaning or consistency, and yet so disposed, as to have been perused, perhaps by one half of their readers, without any suspicion of the deception. Most of those phrases, however, which had thus become sickening, and almost insignificant, to the intelligent readers of poetry in the days of Queen Anne, are in themselves beautiful and expressive, and, no doubt, retain much of their native grace in those ears that have not been alienated by their repetition.

But it is not merely from the use of much excellent diction, that a modern poet is thus debarred by the lavishness of his predecessors. There is a certain range of subjects and characters, and a certain manner and tone, which were probably, in their origin, as graceful and attractive, which have been proscribed by the same dread of imitation. It would be too long to enter, in this place, into any detailed examination of the peculiarities—originating chiefly in this source—which distinguish ancient from modern poetry. It may be enough just to remark, that, as the elements of poetical emotion are necessarily limited, so it was natural for those who first sought to excite it, to avail themselves of those subjects, situations, and images that were most obviously calculated to produce that effect; and to assist them by the use of all those aggravating circumstances that most readily occurred as likely to heighten their operation. In this way, they may be said to have got possession of all the choice materials of their art; and, working without fear of comparisons, fell naturally into a free and graceful style of execution, at the same time that the profusion of their resources made them somewhat careless and inexpert in their application. After-poets were in a very different situation. They could neither take the most natural and general topics of interest, nor treat them with the ease and indifference of those who had the whole store at their command—because this was precisely what had been already done by those who had gone before them: And they were therefore put upon various expedients for attaining their object, and yet preserving their claim to originality. Some of them accordingly set themselves to observe and delineate both characters and external objects with greater minuteness and fidelity,—and others to analyse more carefully the mingling passions of the heart, and to feed and cherish a more limited train of emotion, through a longer and more artful succession of incidents,—while a third sort distorted both nature and passion, according to some fantastical theory of their own; or took such a narrow corner of each, and dissected it with such curious and microscopic accuracy, that its original form was no longer discernible by the eyes of the uninstructed. In this way we think that modern poetry has both been enriched with more exquisite pictures, and deeper and more sustained strains of pathetic, than were known to the less elaborate artists of antiquity; at the same time that it has been defaced with more affectation, and loaded with far more intricacy. But whether they failed or succeeded,—and whether they distinguished themselves from their predecessors by faults or by excellences, the later poets, we conceive, must be admitted to have almost always written in a more constrained and narrow manner than their originals, and to have departed farther from what was obvious, easy and natural. Modern poetry, in this respect, may be compared, perhaps, without any great impropriety, to modern sculpture. It is greatly inferior to the ancient in freedom, grace, and simplicity; but, in return, it frequently possesses a more decided expression, and more fine finishing of less suitable embellishments.

Whatever may be gained or lost, however, by this change of manner, it is obvious, that poetry must become less popular by means of it: For the most natural and obvious manner, is always the most taking;—and whatever costs the author much pains and labour, is usually found to require a corresponding effort on the part of the reader,—which all readers are not disposed to make. That they who seek to be original by means of affectation, should revolt more by their affectation than they attract by their originality, is just and natural; but even the nobler devices that win the suffrages of the judicious by their intrinsic beauty, as well as their novelty, are apt to repel the multitude, and to obstruct the popularity of some of the most exquisite productions of genius. The beautiful but minute delineations of such admirable observers as Crabbe or Cowper, are apt to appear tedious to those who take little interest in their subjects, and have no concern about their art;—and the refined, deep, and sustained pathetic of Campbell, is still more apt to be mistaken for monotony and languor, by those who are either devoid of sensibility, or impatient of quiet reflection. The most popular style undoubtedly is that which has great variety and brilliancy, rather than exquisite finish in its images and descriptions; and which touches lightly on many passions, without raising any so high as to transcend the comprehension of ordinary mortals—or dwelling on it so long as to exhaust their patience.

Whether Mr. Scott holds the same opinion with us upon these matters, and has intentionally conformed his practice to this theory,—or whether the peculiarities in his compositions have been produced merely by following out the natural bent of his genius, we do not presume to determine: But, that he has actually made use of all our recipes for popularity, we think very evident; and conceive, that few things are more curious than the singular skill, or good fortune, with which he has reconciled his claims on the favour of the multitude, with his pretensions to more select admiration. Confident in the force and originality of his own genius, he has not been afraid to avail himself of common-places both of diction and of sentiment, whenever they appeared to be beautiful or impressive,—using them, however, at all times, with the skill and spirit of an inventor; and, quite certain that he could not be mistaken for a plagiarist or imitator, he has made free use of that great treasury of characters, images, and expressions, which had been accumulated by the most celebrated of his predecessors,—at the same time that the rapidity of his transitions, the novelty of his combinations, and the spirit and variety of his own thoughts and inventions, show plainly that he was a borrower from any thing but poverty, and *took* only what he would have *given,* if he had been born in an earlier generation. The great secret of his popularity, however, and the leading characteristic of his poetry, appear to us to consist evidently in this, that he has made more use of common topics, images, and expressions, than any original poet of later times; and, at the same time, displayed more genius and originality than any recent author who has worked in the same materials. By the latter peculiarity, he has entitled himself to the admiration of every description of readers;—by the former, he is recommended in an especial manner to the inexperienced—at the hazard of some little offence to the more cultivated and fastidious.

In the choice of his subjects, for example, he does not attempt to interest merely by fine observation or pathetic sentiment, but takes the assistance of a story, and enlists the reader's curiosity among his motives for attention. Then his characters are all selected from the most common *dramatis personæ* of poetry:—kings, warriors, knights, outlaws, nuns, minstrels, secluded damsels, wizards, and true lovers. He never ventures to carry us into the cottage of the modern peasant, like Crabbe or Cowper; not into the bosom of domestic privacy, like Campbell; nor among creatures of the imagination, like Southey or Darwin. Such personages, we readily admit, are not in themselves so interesting or striking as those to whom Mr. Scott has devoted himself; but they are far less familiar in poetry—and are therefore more likely, perhaps, to engage the attention of those to whom poetry is familiar. In the management of the passions, again, Mr. Scott appears to us to have pursued the same popular, and comparatively easy course. He has raised all the most familiar and poetical emotions, by the most obvious aggrava-tions, and in the most compendious and judicious ways. He has dazzled the reader with the splendour, and even warmed him with the transient heat of various affections; but he has nowhere fairly kindled him with enthusiasm, or melted him into tenderness. Writ-ing for the world at large, he has wisely abstained from attempting to raise any passion to a height to which worldly people could not be transported; and contented himself with giving his reader the chance of feeling, as a brave, kind, and affectionate gentleman must often feel in the ordinary course of his existence, without trying to breathe into him either that lofty enthusiasm which disdains the ordinary business and amusements of life, or that quiet and deep sensibility which unfits for most of its pursuits. With regard to diction and imagery, too, it is quite obvious that Mr. Scott has not aimed at writing either in a very pure or a very consistent style. He seems to have been anxious only to strike, and to be easily and universally understood; and, for this purpose, to have culled the most glittering and conspicuous expressions of the most popular authors, and to have interwoven them in splendid confusion with his own nervous diction and irregular versification. Indifferent whether he coins or borrows, and drawing with equal freedom on his memory and his imagination, he goes boldly forward, in full reliance on a never-failing abundance: and dazzles, with his richness and variety, even those who are most apt to be offended with his glare and irregularity. There is nothing, in Mr. Scott, of the severe and majestic style of Milton—or of the terse and fine composition of Pope—or of the elaborate elegance and melody of Campbell—or even of the flowing and redundant diction of Southey.—But there is a medley of bright images and glowing words, set carelessly and loosely together—a diction, tinged successively with the careless richness of Shakespeare, the harshness and antique simplicity of the old romances, the homeliness of vulgar ballads and anecdotes, and the sentimental glitter of the most modern poetry,—passing from the borders of the ludicrous to those of the sublime—alternately minute and energetic—sometimes artificial, and frequently negligent—but always full of spirit and vivacity,—abounding in images that are striking, at first sight, to minds of every contexture—and never expressing a sentiment which it can cost the most ordinary reader any exertion to comprehend.

Such seem to be the leading qualities that have contributed to Mr. Scott's popularity; and as some of them are obviously of a kind to diminish his merit in the eyes of more fastidious judges, it is but fair to complete this view of his peculiarities by a hasty notice of such of them as entitle him to unqualified admiration;—and here it is impossible not to be struck with that vivifying spirit of strength and animation which pervades all the inequalities of his composition, and keeps constantly on the mind of the reader the impression of great power, spirit and intrepidity. There is nothing cold, creeping or feeble, in all Mr. Scott's poetry;—no laborious littleness, or puling classical affectation. He has his failures, indeed, like other people; but he always attempts vigorously: And never fails in his immediate object, without accomplishing something far beyond the reach of an ordinary writer. Even when he wanders from the paths of pure taste, he leaves behind him the footsteps of a powerful genius; and moulds the most humble of his materials into a form worthy of a nobler substance. Allied to this inherent vigour and animation, and in a great degree derived from it, is that air of facility and freedom which adds so peculiar a grace to most of Mr. Scott's compositions. There is certainly no living poet whose works seem to come from him with so much ease, or who so seldom appears to labour, even in the most burdensome parts of his performance. He seems, indeed, never to think either of himself or his reader, but to be completely identified and lost in the personages with whom he is occupied; and the attention of the reader is consequently either transferred, unbroken, to their adventures, or, if it glance back for a moment to the author, it is only to think how much more might be done, by putting forth that strength at full, which has, without effort, accomplished so many wonders. It is owing partly to these qualities, and partly to the great variety of his style, that Mr. Scott is much less frequently tedious than any other bulky poet with whom we are acquainted. His store of images is so copious, that he never dwells upon one long enough to produce weariness in the reader; and, even where he deals in borrowed or in tawdry wares, the rapidity of his transitions, and the transient glance with which he is satisfied as to each, leave the critic no time to be offended, and hurry him forward, along with the multitude, en-chanted with the brilliancy of the exhibition. Thus, the very fre-quency of his deviations from pure taste, comes, in some sort, to constitute their apology; and the profusion and variety of his faults to afford a new proof of his genius.

These, we think, are the general characteristics of Mr. Scott's poetry. Among his minor peculiarities, we might notice his singular talent for description, and especially for the description of scenes abounding in *motion* or *action* of any kind. In this department, indeed, we conceive him to be almost without a rival, either among modern or ancient poets; and the character and process of his descriptions are as extraordinary as their effect is astonishing. He places before the eyes of his readers a more distinct and complete picture, perhaps, than any other artist ever presented by mere words; and yet he does not (like Crabbe) enumerate all the visible parts of the subject with any degree of minuteness, nor confine himself, by any means, to what is visible. The singular merit of his delineations, on the contrary, consists in this, that, with a few bold and abrupt strokes, he finishes a most spirited outline,—and then instantly kindles it by the sudden light and colour of some moral affection. There are none of his fine descriptions, accordingly, which do not derive a great part of their clearness and picturesque effect, as well as their interest, from the quantity of character and moral expression which is thus blended with their details, and which, so far from interrupting the conception of the external object, very powerfully stimulate the fancy of the reader to complete it; and give a grace and a spirit to the whole representation, of which we do not know where to look for any other example.

Another very striking peculiarity in Mr. Scott's poetry, is the air of freedom and nature which he has contrived to impart to most of his distinguished characters; and with which no poet more modern than Shakespeare has ventured to represent personages of such dignity. We do not allude here merely to the genuine familiarity and homeliness of many of his scenes and dialogues, but to that air of gaiety and playfulness in which persons of high rank seem, from time immemorial, to have thought it necessary to array, not their courtesy only, but their generosity and their hostility. This tone of good society, Mr. Scott has shed over his higher characters with great grace and effect; and has, in this way, not only made his representations much more faithful and true to nature, but has very agreeably relieved the monotony of that tragic solemnity which ordinary writers appear to think indispensable to the dignity of poetical heroes and heroines. We are not sure, however, whether he has not occasionally exceeded a little in the use of this ornament; and given, now and then, too coquetish and trifling a tone to discussions of weight and moment.

[In what follows, Jeffrey concentrates on the poem supposedly under review. He concludes:]

[We] must now take an abrupt leave of Mr. Scott, by expressing our hope, and tolerably confident expectation, of soon meeting with him again. That he may injure his popularity by the mere profusion of his publications, is no doubt possible; though many of the most celebrated poets have been among the most voluminous: but, that the public must gain by this liberality, does not seem to admit of any question. If our poetical treasures were increased by the publication of Marmion and the Lady of the Lake, notwithstanding the existence of great faults in both those works, it is evident that we should be still richer if we possessed fifty poems of the same merit; and, therefore, it is for our interest, whatever it may be as to his, that their author's muse should continue as prolific as she has hitherto been. If Mr. Scott will only vary his subjects a little more, indeed, we think we might engage to insure his own reputation against any material injury from their rapid parturition; and, as we entertain very great doubts whether much greater pains would enable him to write much better poetry, we would rather have two beautiful poems, with the present *quantum* of faults—than one, with only one tenth part less alloy. He will always be a poet, we fear, to whom the fastidious will make great objections; but he may easily find, in his popularity, a compensation for their scruples. He has *the jury* hollow in his favour; and though *the court* may think that its directions have not been sufficiently attended to, it will not quarrel with the verdict.

10. Byron's *The Corsair* and *The Bride of Abydos*

Edinburgh Review, 23, April 1814

Jeffrey discusses Byron's narratives in the context of a broad theory of the history of poetry. For him, something of a revival of the spirit of the primitive is taking place today, but what especially marks the modern is its subjectivity.

Lord Byron has clear titles to applause, in the spirit and beauty of his diction and versification, and the splendour of many of his descriptions: But it is to his pictures of the stronger passions, that he is indebted for the fulness of his fame. He has delineated, with unequalled force and fidelity, the workings of those deep and powerful emotions which alternately enchant and agonize the minds that are exposed to their inroads; and represented, with a terrible energy, those struggles and sufferings and exaltations, by which the spirit is at once torn and transported, and traits of divine inspiration, or demoniacal possession, thrown across the tamer features of humanity. It is by this spell, chiefly, we think, that he has fixed the admiration of the public; and while other poets delight by their vivacity, or enchant by their sweetness, he alone has been able to *command* the sympathy, even of reluctant readers, by the natural magic of his moral sublimity, and the terrors and attractions of those overpowering feelings, the depths and the heights of which he seems to have so successfully explored. All the considerable poets of the present age have, indeed, possessed this gift in a greater or lesser degree: but there is no man, since the time of Shakespeare himself, in whom it has been made manifest with greater fulness and splendour, than in the noble author before us: and there are various considerations that lead us to believe, that it is chiefly by its means that he has attained the supremacy with which he seems now to be invested.

It must have occurred, we think, to every one who has attended to the general history of poetry, and to its actual condition among ourselves, that it is destined to complete a certain cycle, or great revolution, with respect at least to some of its essential qualities; and that we are now coming round to a taste and tone of composition, more nearly akin to that which distinguished the beginning of its progress, than any that has prevailed in the course of it.

In the rude ages, when such compositions originate, men's passions are violent, and their sensibility dull. Their poetry deals therefore in strong emotions, and displays the agency of powerful passions; both because these are the objects with which they are most familiar in real life, and because nothing of a weaker cast could make any impression on the rugged natures for whose entertainment they are devised.

As civilization advances, men begin to be ashamed of the undisguised vehemence of their primitive emotions; and learn to subdue, or at least to conceal, the fierceness of their natural passions. The first triumph of regulated society, is to be able to protect its members from actual violence; and the first trait of refinement in manners, is to exclude the coarseness and offence of unrestrained and selfish emotions. The complacency however with which these achievements are contemplated, naturally leads to too great an admiration of the principle from which they proceed. All manifestation of strong feeling is soon proscribed as coarse and vulgar; and first a cold and ceremonious politeness, and afterwards a more gay and heartless dissipation, represses, and in part eradicates the warmer affections and generous passions of our nature, along with its more dangerous and turbulent emotions. It is needless to trace the effects of this revolution in the manners and opinions of society upon that branch of literature, which necessarily reflects all its variations. It is enough to say, in general, that, in consequence of this change, poetry becomes first pompous and stately—then affectedly refined and ingenious—and finally gay, witty, discursive and familiar.

There is yet another stage, however, in the history of man and his inventions. When the pleasures of security are no longer new, and the dangers of excessive or intemperate vehemence cease to be thought of in the upper ranks of society, it is natural that the utility of the precautions which had been taken against them should be brought into question, and their severity in a great measure relaxed. There is in the human breast a certain avidity for strong sensations, which cannot be long repressed even by the fear of serious disaster. The consciousness of having subdued and disarmed the natural violence of mankind, is sufficiently lively to gratify this propensity,

so long as the triumph is recent, and the hazards still visible from
which it has effected our deliverance. In like manner, while it is a
new thing, and somewhat of a distinction, to be able to laugh
gracefully at all things, the successful derision of affection and
enthusiasm is found to do pretty nearly as well as their possession;
and hearts comfortably hardened by dissipation, feel little want of
gratifications which they have almost lost the capacity of receiving.
When these, however, come to be but vulgar accomplishments—
when generations have passed away, during which all persons of
education have employed themselves in doing the same frivolous
things, with the same despair either of interest or glory, it can
scarcely fail to happen, that the more powerful spirits will awaken to
a sense of their own degradation and unhappiness;—a disdain and
impatience of the petty pretensions and joyless elegancies of fashion
will gradually arise: and strong and natural sensations will again be
sought, without dread of their coarseness, in every scene which
promises to supply them. This is the stage of society in which
fanaticism has its second birth, and political enthusiasm its first true
development—when plans of visionary reform, and schemes of
boundless ambition are conceived, and almost realized by the
energy with which they are pursued—the era of revolutions and
projects—of vast performances, and infinite expectations.

Poetry, of course, reflects and partakes in this great transforma-
tion. It becomes more enthusiastic, authoritative and impassioned;
and feeling the necessity of dealing in more powerful emotions than
suited the tranquil and frivolous age which preceded, naturally goes
back to those themes and characters which animated the energetic
lays of its first rude inventors. The feats of chivalry, and the loves of
romance, are revived with more than their primitive wildness and
ardour. For the sake of the natural feeling they contain, the
incidents and diction of the old vulgar ballads are once more
imitated and surpassed; and poetry does not disdain, in pursuit of
her new idol of strong emotion, to descend to the very lowest
conditions of society, and to stir up the most revolting dregs of utter
wretchedness and depravity.

This is the age to which we are now arrived:—and if we have
rightly seized the principle by which we think its peculiarities are to
be accounted for, it will not be difficult to show, that the poet who
has devoted himself most exclusively, and most successfully, to the
delineation of the stronger and deeper passions, is likely to be its
reigning favourite. Neither do we think that we can have essentially
mistaken that principle:—at least it is a fact, independent of all
theory, not only that all the successful poets of the last twenty years
have dealt much more in powerful sensations, than those of the

century that went before; but that, in order to attain this object, they have employed themselves upon subjects which would have been rejected as vulgar and offensive by the fastidious delicacy of that age of fine writing. Instead of ingenious essays, elegant pieces of gallantry, and witty satires all stuck over with classical allusions, we have, in our popular poetry, the dreams of convicts, and the agonies of Gypsey women,—and the exploits of buccaneers, freebooters, and savages—and pictures to shudder at, of remorse, revenge, and insanity—and the triumph of generous feelings in scenes of anguish and terror—and the heroism of low-born affection and the tragedies of vulgar atrocity. All these various subjects have been found interesting, and have succeeded, in different degrees, in spite of accompaniments which would have disgusted an age more recently escaped from barbarity: And as they agree in nothing but in being the vehicles of strong and natural emotions, and have generally pleased, nearly in proportion to the quantity of that emotion they conveyed, it is difficult not to conclude, that they have pleased only for the sake of that quality—a growing appetite for which may be regarded as the true characteristic of this age of the world.

In selecting subjects and characters for this purpose, it was not only natural, but in a great measure necessary, to go back to the only ages when strong passions were indulged, or at least displayed without controul, by persons in the better ranks of society; in the same way as, in order to get perfect models of muscular force and beauty, we still find that we must go back to the works of those days when men went almost naked, and were raised to the rank of heroes for feats of bodily strength and activity. The savages and barbarians that are still to be found in the world, are, no doubt, very exact likenesses of those whom civilization has driven out of it; and they may be used accordingly for most of the purposes for which their antient prototypes are found serviceable. In poetry, however, it happens again, as in sculpture, that it is safer, at least for a moderate genius, rather to work upon the relics we have of antiquity, than upon what is most nearly akin to it among our own contemporaries; both because there is a certain charm and fascination in what is antient and long remembered, and because those particular modifications of energetic forms and characters, which have already been made the subject of successful art, can be more securely and confidently managed in imitation, than the undefined vastness of a natural condition, however analogous to that from which they were selected.—Mr Southey, accordingly, who has gone in search of strong passions among the savages of America, and the gods and enchanters of India, has had far less success than Mr Scott, who has borrowed his energies from the more familiar scenes of European chivalry, and built his fairy castles with materials already tried and consecrated in the fabric of our old romances. The noble author before us has been obliged, like them, to go out of his own age and country in quest of the same indispensable ingredients; and his lot has fallen among the Turks and Arabs of the Mediterranean;—ruffians and desperadoes, certainly not much more amiable in themselves than the worst subjects of the others,—but capable of great redemption in the hands of a poet of genius, by being placed within the enchanted circle of antient Greece, and preserving among them so many vestiges of Roman pride and magnificence. There is still one general remark, however, to be made, before coming immediately to the merit of the pieces before us.

Although the necessity of finding beings capable of strong passions, thus occasions the revival, in a late stage of civilization, of the characters and adventures which animated the poetry of rude ages, it must not be thought that they are made to act and feel, on this resurrection, exactly as they did in their first natural presentation. They were then produced, not as exotics or creatures of the imagination, but merely as better specimens of the ordinary nature with which their authors were familiar; and the astonishing situations and appalling exploits in which they were engaged, were but a selection from the actual occurrences of the times. Neither the heroes themselves, nor their first celebrators, would have perceived any sublimity in the character itself or the tone of feeling, which such scenes and such exploits indicate to the more reflecting readers of a distant generation; and would still less have thought of analyzing the working of those emotions, or moralizing on the incidents to which they gave birth. In this primitive poetry, accordingly, we have rather the result than the delineation of strong passions—the events which they produce, rather than the energy that produces them. The character of the agent is unavoidably disclosed indeed in short and impressive glimpses—but it is never made the direct subject of exhibition; and the attention of the reader is always directed to what he does—not to what he feels. A more refined, reflecting, and sensitive generation, indeed, in reading these very legends, supposes what *must* have been felt, both before and after the actions that are so minutely recorded; and thus lends to them, from the stores of its own sensibility, a dignity and an interest which they did not possess in the minds of their own rude composers. When the same scenes and characters, however, are ultimately called back to feed the craving of a race disgusted with heartless occupations, for natural passions and overpowering emotions, it would go near to defeat the very object of their revival, if these passions were still left to indicate themselves only by the giant vestiges of outrageous deeds, or acts of daring and desperation. The passion itself must now be pourtrayed—and all its fearful workings displayed in detail before us. The minds of the great agents must be unmasked for us—and all the anatomy of their throbbing bosoms laid open to our gaze. We must be made to understand what they feel and enjoy and endure;—and all the course and progress of their *possession*, and the crossing and mingling of their opposite affections, must be rendered sensible to our touch; till, without regard to their external circumstances, we can enter into all the motions of their hearts, and read, and shudder as we read, the secret characters which stamp the capacity of unlimited suffering on a nature which we feel to be our own.

It is chiefly by these portraitures of the interior of human nature that the poetry of the present day is distinguished from all that preceded it and the difference is perhaps most conspicuous when the persons and subjects are borrowed from the poetry of an earlier age. Not only is all this anatomy of the feelings superadded to the primitive legend of exploits, but in many cases feelings are imputed to the agents, of which persons in their condition were certainly incapable, and which no description could have made intelligible to their contemporaries—while, in others, the want of feeling, probably a little exaggerated beyond nature also, is dwelt upon, and made to produce great effect as a trait of singular atrocity, though far too familiar to have excited any sensation either in the readers or spectators of the times to which the adventures naturally belong. Our modern poets, in short, have borrowed little more than the situations and unrestrained passions of the state of society from which they have taken their characters—and have added all the sensibility and delicacy from the stores of their own experience. They have lent their knights and squires of the fifteenth century the deep reflection and considerate delicacy of the nineteenth,—and combined the desperate and reckless valour of a Buccaneer or Corsair of any age, with the refined gallantry and sentimental generosity of an English gentleman of the present day. The combination we believe to be radically incongruous; but it was almost indispensable to the poetical effect that was in contemplation. The point was, to unite all the fine and strong feelings to which cultivation and reflection alone can give birth, with those manners and that condition of society, in which passions are uncontrouled, and their natural indications manifested without reserve. It was necessary, therefore, to unite two things that never did exist together in any period of society; and the union, though it may startle sober thinkers a little, is perhaps within the legitimate prerogatives of poetry. The most outrageous, and the least successful attempt of

this sort we remember, is that of Mr Southey, who represents a
wild Welch chieftain, who goes a buccaneering to America in the
twelfth century, with all the softness, decorum, and pretty behaviour
of Sir Charles Grandison. But the incongruity itself is universal—
from Campbell, who invests a Pensylvanian farmer with the wisdom
and mildness of Socrates, and the dignified manners of an old Croix
de St Louis—to Scott, who makes an old, bloody-minded and
mercenary ruffian talk like a sentimental hero and poet, in his latter
days—or the author before us, who has adorned a mercilesss corsair
on a rock in the Mediterranean, with every virtue under heaven—
except common honesty.

Of that noble author, and the peculiarity of his manner, we have
not much more to say, before proceeding to give an account of the
pieces now before us. His object obviously is, to produce a great
effect, partly by the novelty of his situations, but chiefly by the force
and energy of his sentiments and expressions; and the themes which
he has selected, though perhaps too much resembling each other,
are unquestionably well adapted for this purpose. There is something grand and imposing in the unbroken stateliness, courage, and
heroic bigotry of a Turk of the higher order; and a certain voluptuous and barbaric pomp about his establishment, that addresses
itself very forcibly to the imagination. His climate too, and most of
its productions, are magnificent—and glow with a raised and exotic
splendour; but the ruins of Grecian art, and of Grecian liberty and
glory with which he is surrounded, form by far the finest of his
accompaniments. There is nothing, we admit, half so trite in poetry
as commonplaces of classical enthusiasm; but it is for this very
reason that we admire the force of genius by which Lord Byron has
contrived to be original, natural, and pathetic, upon a subject so un-
promising, and apparently so long exhausted. How he has managed
it, we do not yet exactly understand; though it is partly, we have no
doubt, by placing us in the midst of the scene as it actually exists, and
superadding the charm of enchanting landscape to that of interesting
recollections. Lord Byron, we think, is the only modern poet who
has set before our eyes a visible picture of the present aspect of
scenes so famous in story; and, instead of feeding us with the
unsubstantial food of historical associations, has spread around us
the blue waters and dazzling skies—the ruined temples and dusky
olives—the desolate cities, and turbaned population, of modern
Attica. We scarcely knew before that Greece was still a beautiful
country.

He has also made a fine use of the gentleness and submission of
the females of these regions, as contrasted with the lordly pride and
martial ferocity of the men: and though we suspect he has lent them

more *soul* than of right belongs to them, as well as more delicacy and reflection; yet there is something so true to female nature in general, in his representations of this sort, and so much of the Oriental softness and acquiescence in his particular delineations, that it is scarcely possible to refuse the picture the praise of being characteristic and harmonious, as well as eminently sweet and beautiful in itself.

The other merits of his composition are such as his previous publications had already made familiar to the public,—an unparalleled rapidity of narrative, and condensation of thoughts and images—a style always vigorous and original, though sometimes quaint and affected, and more frequently strained, harsh, and abrupt—a diction and versification invariably spirited, and almost always harmonious and emphatic: Nothing diluted in short, or diffused into weakness, but full of life, and nerve, and activity—expanding only in the eloquent expression of strong and favourite affections, and everywhere else concise, energetic, and impetuous—hurrying on with a disdain of little ornaments and accuracies, and not always very solicitous about being comprehended by readers of inferior capacity.

The more considerable of the two poems now before us, entitled 'The Corsair,' exhibits all those qualities, perhaps, in a more striking light than any of the author's other publications. It is written in the regular heroic couplet, with a spirit, freedom, and variety of tone, of which, notwithstanding the example of Dryden, we scarcely believed that measure susceptible. In all the descriptive and serious pieces of Dryden, and in all his writings, indeed, except his Political Satires and his immortal Ode, there are innumerable flat, dull, and prosaic passages;—lines without force, spirit, or energy, and in fact without any other merit than that of accurate versification, and easy and natural diction. Nothing can be more exquisite than the couplets of Pope, for the expression of pointed remark, wit, sarcasm, or epigram; but there is nothing in Pope of impetuous passion or enthusiastic vehemence; and his acknowledged mastery in the species of versification, had almost brought it to be considered as appropriate to such subjects,—when Goldsmith, and after him Rogers and Campbell, came to show that it was also capable of strains of the deepest tenderness and sweetest simplicity. Still, however, all these were compositions of a measured and uniform structure—and it was yet to be proved that this, the most ponderous and stately verse in our language, could be accommodated to the variations of a tale of passion and of pity, and to all the breaks, starts and transitions of an adventurous and dramatic narration. This experiment Lord Byron has made, with equal boldness and success—and has satisfied us, at least, that the oldest and most respectable measure that is known among us, is at least as flexible as any other—and capable, in the hands of a master, of vibrations as strong and rapid as those of a lighter structure. We shall not be positive that the charm may not be partly at least in the subject— but we certainly never read so many ten-syllabled couplets together before, with so little feeling of heaviness or monotony.

11. Byron's *Childe Harold's Pilgrimage,* canto 3, and *The Prisoner of Chillon, and other Poems*

Edinburgh Review, 27, December 1816; *Contributions,* 3

This is the fourth of Jeffrey's eight articles on Byron. He ranks this evidently fascinating poet highly amongst the moderns, though he regrets that he falls into the Lakist error of egocentricity. As with Scott, Byron's popularity with the reading public shows his merit. On the other hand, in Jeffrey's view Byron at present lacks the pre-eminent quality of genius, that is, moral health.

If the finest poetry be that which leaves the deepest impression on the minds of its readers—and this is not the worst test of its excellence—Lord Byron, we think, must be allowed to take precedence of all his distinguished contemporaries. He has not the variety of Scott—nor the delicacy of Campbell—nor the absolute truth of Crabbe—nor the polished sparkling of Moore; but in force of diction, and inextinguishable energy of sentiment, he clearly surpasses them all. 'Words that breathe, and thoughts that burn,' are not merely the ornaments, but the common staple of his poetry; and he is not inspired or impressive only in some happy passages, but through the whole body and tissue of his composition. It was an unavoidable condition, perhaps, of this higher excellence, that his scene should be narrow, and his persons few. To compass such ends as he had in view, it was necessary to reject all ordinary agents, and all trivial combinations. He could not possibly be amusing, or ingenious, or playful; or hope to maintain the requisite pitch of interest by the recitation of sprightly adventures, or the opposition of common characters. To produce great effects, in short, he felt that it was necessary to deal only with the greater passions—with the exaltations of a daring fancy, and the errors of a lofty intellect— with the pride, the terrors, and the agonies of strong emotion—the fire and air alone of our human elements.

In this respect, and in his general notion of the end and the means of poetry, we have sometimes thought that his views fell more in with those of the Lake poets, than of any other existing party in the poetical commonwealth: And, in some of his later productions especially, it is impossible not to be struck with his occasional approaches to the style and manner of this class of writers. Lord Byron, however, it should be observed, like all other persons of a quick sense of beauty, and sure enough of their own originality to be in no fear of paltry imputations, is a great mimic of styles and manners, and a great borrower of external character. He and Scott, accordingly, are full of imitations of all the writers from whom they have ever derived gratification; and the two most original writers of the age might appear, to superficial observers, to be the most deeply indebted to their predecessors. In this particular instance, we have no fault to find with Lord Byron: For undoubtedly the finer passages of Wordsworth and Southey have in them wherewithal to lend an impulse to the utmost ambition of rival genius; and their diction and manner of writing is frequently both striking and original. But we must say, that it would afford us still greater pleasure to find these tuneful gentlemen returning the compliment which Lord Byron has here paid to their talents; and forming themselves on the model rather of his imitations, than of their own originals. In those imitations they will find that, though he is sometimes abundantly mystical, he never, or at least very rarely, indulges in absolute nonsense—never takes his lofty flights upon mean or ridiculous occasions—and, above all, never dilutes his strong conceptions, and magnificent imaginations, with a flood of oppressive verbosity. On the contrary, he is, of all living writers, the most concise and condensed; and, we would fain hope, may go far, by his example, to redeem the great reproach of our modern literature—its intolerable prolixity and redundance. In his nervous and manly lines, we find no elaborate amplification of common sentiments—no ostentatious polishing of pretty expressions; and we really think that the brilliant success which has rewarded his disdain of those paltry artifices, should put to shame for ever that puling and self-admiring race, who can live through half a volume on the stock of a single thought, and expatiate over diverse fair quarto pages with the details of one tedious description. In Lord Byron, on the contrary, we have a perpetual stream of thick-coming fancies—an eternal spring of fresh-blown images, which seem called into existence by the sudden flash of those glowing thoughts and overwhelming emotions, that struggle for expression through the whole flow of his poetry—and impart to a diction that is often abrupt and irregular, a force and a charm which frequently realise all that is said of inspiration.

With all these undoubted claims to our admiration, however, it is impossible to deny that the noble author before us has still something to learn, and a good deal to correct. He is frequently abrupt and careless, and sometimes obscure. There are marks, occasionally, of effort and straining after an emphasis, which is generally spontaneous; and, above all, there is far too great a monotony in the moral colouring of his pictures, and too much repetition of the same sentiments and maxims. He delights too exclusively in the delineation of a certain morbid exaltation of character and of feeling—a sort of demoniacal sublimity, not without some traits of the ruined Archangel. He is haunted almost perpetually with the image of a being feeding and fed upon by violent passions, and the recollections of the catastrophes they have occasioned: And, though worn out by their past indulgence, unable to sustain the burden of an existence which they do not continue to animate:—full of pride, and revenge, and obduracy—disdaining life and death, and mankind and himself—and trampling, in his scorn, not only upon the falsehood and formality of polished life, but upon its tame virtues and slavish devotion: Yet envying, by fits, the very beings he despises, and melting into mere softness and compassion, when the helplessness of childhood or the frailty of woman make an appeal to his generosity. Such is the person with whom we are called upon almost exclusively to sympathise in all the greater productions of this distinguished writer:—In Childe Harold—in the Corsair—in Lara—in the Siege of Corinth—in Parisina, and in most of the smaller pieces.

It is impossible to represent such a character better than Lord Byron has done in all these productions—or indeed to represent any thing more terrible in its anger, or more attractive in its relenting. In point of effect, we readily admit, that no one character can be more poetical or impressive:—But it is really too much to find the scene perpetually filled by one character—not only in all the acts of each several drama, but in all the different dramas of the series;—and, grand and impressive as it is, we feel at last that these very qualities make some relief more indispensable, and oppress the spirits of ordinary mortals with too deep an impression of awe and repulsion. There is too much guilt, in short, and too much gloom, in the leading character;—and though it be a fine thing to gaze, now and then, on stormy seas, and thunder-shaken mountains, we should prefer passing our days in sheltered valleys, and by the murmur of calmer waters.

We are aware that these metaphors may be turned against us—and that, without metaphor, it may be said that men do not *pass their days* in reading poetry—and that, as they may look into Lord Bryon only about as often as they look abroad upon tempests, they have no more reason to complain of him for being grand and gloomy, than to complain of the same qualities in the glaciers and volcanoes which they go so far to visit. Painters, too, it may be said, have often gained great reputation by their representations of tigers and other ferocious animals, or of caverns and banditti—and poets should be allowed, without reproach, to indulge in analogous exercises. We are far from thinking that there is no weight in these considerations; and feel how plausibly it may be said, that we have no better reason for a great part of our complaint, than that an author, to whom we are already very greatly indebted, has chosen rather to please himself, than us, in the use he makes of his talents.

This, no doubt, seems both unreasonable and ungrateful: But it is nevertheless true, that a public benefactor becomes a debtor to the public; and is, in some degree, responsible for the employment of those gifts which seem to be conferred upon him, not merely for his own delight, but for the delight and improvement of his fellows through all generations. Independent of this, however, we think there is a reply to the apology. A great living poet is not like a distant volcano, or an occasional tempest. He is a volcano in the heart of our land, and a cloud that hangs over our dwellings; and we have some reason to complain, if, instead of genial warmth and grateful shade, he voluntarily darkens and inflames our atmosphere with perpetual fiery explosions and pitchy vapours. Lord Byron's poetry, in short, is too attractive and too famous to lie dormant or inoperative; and, therefore, if it produce any painful or pernicious effects, there will be murmurs, and ought to be suggestions of alteration. Now, though an artist may draw fighting tigers and hungry lions in as lively and natural a way as he can, without giving any encouragement to human ferocity, or even much alarm to human fear, the case is somewhat different, when a poet represents men with tiger-like dispositions:—and yet more so, when he exhausts the resources of his genius to make this terrible being interesting and attractive, and to represent all the lofty virtues as the natural allies of his ferocity. It is still worse when he proceeds to show, that all these precious gifts of dauntless courage, strong affection, and high imagination, are not only akin to guilt, but the parents of misery;—and that those only have any chance of tranquillity or happiness in this world, whom it is the object of his poetry to make us shun and despise.

These, it appears to us, are not merely errors in taste, but perversions of morality; and, as a great poet is necessarily a moral teacher, and gives forth his ethical lessons, in general with far more effect and authority than any of his graver brethren, he is peculiarly liable to the censures reserved for those who turn the means of improvement to purposes of corruption.

It may no doubt be said, that poetry in general tends less to the useful than the splendid qualities of our nature—that a character poetically good has long been distinguished from one that is morally so—and that, ever since the time of Achilles, our sympathies, on such occasions, have been chiefly engrossed by persons whose deportment is by no means exemplary; and who in many points approach to the temperament of Lord Byron's ideal hero. There is some truth in this suggestion also. But other poets, in the *first* place, do not allow their favourites so outrageous a monopoly of the glory and interest of the piece—and sin less therefore against the laws either of poetical or distributive justice. In the *second* place, their heroes are not, generally, either so bad or so good as Lord Byron's—and do not indeed very much exceed the standard of truth and nature, in either of the extremes. His, however, are as monstrous and unnatural as centaurs, and hippogriffs—and must ever figure in the eye of sober reason as so many bright and hateful impossibilities. But the most important distinction is, that the other poets who deal in peccant heroes, neither feel nor express that ardent affection for them, which is visible in the whole of this author's delineations; but merely make use of them as necessary agents in the extraordinary adventures they have to detail, and persons whose mingled vices and virtues are requisite to bring about the catastrophe of their story. In Lord Byron, however, the interest of the story, where there happens to be one, which is not always the case, is uniformly postponed to that of the character itself—into which he enters so deeply, and with so extraordinary a fondness, that he generally continues to speak in its language, after it has been dismissed from the stage; and to inculcate, on his own authority, the same sentiments which had been previously recommended by its example. We do not consider it as unfair, therefore, to say that Lord Byron appears to us to be the zealous apostle of a certain fierce and magnificent misanthropy; which has already saddened his poetry with too deep a shade, and not only led to a great misapplication of great talents, but contributed to render popular some very false estimates of the constituents of human happiness and merit.

[After many pages of examination of particular texts, Jeffrey concludes:]

Beautiful as this poetry is, it is a relief at last to close the volume. We cannot maintain our accustomed tone of levity, or even speak like calm literary judges, in the midst of these agonizing traces of a wounded and distempered spirit. Even our admiration is at last swallowed up in a most painful feeling of pity and of wonder. It is impossible to mistake these for fictitious sorrows, conjured up for the purpose of poetical effect. There is a dreadful tone of sincerity, and an energy that cannot be counterfeited, in the expression of wretchedness and alienation from human kind, which occurs in every page of this publication; and as the author has at last spoken out in his own person, and unbosomed his griefs a great deal too freely to his readers, the offence now would be to entertain a doubt of their reality. We certainly have no hope of preaching him into philanthropy and cheerfulness; but it is impossible not to mourn over such a catastrophe of such a mind; or to see the prodigal gifts of Nature, Fortune, and Fame, thus turned to bitterness, without an oppressive feeling of impatience, mortification and surprise. Where there are such elements, however, it is equally impossible to despair that they may yet enter into happier combinations,—or not to hope that 'this puissant spirit'

> yet shall reascend
> Self-rais'd, and repossess its native seat.

12. Keats's *Endymion* and *Lamia* volume

Edinburgh Review, 34, August 1820; *Contributions*, 3

In comparison with Jeffrey's treatment of another great poet, Wordsworth, his view of Keats is remarkably sympathetic. His article followed the attack of Croker in the *Quarterly Review*, but it appeared too late to be appreciated by the poet himself. It is noteworthy that Monckton Milnes's life of Keats (1848) was dedicated to Jeffrey.

We had never happened to see either of these volumes till very lately—and have been exceedingly struck with the genius they display, and the spirit of poetry which breathes through all their extravagance. That imitation of our older writers, and especially of our older dramatists, to which we cannot help flattering ourselves that we have somewhat contributed, has brought on, as it were, a second spring in our poetry;—and few of its blossoms are either more profuse of sweetness, or richer in promise, that this which is now before us. Mr. Keats, we understand, is still a very young man; and his whole works, indeed, bear evidence enough of the fact. They are full of extravagance and irregularity, rash attempts at originality, interminable wanderings, and excessive obscurity. They manifestly require, therefore, all the indulgence that can be claimed for a first attempt:—But we think it no less plain that they deserve it: For they are flushed all over with the rich lights of fancy; and so coloured and bestrewn with the flowers of poetry, that even while perplexed and bewildered in their labyrinths, it is impossible to resist the intoxication of their sweetness, or to shut our hearts to the enchantments they so lavishly present. The models upon which he has formed himself, in the Endymion, the earliest and by much the most considerable of his poems, are obviously The Faithful Shepherdess of Fletcher, and The Sad Shepherd of Ben Jonson;— the exquisite metres and inspired diction of which he has copied with great boldness and fidelity—and, like his great originals, has also contrived to impart to the whole piece that true rural and poetical air—which breathes only in them, and in Theocritus— which is at once homely and majestic, luxurious and rude, and sets before us the genuine sights and sounds and smells of the country, with all the magic and grace of Elysium. His subject has the disadvantage of being Mythological; and in this respect, as well as on account of the raised and rapturous tone it consequently assumes, his poem, it may be thought, would be better compared to the Comus and the Arcades of Milton, of which, also, there are many traces of imitation. The great distinction, however, between him and these divine authors, is, that imagination in them is subordinate to reason and judgment, while, with him, it is para- mount and supreme—that their ornaments and images are em- ployed to embellish and recommend just sentiments, engaging inci- dents, and natural characters, while his are poured out without measure or restraint, and with no apparent design but to unburden the breast of the author, and give vent to the overflowing vein of his fancy. The thin and scanty tissue of his story is merely the light framework on which his florid wreaths are suspended; and while his imaginations go rambling and entangling themselves every where, like wild honeysuckles, all idea of sober reason, and plan, and consistency, is utterly forgotten, and 'strangled in their waste fertil- ity.' A great part of the work, indeed, is written in the strangest and most fantastical manner than can be imagined. It seems as if the author had ventured every thing that occurred to him in the shape of a glittering image or striking expression—taken the first word that presented itself to make up a rhyme, and then made that word the germ of a new cluster of images—a hint for a new excursion of the fancy—and so wandered on, equally forgetful whence he came, and heedless whither he was going, till he had covered his pages with an interminable arabesque of connected and incongruous figures, that multiplied as they extended, and were only harmonised by the brightness of their tints, and the graces of their forms. In this rash and headlong career he has of course many lapses and failures. There is no work, accordingly, from which a malicious critic could cull more matter for ridicule, or select more obscure, unnatural, or absurd passages. But we do not take *that* to be our office;—and must beg leave, on the contrary, to say, that any one who, on this account, would represent the whole poem as despicable, must either have no notion of poetry, or no regard to truth.

It is, in truth, at least as full of genius as of absurdity; and he who does not find a great deal in it to admire and to give delight, cannot in his heart see much beauty in the two exquisite dramas to which we have already alluded; or find any great pleasure in some of the finest creations of Milton and Shakespeare. There are very many such persons, we verily believe, even among the reading and judicious part of the community—correct scholars, we have no doubt, many of them, and, it may be, very classical composers in prose and in verse—but utterly ignorant, on our view of the matter, of the true genius of English poetry, and incapable of estimating its appropriate and most exquisite beauties. With that spirit we have no hesitation in saying that Mr. Keats is deeply imbued—and of those beauties he has presented us with many striking examples. We are very much inclined indeed to add, that we do not know any book which we would sooner employ as a test to ascertain whether any one had in him a native relish for poetry, and a genuine sensibility to its intrinsic charm. The greater and more distinguished poets of our country have so much else in them, to gratify other tastes and propensities, that they are pretty sure to captivate and amuse those to whom their poetry may be but an hindrance and obstruction, as well as those to whom it constitutes their chief attraction. The interest of the stories they tell—the vivacity of the characters they delineate—the weight and force of the maxims and sentiments in which they abound—the very pathos, and wit and humour they display, which may all and each of them exist apart from their poetry, and independent of it, are quite sufficient to account for their popularity, without referring much to that still higher gift, by which they subdue to their enchantments those whose souls are truly attuned to the finer impulses of poetry. It is only, therefore, where those other recommendations are wanting, or exist in a weaker degree, that the true force of the attraction, exercised by the pure poetry with which they are so often combined, can be fairly appreciated:—where, without much incident or many characters, and with little wit, wisdom, or arrangement, a number of bright pictures are presented to the imagination, and a fine feeling expressed of those mysterious relations by which visible external things are assimilated with inward thoughts and emotions, and become the images and exponents of all passions and affections. To an unpoetical reader such passages will generally appear mere raving and absurdity—and to this censure a very great part of the volumes before us will certainly be exposed, with this class of readers. Even in the judgment of a fitter audience, however, it must we fear, be admitted, that, besides the riot and extravagance of his fancy, the scope and substance of Mr. Keats's poetry is rather too dreamy and abstracted to excite the strongest interest, or to sustain the attention through a work of any great compass or extent. He deals too much with shadowy and incomprehensible beings, and is too constantly rapt into an extramundane Elysium, to command a lasting interest with ordinary mortals—and must employ the agency of more varied and coarser emotions, if he wishes to take rank with the enduring poets of this or of former generations. There is something very curious, too, we think, in the way in which he, and Mr. Barry Cornwall also, have dealt with the Pagan mythology, of which they have made so much use in their poetry. Instead of presenting its imaginary persons under the trite and vulgar traits that belong to them in the ordinary systems, little more is borrowed from these than the general conception of their condition and relations; and an original character and distinct individuality is then bestowed upon them, which has all the merit of invention, and all the grace and attraction of the fictions on which it is engrafted. The ancients, though they probably did not stand in any great awe of their deities, have yet abstained very much from any minute or dramatic representation of their feelings and affections. In Hesiod and Homer, they are broadly delineated by some of their actions and adventures, and introduced to us merely as the agents in those particular transactions; while in the Hymns, from those ascribed to Orpheus and Homer, down to those of Callimachus, we have little but pompous epithets and invocations, with a flattering commemoration of their most famous exploits—and are never allowed to enter into their bosoms, or follow out the train of their feelings, with the presumption of our human sympathy. Except the love-song of the Cyclops to his Sea Nymph in Theocritus—the Lamentation of Venus for Adonis in Moschus—and the more recent Legend of Apuleius, we scarcely recollect a passage in all the writings of antiquity in which the passions of an immortal are fairly disclosed to the scrutiny and observation of men. The author before us, however, and some of his contemporaries, have dealt differently with the subject;—and, sheltering the violence of the fiction under the ancient traditionary fable, have in reality created and imagined an entire new set of characters; and brought closely and minutely before us the loves and sorrows and perplexities of beings, with whose names and supernatural attributes we had long been familiar, without any sense or feeling of their personal charac-ter. We have more than doubts of the fitness of such personages to maintain a permanent interest with the modern public;—but the way in which they are here managed certainly gives them the best chance that now remains for them; and, at all events, it cannot be denied that the effect is striking and graceful.

13. The state of modern poetry, introducing a review of Atherstone's *Fall of Nineveh*.

Edinburgh Review, 48, September 1828

We have been rather in an odd state for some years, we think, both as to Poets and Poetry. Since the death of Lord Byron there has been no king in Israel; and none of his former competitors now seem inclined to push their pretensions to the vacant throne. Scott, and Moore, and Southey, appear to have nearly renounced verse, and finally taken service with the Muses of prose:—Crabbe, and Coleridge, and Wordsworth, we fear, are burnt out:—and Campbell and Rogers repose under their laurels, and, contented each with his own elegant little domain, seem but little disposed either to extend its boundaries, or to add new provinces to their rule. Yet we cannot say either that this indifference may be accounted for by the impoverished state of the kingdom whose sovereignty is thus in abeyance, or that the *interregnum* has as yet given rise to any notable disorders. On the contrary, we do not remember a time when it would have been a prouder distinction to be at the head of English poetry, or when the power which every man has to do what is good in his own eyes, seemed less in danger of being abused. Three poets of great promise have indeed been lost, 'in the morn and liquid dew of their youth'—in Kirke White, in Keats, and in Pollok; and a powerful, though more uncertain genius extinguished, less prematurely, in Shelley. Yet there still survive writers of great talents and attraction. The elegance, the tenderness, the feminine sweetness of Felicia Hemans—the classical copiousness of Milman— the facility and graceful fancy of Hunt, though defrauded of half its praise by carelessness and presumption and, besides many others, the glowing pencil and gorgeous profusion of the author more immediately before us.

There is no want, then, of poetry among us at the present day; nor even of very good and agreeable poetry. But there are no miracles of the art—nothing that marks its descent from 'the highest heaven of invention'—nothing visibly destined to inherit immortality. Speaking very generally, we would say, that our poets never showed a better or less narrow taste, or a juster relish of what is truly excellent in the models that lie before them, and yet have seldom been more deficient in the powers of creative genius; or rather, perhaps, that with an unexampled command over the raw materials of poetry, and a true sense of their value, they have rarely been so much wanting in the skill to work them up to advantage—in the power of attaching human interests to sparkling fancies, making splendid descriptions subservient to intelligible purposes, or fixing the fine and fugitive spirit of poetry in some tangible texture of exalted reason or sympathetic emotion. The improvement in all departments is no doubt immense, since the days when Hoole and Hayley were thought great poets. But it is not quite clear to us, that the fervid and florid Romeos of the present day, may not be gathered, in no very long course of years, to the capacious tomb of these same ancient Capulets. They are but shadows, we fear, that have no independent or substantial existence—and though reflected from grand and beautiful originals, have but little chance to maintain their place in the eyes of the many generations by whom those originals will yet be worshipped—but who will probably prefer, each in their turn, shadows of their own creating.

The present age, we think, has an hundred times more poetry, and more true taste for poetry, than that which immediately preceded it,—and of which, reckoning its duration from the extinction of the last of Queen Anne's wits down to about thirty odd years ago, we take leave to say that it was, beyond all dispute, the most unpoetical age in the annals of this or any other considerable nation. Nothing, indeed, can be conceived more dreary and sterile than the aspect of our national poetry from the time of Pope and Thomson, down to that of Burns and Cowper. With the exception of a few cold and scattered lights—Gray, Goldsmith, Warton, Mason, and Johnson—men of sense and eloquence occasionally exercising themselves in poetry out of scholar-like ambition, but not poets in any genuine sense of the word—the whole horizon was dark, silent, and blank; or only presented objects upon which it is now impossible to look seriously without shame. These were the happy days of Pye and Whitehead—of Hoole and of Hayley—and then, throughout the admiring land, resounded the mighty names of Jerningham and Jage, of Edwards, of Murphy, of Moore, and of others whom we cannot but feel it is a baseness to remember.

The first man who broke 'the numbing spell' was Cowper,—(for Burns was not generally known till long after,)—and, though less highly gifted than several who came after him, this great praise should always be remembered in his epitaph. He is entitled, in our estimation, to a still greater praise; and that is, to the praise of absolute and entire originality. Whatever he added to the resources of English poetry, was drawn directly from the fountains of his own genius, or the stores of his own observation. He was a copyist of no style—a restorer of no style; and did not, like the eminent men who succeeded him, merely recall the age to the treasures it had almost forgotten, open up anew a vein that had been long buried in rubbish, or revive a strain which had already delighted the ears of a more aspiring generation. That this, however, was the case with the poets who immediately followed, cannot, we think, be reasonably doubted; and the mere statement of the fact, seems to us sufficiently to explain the present state of our poetry—its strength and its weakness—its good taste and its deficient power—its resemblance to works that can never die—and its own obvious liability to the accidents of mortality.

It has advanced beyond the preceding age, simply by going back to one still older; and has put *its* poverty to shame only by unlocking the hoards of a remoter ancestor. It has reformed merely by restoring; and innovated by a systematic recurrence to the models of antiquity. Scott went back as far as to the Romances of Chivalry: and the poets of the lakes to the humbler and more pathetic simplicity of our early ballads; and both, and all who have since adventured in poetry, have drawn, without measure or disguise, from the living springs of Shakespeare and Spenser, and the other immortal writers who adorned the glorious era of Elizabeth and James.

It is impossible to value more highly than we do the benefits of this restoration. It is a great thing to have rendered the public once more familiar with these mighty geniuses—and, if we must be copyists, there is nothing certainly that deserves so well to be copied. The consequence, accordingly, has been, that, even in our least inspired writers, we can again reckon upon freedom and variety of style, some sparks of fancy, some traits of nature, and some echo, however feeble, of that sweet melody of rhythm and of diction, which must linger for ever in every ear which has once drank in the music of Shakespeare; while, in authors of greater vigour, we are sure to meet also with gorgeous descriptions and splendid imagery, tender sentiments expressed in simple words, and vehement passions pouring themselves out in fearless and eloquent declamation.

But with all this, it is but too true that we have still a feeling that we are glorying but in secondhand finery and counterfeit inspiration;

and that the poets of the present day, though they have not only Taste enough to admire, but skill also to imitate, the great masters of an earlier generation, have not inherited the Genius that could have enabled them either to have written as they wrote, or even to have come up, without their example, to the level of their own imitations. The heroes of our modern poetry, indeed, are little better, as we take it, than the heroes of the modern theatres—attired, no doubt, in the exact costume of the persons they represent, and wielding their gorgeous antique arms with an exact imitation of heroic movements and deportment—nay, even evincing in their tones and gestures, a full sense of inward nobleness and dignity—and yet palpably unfit to engage in any feat of actual prowess, and incapable, in their own persons, even of conceiving what they have been so well taught to personate. We feel, in short, that our modern poetry is substantially derivative, and, as geologists say of our present earth, of secondary formation—made up of the *debris* of a former world, and composed, in its loftiest and most solid parts, of the fragments of things far more lofty and solid.

The consequence, accordingly, is, that we have abundance of admirable descriptions, ingenious similitudes, and elaborate imitations—but little invention, little direct or overwhelming passion, and little natural simplicity. On the contrary, every thing almost now resolves into description,—descriptions not only of actions and external objects, but of characters, and emotions, and the signs and accompaniments of emotion—and all given at full length, ostentatious, elaborate, and highly finished, even in their counterfeit carelessness and disorder. But no sudden unconscious bursts, either of nature or of passion—no casual flashes of fancy, no slight passing intimations of deep but latent emotions, no rash darings of untutored genius, soaring proudly up into the infinite unknown! The chief fault, however, is the want of subject and of matter—the absence of real persons, intelligible interests, and conceivable incidents, to which all this splendid apparatus of rhetoric and fancy may attach itself, and thus get a purpose and a meaning, which it never can possess without them. To satisfy a rational being, even in his most sensitive mood, we require not only a just representation of passion in the abstract, but also that it shall be embodied in some individual person whom we can understand and sympathize with—and cannot long be persuaded to admire splendid images and ingenious allusions which bear upon no comprehensible object, and seem to be introduced for no other purpose than to be admired.

Without going the full length of the mathematician, who could see no beauty in poetry because it *proved* nothing, we cannot think it quite unreasonable to insist on knowing a little what it is about; and must be permitted to hold it a good objection to the very finest composition, that it gives us no distinct conceptions, either of character, of action, of passion, or of the author's design in laying it before us. Now this, we think, is undeniably the prevailing fault of our modern poets. What they do best is description—in a story certainly they do not excel—their pathos is too often overstrained and rhetorical, and their reflections mystical and bombastic. The great want, however, as we have already said, is the want of solid subject, and of persons who can be supposed to have existed. There is plenty of splendid drapery and magnificent localities—but nobody to put on the one, or to inhabit and vivify the other. Instead of living persons, we have commonly little else than mere puppets or academy figures—and very frequently are obliged to be contented with scenes of still life altogether—with gorgeous dresses tossed into glittering heaps, or suspended in dazzling files—and enchanted solitudes, where we wait in vain for some beings like ourselves, to animate its beauties with their loves, or to aggravate its horrors by their contentions.

The consequence of all this is, that modern poems, with great beauty of diction, much excellent description, and very considerable displays of taste and imagination, are generally languid, obscure, and tiresome. Short pieces, however, it should be admitted, are frequently very delightful—elegant in composition, sweet and touching in sentiment, and just and felicitous in expressing the most delicate shades both of character and emotion. Where a single scene, thought, or person, is to be represented, the improved taste of the age, and its general familiarity with beautiful poetry, will generally ensure, from our better artists, not only a creditable, but a very excellent production. What used to be true of *female* poets only, is now true of all. We have not wings, it would seem, for a long flight—and the larger works of those who pleased us most with their small ones, scarcely ever fail of exhibiting the very defects from which we should have thought them most secure—and turn out insipid, verbose, and artificial, like their neighbours. In little poems, in short, which do not require any choice or management of subject, we succeed very well; but where a story is to be told, and an interest to be sustained, through a considerable train of incidents and variety of characters, our want of vigour and originality is but too apt to become apparent; and is only the more conspicuous from our skilful and familiar use of that inspired diction, and those poetical materials which we have derived from the mighty masters to whose vigour and originality they were subservient, and on whose genius they waited but as 'servile ministers.'

14. Felicia Hemans's *Records of Woman* and
The Forest Sanctuary

Edinburgh Review, 50, October 1829; *Contributions*, 3

In his final literary review, Jeffrey declares with characteristic emphasis that the 'essence of poetry' is 'the fine perception and vivid expression of that subtle and vivid Analogy which exists between the physical and the moral world.' However, he also comments on the 'perishable nature of modern literary fame.' He himself now prefers the elegance without passion of the Whigs Rogers and Campbell and, with more than a touch of gallantry, this quality in Mrs. Hemans herself.

Women, we fear, cannot do every thing; nor even every thing they attempt. But what they can do, they do, for the most part, excellently—and much more frequently with an absolute and perfect success, than the aspirants of our rougher and more ambitious sex. They cannot, we think, represent naturally the fierce and sullen passions of men—nor their coarser vices—nor even scenes of actual business or contention—nor the mixed motives, and strong and faulty characters, by which affairs of moment are usually conducted on the great theatre of the world. For much of this they are disqualified by the delicacy of their training and habits, and the still more disabling delicacy which pervades their conceptions and feelings; and from much they are excluded by their necessary inexperience of the realities they might wish to describe—by their substantial and incurable ignorance of business—of the way in which serious affairs are actually managed—and the true nature of the agents and impulses that give movement and direction to the stronger currents of ordinary life. Perhaps they are also incapable of long moral or political investigations, where many complex and indeterminate elements are to be taken into account, and a variety of opposite probabilities to be weighed before coming to a conclusion. They are generally too impatient to get at the ultimate results, to go well through with such discussions; and either stop short at some imperfect view of the truth, or turn aside to repose in the shade of some plausible error. This, however, we are persuaded, arises entirely from their being seldom set on such tedious tasks. Their proper and natural business is the practical regulation of private life, in all its bearings, affections, and concerns; and the questions with which they have to deal in that most important department, though often of the utmost difficulty and nicety, involve, for the most part, but few elements; and may generally be better described as delicate than intricate;—requiring for their solution rather a quick tact and fine perception, than a patient or laborious examination. For the same reason, they rarely succeed in long works, even on subjects the best suited to their genius; their natural training rendering them equally averse to long doubt and long labour.

For all other intellectual efforts, however, either of the understanding or the fancy, and requiring a thorough knowledge either of man's strength or his weakness, we apprehend them to be, in all respects, as well qualified as their brethren of the stronger sex: While, in their perceptions of grace, propriety, ridicule—their power of detecting artifice, hypocrisy, and affectation—the force and promptitude of their sympathy, and their capacity of noble and devoted attachment, and of the efforts and sacrifices it may require, they are, beyond all doubt, our Superiors.

Their business being, as we have said, with actual or social life, and the colours it receives from the conduct and dispositions of individuals, they unconsciously acquire, at a very early age, the finest perception of character and manners, and are almost as soon instinctively schooled in the deep and more dangerous learning of feeling and emotion; while the very minuteness with which they make and meditate on these interesting observations, and the finer shades and variations of sentiment which are thus treasured and recorded, trains their whole faculties to a nicety and precision of operation, which often discloses itself to advantage in their application to studies of a different character. When women, accordingly, have turned their minds—as they have done but too seldom—to the exposition or arrangement of any branch of knowledge, they have commonly exhibited, we think, a more beautiful accuracy, and a more uniform and complete justness of thinking, than their less discriminating brethren. There is a finish and completeness, in short, about every thing they put out of their hands, which indicates not only an inherent taste for elegance and neatness, but a habit of nice observation, and singular exactness of judgment.

It has been so little the fashion, at any time, to encourage women to write for publication, that it is more difficult than it should be, to prove these truths by examples. Yet there are enough, within the reach of a very careless and superficial glance over the open field of literature, to enable us to explain, at least, and illustrate, if not entirely to verify, our assertions. No *Man,* we will venture to say, could have written the Letters of Madame de Sevigné, or the Novels of Miss Austin [*sic*], or the Hymns and Early Lessons of Mrs. Barbauld, or the Conversations of Mrs. Marcet. Those performances, too, are not only essentially and intensely feminine; but they are, in our judgment, decidedly more perfect than any masculine productions with which they can be brought into comparison. They accomplish more completely all the ends at which they aim; and are worked out with a gracefulness and felicity of execution which excludes all idea of failure, and entirely satisfies the expectations they may have raised. We might easily have added to these instances. There are many parts of Miss Edgeworth's earlier stories, and of Miss Mitford's sketches and descriptions, and not a little of Mrs. Opie's, that exhibit the same fine and penetrating spirit of observation, the same softness and delicacy of hand, and unerring truth of delineation, to which we have alluded as characterising the purer specimens of female art. The same distinguishing traits of woman's spirit are visible through the grief and piety of Lady Russel, and the gaiety, the spite, and the venturesomeness of Lady Mary Wortley. We have not as yet much female poetry; but there is a truly feminine tenderness, purity, and elegance, in the Psyche of Mrs. Tighe, and in some of the smaller pieces of Lady Craven. On some of the works of Madame de Staël—her Corinne especially—there is a still deeper stamp of the genius of her sex. Her pictures of its boundless devotedness—its depth and capacity of suffering—its high aspirations—its painful irritability, and inextinguishable thirst for emotion, are powerful specimens of that morbid anatomy of the heart, which no hand but that of a woman was fine enough to have laid open, or skilful enough to have recommended to our sympathy and love. There is the same exquisite and inimitable delicacy, if not the same power, in many of the happier passages of Madame de Souza and Madame Cottin—to say nothing of the more lively and yet melancholy records of Madame de Staël, during her long penance in the court of the Duchesse de Maine.

[Jeffrey now turns directly to the poetry of Mrs. Hemans, but he interjects the following general observations.]

It has always been our opinion, that the very essence of poetry—apart from the pathos, the wit, or the brilliant description which may be embodied in it, but may exist equally in prose—consists in the fine perception and vivid expression of that subtle and mysterious Analogy which exists between the physical and the moral world—which makes outward things and qualities the natural types and emblems of inward gifts and emotions, or leads us to ascribe life and sentiment to every thing that interests us in the aspects of external nature. The feeling of this analogy, obscure and inexplicable as the theory of it may be, is so deep and universal in our nature, that it has stamped itself on the ordinary language of men of every kindred and speech: and that to such an extent, that one half of the epithets by which we familiarly designate moral and physical qualities, are in reality so many metaphors, borrowed reciprocally, upon this analogy, from those opposite forms of existence. The very familiarity, however, of the expression, in these instances, takes away its poetical effect—and indeed, in substance, its metaphorical character. The original sense of the word is entirely forgotten in the derivative one to which it has succeeded; and it requires some etymological recollection to convince us that it was originally nothing else than a typical or analogical illustration. Thus we talk of a sparkling wit, and a furious blast—a weighty argument, and a gentle stream—without being at all aware that we are speaking in the language of poetry, and transferring qualities from one extremity of the sphere of being to another. In these cases, accordingly, the metaphor, by ceasing to be felt, in reality ceases to exist, and the analogy being no longer intimated, of course can produce no effect. But whenever it is intimated, it does produce an effect; and that effect we think is poetry.

It has substantially two functions, and operates in two directions. In the *first* place, when material qualities are ascribed to mind, it strikes vividly out, and brings at once before us the conception of an inward feeling or emotion, which it might otherwise have been difficult to convey, by the presentment of some bodily form or quality, which is instantly felt to be its true representative, and enables us to fix and comprehend it with a force and clearness not otherwise attainable; and, in the *second* place, it vivifies dead and inanimate matter with the attributes of living and sentient mind, and fills the whole visible universe around us with objects of interest and sympathy, by tinting them with the hues of life, and associating them with our own passions and affections. This magical operation the poet too performs, for the most part, in one of two ways—either by the direct agency of similes and metaphors, more or less condensed or developed, or by the mere graceful presentment of such visible objects on the scene of his passionate dialogues or adventures, as partake of the character of the emotion he wishes to excite, and thus form an appropriate accompaniment or preparation for its direct indulgence or display. The former of those methods has perhaps been most frequently employed, and certainly has most attracted attention. But the latter, though less obtrusive, and perhaps less frequently resorted to of set purpose, is, we are inclined to think, the most natural and efficacious of the two; and is often adopted, we believe unconsciously, by poets of the highest order;—the predominant emotion of their minds overflowing spontaneously on all the objects which present themselves to their fancy, and calling out from them, and colouring with their own hues, those that are naturally emblematic of its character, and in accordance with its general expression. It would be easy to show how habitually this is done, by Shakespeare and Milton especially, and how much many of their finest passages are indebted, both for force and richness of effect, to this general and diffusive harmony of the external character of their scenes with the passions of their living agents—this harmonising and appropriate glow with which they kindle the whole surrounding atmosphere, and bring all that strikes the sense into unison with all that touches the heart.

[Jeffrey concludes:]

We have seen too much of the perishable nature of modern literary fame, to venture to predict to Mrs. Hemans that hers will be immortal, or even of very long duration. Since the beginning of our critical career we have seen a vast deal of beautiful poetry pass into oblivion, in spite of our feeble efforts to recall or retain it in remembrance. The tuneful quartos of Southey are already little better than lumber:—and the rich melodies of Keats and Shelley,—and the fantastical emphasis of Wordsworth,—and the plebeian pathos of Crabbe, are melting fast from the field of our vision. The novels of Scott have put out his poetry. Even the splendid strains of Moore are fading into distance and dimness, except where they have been married to immortal music; and the blazing star of Byron himself is receding from its place of pride. We need say nothing of Milman, and Croly, and Atherstone, and Hood, and a legion of others, who, with no ordinary gifts of taste and fancy, have not so properly survived their fame, as been excluded by some hard fatality, from what seemed their just inheritance. The two who have the longest withstood this rapid withering of the laurel, and with the least marks of decay on their branches, are Rogers and Campbell; neither of them, it may be remarked, voluminous writers, and both distinguished rather for the fine taste and consummate elegance of their writings, than for that fiery passion, and disdainful vehemence, which seemed for a time to be so much more in favour with the public.

English Literature—Drama

Jeffrey had a firm view of the distance between the artistically polished drama of the Continent and the natural drama of England. The former extended in range from ancient Greece to modern France and Italy. The latter was epitomized in the work of Shakespeare and his contemporaries. Jeffrey sympathized with the diverse views of Shakespeare expressed by Bowdler and Hazlitt. Like Hazlitt, he appreciated particularly the poetic liaison which the universal genius of Shakespeare establishes between emotion and external nature. With regard to contemporary drama, Jeffrey's preoccupation with Byron's character and morality overshadowed his assessment of his artistic achievement as a dramatist. This was the preoccupation which disfigured the review of Swift.

15. The Continental and the English drama, from a review of Joanna Baillie's *Plays on the Passions*

Edinburgh Review, 19, February 1812

There are two sorts of dramatic composition, or at least of tragedy, known in this country:—one, the old classical tragedy of the Grecian stage, modernized according to the French or Continental model; the other, the bold, free, irregular and miscellaneous drama of our own older writers,—or, to speak it more shortly and intelligibly, of Shakespeare. Miss Baillie, it appears to us, has attempted to unite the excellences of both these styles;—and has produced a combination of their defects.

The old Greek tragedy consisted of the representation of some one great, simple, and touching event, brought about by the agency of a very few persons, and detailed in grave, stately, and measured language, interspersed with choral songs and movements to music. In this primitive form of the drama, the story was commonly unfolded by means of a good deal of plain statement, direct inquiry, and detailed narration;—while the business was helped forward by means of short and pointed, though frequently very simple and obvious argumentation,—and the interest maintained by pathetic exclamations, and reflections apparently artless and unostentatious.

Such, we conceive, was the character of the ancient drama; upon the foundation of which, the French, or Continental school, appears obviously to have been built. The chief variations (besides the extinction of the Chorus) seem to be, first, that love has been made to supplant almost all other passions,—and the tone, accordingly, has become less solemn and severe; secondly, that there is less simple narrative and inquiry, and a great deal more argument or debate—every considerable scene, in fact, being now required to contain a complete and elaborate discussion, to which all the parties must come fully prepared to maintain their respective theses; and, thirdly, that the topics are drawn, in general, from more extended and philosophical views of human nature; and the state of the feelings set forth with more rhetorical amplification, and with a more anxious and copious minuteness. Notwithstanding those very important distinctions, however, we think ourselves justified in arranging the tragic drama of ancient Greece, and that of the continent of modern Europe, as productions of the same school; because they will be found to agree in their main and characteristic attributes; because they both require the style and tone to be uniformly grave, lofty, and elaborate—the fable to be simple and direct—and the subject represented, to be weighty and important. Neither of them, consequently, admits of those minute touches of character, which give life and individuality to such delineations; and the interest, in both, rests either on the greatness of the action, and the general propriety and congruity of the sentiments by which it is accompanied—or on the beauty and completeness of the discussion—the poetical graces, the purity and elevation of the language—and the accumulation of bright thoughts and happy expressions which are brought to bear upon the same subject.

Such, we believe, is the idea of dramatic excellence that prevails over the continent of Europe, and such the chief elements which are there admitted to compose it. In this country, however, we are fortunate enough to have a drama of a different description—a drama which aims at a far more exact imitation of nature, and admits of an appeal to a far greater variety of emotions—which requires less dignity or grandeur in its incidents, but deals them out with infinitely greater complication and profusion—which peoples its busy scenes with innumerable characters, and varies its style as freely as it multiplies its persons—which frequently remits the main action, and never exhausts any matter of controversy or discussion—indulges in flights of poetry too lofty for sober interlocutors, and sinks into occasional familiarities too homely for lofty representation—but, still pursuing nature and truth of character and of passion, is perpetually setting before us the express image of individuals whose reality it seems impossible to question, and the thrilling echo of emotions in which we are compelled to sympathize. In illustration of this style, it would be mere pedantry to refer to any other name than that of Shakespeare; who has undoubtedly furnished the most perfect, as well as the most popular examples of its excellence; and who will be found to owe much of his unrivalled power over the attention, the imagination, and the feelings of his readers, to the rich variety of his incidents and images, and to the inimitable truth and minuteness of his crowded characters.

Nothing then, it appears, can be more radically different than the modern French and the old English tragedy. The one is the offspring of genius and original observation—the other of judgment and skill. The one aims at pleasing chiefly by a faithful representation of nature, and character, and passion—the other by a display of poetical and elaborate beauties. The style of the latter, therefore, requires a continual elevation, and its characters a certain dignified uniformity, which are necessarily rejected by the former;—while our old English drama derives no small share of its interest from the rapidity and profusion of the incidents, and the multitude of the persons and images which it brings before the fancy;—all which are excluded from the more solemn and artificial stage of our continental neighbours.

16. Ford's *Dramatic Works,* edited by Henry Weber

Edinburgh Review, 18, August 1811; *Contributions, 2*

Jeffrey welcomes the revival in the appreciation of Elizabethan and Jacobean poetic drama as the expression of a great literary age. Surveying the history of poetry in general since then, he deplores the Restoration as introducing a corrupt 'French taste,' but he feels that in the eighteenth century a revival took place, culminating in the work of the present day. This modern writing is both imitative of the older poets and original; it is marred by affectation.

In his admiration of the Elizabethan drama Jeffrey is following Lamb in *Specimens of English Dramatic Poets* (1808). The work under review, Weber's edition of Ford, preceded that of Gifford (1827). The article shows Jeffrey's influential, revised view of English literary history and of the place of modern poetry in relation to it.

All true lovers of English poetry have been long in love with the dramatists of the time of Elizabeth and James; and must have been sensibly comforted by their late restoration to some degree of favour and notoriety. If there was any good reason, indeed, to believe that the notice which they have recently attracted proceeded from any thing but that indiscriminate rage for editing and annotating by which the present times are so happily distinguished, we should be disposed to hail it as the most unequivocal symptom of improvement in public taste that has yet occurred to reward and animate our labours. At all events, however, it gives us a chance for such an improvement; by placing in the hands of many, who would not otherwise have heard of them, some of those beautiful performances which we have always regarded as among the most pleasing and characteristic productions of our native genius.

Ford certainly is not the best of those neglected writers,—nor Mr. Weber by any means the best of their recent editors: But we cannot resist the opportunity which this publication seems to afford, of saying a word or two of a class of writers, whom we have long worshipped in secret with a sort of idolatrous veneration, and now find once more brought forward as candidates for public applause. The æra to which they belong, indeed, has always appeared to us by far the brightest in the history of English literature,—or indeed of human intellect and capacity. There never was, any where, any thing like the sixty or seventy years that elapsed from the middle of Elizabeth's reign to the period of the Restoration. In point of real force and originality of genius, neither the age of Pericles, nor the age of Augustus, nor the times of Leo X., nor of Louis XIV., can come at all into comparison: For, in that short period, we shall find the names of almost all the very great men that this nation has ever produced,—the names of Shakespeare, and Bacon, and Spenser, and Sydney,—and Hooker, and Taylor, and Barrow, and Raleigh,—and Napier, and Milton, and Cudworth, and Hobbes, and many others;—men, all of them, not merely of great talents and accomplishments, but of vast compass and reach of understanding, and of minds truly creative and original;—not perfecting art by the delicacy of their taste, or digesting knowledge by the justness of their reasonings; but making vast and substantial additions to the materials upon which taste and reason must hereafter be employed,—and enlarging, to an incredible and unparalleled extent, both the stores and the resources of the human faculties.

Whether the brisk concussion which was given to men's minds by the force of the Reformation had much effect in producing this sudden development of British genius, we cannot undertake to determine. For our own part, we should be rather inclined to hold, that the Reformation itself was but one symptom or effect of that great spirit of progression and improvement which had been set in operation by deeper and more general causes; and which afterwards blossomed out into this splendid harvest of authorship. But whatever may have been the causes that determined the appearance of those great works, the fact is certain, not only that they appeared together in great numbers, but that they possessed a common character, which, in spite of the great diversity of their subjects and designs, would have made them be classed together as the works of the same order or description of men, even if they had appeared at the most distant intervals of time. They are the works of Giants, in short—and of Giants of one nation and family;—and their characteristics are, great force, boldness, and originality; together with a certain raciness of English peculiarity, which distinguishes them from all those performances that have since been produced among ourselves, upon a more vague and general idea of European excellence. Their sudden appearance, indeed, in all this splendour of native luxuriance, can only be compared to what happens on the breaking up of a virgin soil,—where all indigenous plants spring up at once with a rank and irrepressible fertility, and display whatever is peculiar or excellent in their nature, on a scale the most conspicuous and magnificent. The crops are not indeed so clean, as where a more exhausted mould has been stimulated by systematic cultivation; nor so profitable, as where their quality has been varied by a judicious admixture of exotics, and accommodated to the demands of the universe by the combinations of an unlimited trade. But to those whose chief object of admiration is the living power and energy of vegetation, and who take delight in contemplating the various forms of her unforced and natural perfection, no spectacle can be more rich, splendid or attractive.

In the times of which we are speaking, classical learning, though it had made great progress, had by no means become an exclusive study; and the ancients had not yet been permitted to subdue men's minds to a sense of hopeless inferiority, or to condemn the moderns to the lot of humble imitators. They were resorted to, rather to furnish materials and occasional ornaments, than as models for the general style of composition; and, while they enriched the imagination, and insensibly improved the taste of their successors, they did not at all restrain their freedom, or impair their originality. No common standard had yet been erected, to which all the works of European genius were required to conform; and no general authority was acknowledged, by which all private or local ideas of excellence must submit to be corrected. Both readers and authors were comparatively few in number. The former were infinitely less critical and difficult than they have since become; and the latter, if they were not less solicitous about fame, were at least much less jealous and timid as to the hazards which attended its pursuit. Men, indeed, seldom took to writing in those days, unless they had a great deal of matter to communicate; and neither imagined that they could make a reputation by delivering commonplaces in an elegant manner, or that the substantial value of their sentiments would be disregarded for a little rudeness or negligence in the finishing. They were habituated, therefore, both to depend upon their own resources, and to draw upon them without fear or anxiety; and followed the dictates of their own taste and judgment, without standing much in awe of the ancients, of their readers, or of each other.

The achievements of Bacon, and those who set free our under-standings from the shackles of Papal and of tyrannical imposition, afford sufficient evidence of the benefit which resulted to the reasoning faculties from this happy independence of the first great writers of this nation. But its advantages were, if possible, still more conspicuous in the mere literary character of their productions. The quantity of bright thoughts, of original images, and splendid ex-pressions, which they poured forth upon every occasion, and by which they illuminated and adorned the darkest and most rugged topics to which they had happened to turn themselves, is such as has never been equalled in any other age or country; and places them at least as high, in point of fancy and imagination, as of force of reason, or comprehensiveness of understanding. In this highest and most comprehensive sense of the word, a great proportion of the writers we have alluded to were *Poets:* and, without going to those who composed in metre, and chiefly for purposes of delight, we will venture to assert, that there is in any one of the prose folios of Jeremy Taylor more fine fancy and original imagery—more brilliant conceptions and glowing expressions—more new figures, and new applications of old figures—more, in short, of the body and the soul of poetry, than in all the odes and the epics that have since been produced in Europe. There are large portions of Barrow, and of Hooker and Bacon, of which we may say nearly as much: nor can any one have a tolerably adequate idea of the riches of our language and our native genius, who has not made himself acquainted with the prose writers, as well as the poets, of this memorable period.

The civil wars, and the fanaticism by which they were fostered, checked all this fine bloom of the imagination, and gave a different and less attractive character to the energies which they could not extinguish. Yet, those were the times that matured and drew forth the dark, but powerful genius of such men as Cromwell, and Harrison, and Fleetwood, &c.—the milder and more generous enthusiasm of Blake, and Hutchison, and Hampden—and the stir-ring and indefatigable spirit of Pym, and Hollis, and Vane—and the chivalrous and accomplished loyalty of Strafford and Falkland; at the same time that they stimulated and repaid the severer studies of Coke, and Selden, and Milton. The Drama, however, was entirely destroyed, and has never since regained its honours; and Poetry, in general, lost its ease, and its majesty and force, along with its copiousness and originality.

The Restoration made things still worse: for it broke down the barriers of our literary independence, and reduced us to a province of the great republic of Europe. The genius and fancy which lingered through the usurpation, though soured and blighted by the severities of that inclement season, were still genuine English genius and fancy; and owned no allegiance to any foreign authorities. But the Restoration brought in a French taste upon us, and what was called a classical and a polite taste; and the wings of our English Muses were clipped and trimmed, and their flights regulated at the expense of all that was peculiar, and much of what was brightest in their beauty. The King and his courtiers, during their long exile, had of course imbibed the taste of their protectors; and, coming from the gay court of France, with something of that additional profligacy that belonged to their outcast and adventurer character, were likely enough to be revolted by the peculiarities, and by the very excellences, of our native literature. The grand and sublime tone of our greater poets, appeared to them dull, morose, and gloomy; and the fine play of their rich and unrestrained fancy, mere childishness and folly: while their frequent lapses and perpetual irregularity were set down as clear indications of barbarity and ignorance. Such sentiments, too, were natural, we must admit, for a few dissipated and witty men, accustomed all their days to the regulated splendour of a court—to the gay and heartless gallantry of French manners—and to the imposing pomp and brilliant regularity of French poetry. But, it may appear somewhat more unaccountable that they should have been able to impose their sentiments upon the great body of the nation. A court, indeed, never has so much influence as at the moment of a restoration: but the influence of an English court has been but rarely discernible in the literature of the country; and had it not been for the peculiar circumstances in which the nation was then placed, we believe it would have resisted this attempt to naturalise foreign notions, as sturdily as it was done on almost every other occasion.

At this particular moment, however, the native literature of the country had been sunk into a very low and feeble state by the rigours of the usurpation,—the best of its recent models laboured under the reproach of republicanism,—and the courtiers were not only disposed to see all its peculiarities with an eye of scorn and aversion, but had even a good deal to say in favour of that very opposite style to which they had been habituated. It was a witty, and a grand, and a splendid style. It showed more scholarship and art, than the luxuriant negligence of the old English school; and was not only free from many of its hazards and some of its faults, but possessed merits of its own, of a character more likely to please those who had then the power of conferring celebrity, or condemning to derision. Then it was a style which it was peculiarly easy to justify by argument; and in support of which great authorities, as well as imposing reasons, were always ready to be produced. It came upon us with the air and the pretension of being the style of cultivated Europe, and a true copy of the style of polished antiquity. England, on the other hand, had had but little intercourse with the rest of the world for a considerable period of time: Her language was not at all studied on the Continent, and her native authors had not been taken into acccount in forming those ideal standards of excellence which had been recently constructed in France and Italy upon the authority of the Roman classics, and of their own most celebrated writers. When the comparison came to be made, therefore, it is easy to imagine that it should generally be thought to be very much to our disadvantage, and to understand how the great multitude, even among ourselves, should be dazzled with the pretensions of the fashionable style of writing, and actually feel ashamed of their own richer and more varied productions.

It would greatly exceed our limits to describe accurately the particulars in which this new Continental style differed from our old insular one: But, for our present purpose, it may be enough perhaps to say, that it was more worldly, and more townish,—holding more of reason, and ridicule, and authority—more elaborate and more assuming—addressed more to the judgment than to the feelings, and somewhat ostentatiously accommodated to the habits, or supposed habits, of persons in fashionable life. Instead of tenderness and fancy, we had satire and sophistry—artificial declamation, in place of the spontaneous animations of genius—and for the universal language of Shakespeare, the personalities, the party politics, and the brutal obscenities of Dryden. Nothing, indeed, can better characterize the change which had taken place in our national taste, than the alterations and additions which this eminent person presumed—and thought it necessary—to make on the productions of Shakespeare and Milton. The heaviness, the coarseness, and the bombast of that abominable travestie, in which he has exhibited the Paradise Lost in the form of an opera, and the atrocious indelicacy and compassionable stupidity of the new characters with which he has polluted the enchanted solitude of Miranda and Prospero in the Tempest, are such instances of degeneracy as we would be apt to impute rather to some transient hallucination in the author himself, than to the general prevalence of any systematic bad taste in the public, did we not know that Wycherly and his coadjutors were in the habit of converting the neglected dramas of Beaumont and Fletcher into popular plays, merely by leaving out all the romantic sweetness of their characters—turning their melodious blank verse into vulgar prose—and aggravating the indelicacy of their lower characters, by lending a more disgusting indecency to the whole *dramatis personæ*.

Dryden was, beyond all comparison, the greatest poet of his own day; and, endued as he was with a vigorous and discursive imagination, and possessing a mastery over his language which no later writer has attained, if he had known nothing of foreign literature, and been left to form himself on the models of Shakespeare, Spenser and Milton; or if he had lived in the country, at a distance from the pollutions of courts, factions, and playhouses, there is reason to think that he would have built up the pure and original school of English poetry so firmly, as to have made it impossible for fashion, or caprice, or prejudice of any sort, ever to have rendered any other popular among our own inhabitants. As it is, he has not written one line that is pathetic, and very few that can be considered as sublime.

Addison, however, was the consummation of this Continental style; and if it had not been redeemed about the same time by the fine talents of Pope, would probably have so far discredited it, as to have brought us back to our original faith half a century ago. The extreme caution, timidity, and flatness of this author in his poetical compositions—the narrowness of his range in poetical sentiment and diction, and the utter want either of passion or of brilliancy, render it difficult to believe that he was born under the same sun with Shakespeare, and wrote but a century after him. His fame, at this day, stands solely upon the delicacy, the modest gaiety, and ingenious purity of his prose style;—for the occasional elegance and small ingenuity of his poems can never redeem the poverty of their diction, and the tameness of their conception. Pope has incomparably more spirit and taste and animation: but Pope is a satirist, and a moralist, and a wit, and a critic, and a fine writer, much more than he is a poet. He has all the delicacies and proprieties and felicities of diction—but he has not a great deal of fancy, and scarcely ever touches any of the greater passions. He is much the best, we think, of the classical Continental school; but he is not to be compared with the masters—nor with the pupils—of that Old English one from which there had been so lamentable an apostacy. There are no pictures of nature or of simple emotion in all his writings. He is the poet of town life, and of high life, and of literary life; and seems so much afraid of incurring ridicule by the display of natural feeling or unregulated fancy, that it is difficult not to imagine that he would have thought such ridicule very well directed.

The best of what we copied from the Continental poets, on this desertion of our own great originals, is to be found, perhaps, in the lighter pieces of Prior. That tone of polite raillery—that airy, rapid, picturesque narrative, mixed up with wit and *naïveté*—that style, in short, of good conversation concentrated into flowing and polished verses, was not within the vein of our native poets; and probably never would have been known among us, if we had been left to our own resources. It is lamentable that this, which alone was worth borrowing, is the only thing which has not been retained. The tales and little apologues of Prior are still the only examples of this style in our language.

With the wits of Queen Anne this foreign school attained the summit of its reputation; and has ever since, we think, been declining, though by slow and almost imperceptible gradations. Thomson was the first writer of any eminence who seceded from it, and made some steps back to the force and animation of our original poetry. Thomson, however, was educated in Scotland, where the new style, we believe, had not yet become familiar; and lived, for a long time, a retired and unambitious life, with very little intercourse with those who gave the tone in literature at the period of his first appearance. Thomson, accordingly, has always been popular with a much wider circle of readers, than either Pope or Addison; and, in spite of considerable vulgarity and signal cumbrousness of diction, has drawn, even from the fastidious, a much deeper and more heartfelt admiration.

Young exhibits, we think, a curious combination, or contrast rather, of the two styles of which we have been speaking. Though incapable either of tenderness or passion, he had a richness and activity of fancy that belonged rather to the days of James and Elizabeth, than to those of George and Anne:—But then, instead of indulging it, as the older writers would have done, in easy and playful inventions, in splendid descriptions, or glowing illustrations, he was led, by the restraints and established taste of his age, to work it up into strained and fantastical epigrams, or into cold and revolting hyperboles. Instead of letting it flow gracefully on, in an easy and sparkling current, he perpetually forces it out in jets, or makes it stagnate in formal canals;—and thinking it necessary to write like Pope, when the bent of his genius led him rather to copy what was best in Cowley and most fantastic in Shakespeare, he has produced something which excites wonder instead of admiration, and is felt by every one to be at once ingenious, incongruous and unnatural.

After Young, there was a plentiful lack of poetical talent, down to a period comparatively recent. Akenside and Gray, indeed, in the interval, discovered a new way of imitating the ancients;—and Collins and Goldsmith produced some small specimens of exquisite and original poetry. At last, Cowper threw off the whole trammels of French criticism and artificial refinement; and, setting at defiance all the imaginary requisites of poetical diction and classical imagery—dignity of style, and politeness of phraseology—ventured to write again with the force and the freedom which had characterised the old school of English literature, and been so unhappily sacrificed, upwards of a century before. Cowper had many faults, and some radical deficiencies;—but this atoned for all. There was something so delightfully refreshing, in seeing natural phrases and natural images again displaying their unforced graces, and waving their unpruned heads in the enchanted gardens of poetry, that no one complained of the taste displayed in the selection;—and Cowper is, and is likely to continue, the most popular of all who have written for the present or the last generation.

Of the poets who have come after him, we cannot, indeed, say that they have attached themselves to the school of Pope and Addison; or that they have even failed to show a much stronger predilection for the native beauties of their great predecessors. Southey, and Wordsworth, and Coleridge, and Miss Baillie, have all of them copied the manner of our older poets; and, along with this indication of good taste, have given great proofs of original genius. The misfortune is, that their copies of those great originals are liable to the charge of extreme affectation. They do not write as those great poets would have written: they merely mimic their manner, and ape their peculiarities;—and consequently, though they profess to imitate the freest and most careless of all versifiers, their style is more remarkable and offensively artificial than that of any other class of writers. They have mixed in, too, so much of the maukish tone of pastoral innocence and babyish simplicity, with a sort of pedantic emphasis and ostentatious glitter, that it is difficult not to be disgusted with their perversity, and with the solemn self-complacency, and keen and vindictive jealousy, with which they have put in their claims on public admiration. But we have said enough elsewhere of the faults of those authors; and shall only add, at present, that, notwithstanding all these faults, there is a fertility and a force, a warmth of feeling and an exaltation of imagination about them, which classes them, in our estimation, with a much higher order of poets than the followers of Dryden and Addison;

and justifies an anxiety for their fame, in all the admirers of Milton and Shakespeare.

Of Scott, or of Campbell, we need scarcely say any thing, with reference to our present object, after the very copious accounts we have given of them on former occasions. The former professes to copy something a good deal older than what we consider as the golden age of English poetry,—and, in reality, has copied every style, and borrowed from every manner that has prevailed, from the times of Chaucer to his own;—illuminating and uniting, if not harmonizing them all, by a force of colouring, and a rapidity of succession, which is not to be met with in any of his many models. The latter, we think, can scarcely be said to have copied his pathos, or his energy, from any models whatever, either recent or early. The exquisite harmony of his versification is elaborated, perhaps, from the Castle of Indolence of Thomson, and the serious pieces of Goldsmith;—and it seems to be his misfortune, not to be able to reconcile himself to any thing which he cannot reduce within the limits of this elaborate harmony. This extreme fastidiousness, and the limitation of his efforts to themes of unbroken tenderness or sublimity, distinguish him from the careless, prolific, and miscellaneous authors of our primitive poetry;—while the enchanting softness of his pathetic passages, and the power and originality of his more sublime conceptions, place him at a still greater distance from the wits, as they truly called themselves, of Charles II. and Queen Anne.

We do not know what other apology to offer for this hasty, and, we fear, tedious sketch of the history of our poetry, but that it appeared to us to be necessary, in order to explain the peculiar merit of that class of writers to which the author before us belongs; and that it will very greatly shorten what we have still to say on the characteristics of our older dramatists. An opinion prevails very generally on the Continent, and with foreign-bred scholars among ourselves, that our national taste has been corrupted chiefly by our idolatry of Shakespeare;—and that it is our patriotic and traditional admiration of that singular writer, that reconciles us to the monstrous compound of faults and beauties that occur in his performances, and must to all impartial judges appear quite absurd and unnatural. Before entering upon the character of a contemporary dramatist, it was of some importance, therefore, to show that there was a distinct, original, and independent school of literature in England in the time of Shakespeare; to the general tone of whose productions his works were sufficiently conformable; and that it was owing to circumstances in a great measure accidental, that this native school was superseded about the time of the Restoration, and a foreign standard of excellence intruded on us, not in the drama only, but in every other department of poetry. This new style of composition, however, though adorned and recommended by the splendid talents of many of its followers, was never perfectly naturalised, we think, in this country; and has ceased, in a great measure, to be cultivated by those who have lately aimed with the greatest success at the higher honours of poetry. Our love of Shakespeare, therefore, is not a *monomania* or solitary and unaccountable infatuation; but is merely the natural love which all men bear to those forms of excellence that are accommodated to their peculiar character, temperament, and situation; and which will always return, and assert its power over their affections, long after authority has lost its reverence, fashions been antiquated, and artificial tastes passed away. In endeavouring, therefore, to bespeak some share of favour for such of his contemporaries as had fallen out of notice, during the prevalence of an imported literature, we conceive that we are only enlarging that foundation of native genius on which alone any lasting superstructure can be raised, and invigorating that deep-rooted stock upon which all the perennial blossoms of our literature must still be engrafted.

The notoriety of Shakespeare may seem to make it superfluous to speak of the peculiarities of those old dramatists, of whom he will be admitted to be so worthy a representative. Nor shall we venture to say any thing of the confusion of their plots, the disorders of their chronology, their contempt of the unities, or their imperfect discrimination between the provinces of Tragedy and Comedy. Yet there are characteristics which the lovers of literature may not be displeased to find enumerated, and which may constitute no dishonourable distinction for the whole fraternity, independent of the splendid talents and incommunicable graces of their great chieftain.

Of the old English dramatists, then, including under this name (besides Shakespeare), Beaumont and Fletcher, Massinger, Jonson, Ford, Shirley, Webster, Dekkar, Field and Rowley, it may be said, in general, that they are more poetical, and more original in their diction, than the dramatists of any other age or country. Their scenes abound more in varied images, and gratuitous excursions of fancy. Their illustrations, and figures of speech, are more borrowed from rural life, and from the simple occupations or universal feelings of mankind. They are not confined to a certain range of dignified expressions, nor restricted to a particular assortment of imagery, beyond which it is not lawful to look for embellishments. Let any one compare the prodigious variety, and wide-ranging freedom of Shakespeare, with the narrow round of flames, tempests, treasons, victims and tyrants, that scantily adorn the sententious pomp of the French drama, and he will not fail to recognise the vast superiority of the former, in the excitement of the imagination, and all the diversities of poetical delight. That very mixture of styles, of which the French critics have so fastidiously complained, forms, when not carried to any height of extravagance, one of the greatest charms of our ancient dramatists. It is equally sweet and natural for personages toiling on the barren heights of life, to be occasionally recalled to some vision of pastoral innocence and tranquillity, as for the victims or votaries of ambition to cast a glance of envy and agony on the joys of humble content.

Those charming old writers, however, have a still more striking peculiarity in their conduct of the dialogue. On the modern stage, every scene is *visibly* studied and digested beforehand,—and every thing from beginning to end, whether it be description, or argument, or vituperation, is very obviously and ostentatiously set forth in the most advantageous light, and with all the decorations of the most elaborate rhetoric. Now, for mere rhetoric, and fine composition, this is very right;—but, for an imitation of nature, it is not quite so well: And however we may admire the skill of the artist, we are not very likely to be moved with any very lively sympathy in the emotions of those very rhetorical interlocutors. When we come to any important part of the play, on the Continental or modern stage, we are sure to have a most complete, formal, and exhausting discussion of it, in long flourishing orations;—argument after argument propounded and answered with infinite ingenuity, and topic after topic brought forward in well-digested method, without any deviation that the most industrious and practised pleader would not approve of,—till nothing more remains to be said, and a new scene introduces us to a new set of gladiators, as expert and persevering as the former. It is exactly the same when a story is to be told,—a tyrant to be bullied,—or a princess to be wooed. On the old English stage, however, the proceedings were by no means so regular. There the discussions always appear to be casual, and the argument quite artless and disorderly. The persons of the drama, in short, are made to speak like men and women who meet without preparation, in real life. Their reasonings are perpetually broken by passion, or left imperfect for want of skill. They constantly wander from the point in hand, in the most unbusinesslike manner in the world;— and after hitting upon a topic that would afford a judicious playwright room for a magnificent see-saw of pompous declamation, they have generally the awkwardness to let it slip, as if perfectly unconscious of its value; and uniformly leave the scene without exhausting the controversy, or stating half the plausible things for themselves that any ordinary advisers might have suggested—after a few weeks' reflection. As specimens of eloquent argumentation, we must admit the signal inferiority of our native favourites; but as true copies of nature,—as vehicles of passion, and representations of character, we confess we are tempted to give them the preference. When a dramatist brings his chief characters on the stage, we readily admit that he must give them something to say,—and that this something must be interesting and characteristic;—but he should recollect also, that they are supposed to come there without having anticipated all they were to hear, or meditated on all they were to deliver; and that it cannot be characteristic, therefore, because it must be glaringly unnatural, that they should proceed regularly through every possible view of the subject, and exhaust, in set order, the whole magazine of reflections that can be brought to bear upon their situation.

It would not be fair, however, to leave this view of the matter, without observing, that this unsteadiness and irregularity of dialogue, which gives such an air of nature to our older plays, and keeps the curiosity and attention so perpetually awake, is frequently carried to a most blameable excess; and that, independent of their passion for verbal quibbles, there *is* an inequality and a capricious uncertainty in the taste and judgment of these good old writers, which excites at once our amazement and our compassion. If it be true, that no other man has ever written so finely as Shakespeare has done in his happier passages, it is no less true that there is not a scribbler now alive who could possibly write worse than he has sometimes written,—who could, on occasion, devise more contemptible ideas, or misplace them so abominably, by the side of such incomparable excellence. That there were no critics, and no critical readers in those days, appears to us but an imperfect solution of the difficulty. He who could write so admirably, must have been a critic to himself. *Children,* indeed, may play with the most precious gems, and the most worthless pebbles, without being aware of any difference in their value; but the very powers which are necessary to the production of intellectual excellence, must enable the possessor to recognize it as excellence; and he who knows when he succeeds, can scarcely be unconscious of his failures. Unaccountable, however, as it is, the fact is certain, that almost all the dramatic writers of this age appear to be alternately inspired, and bereft of understanding; and pass, apparently without being conscious of the change, from the most beautiful displays of genius to the most melancholy exemplifications of stupidity.

There is only one other peculiarity which we shall notice in those ancient dramas; and that is, the singular, though very beautiful style, in which the greater part of them are composed,—a style which we think must be felt as peculiar by all who peruse them, though it is by no means easy to describe in what its peculiarity consists. It is not, for the most part, a lofty or sonorous style,—nor can it be said generally to be finical or affected,—or strained, quaint, or pedantic:—But it is, at the same time, a style full of turn and contrivance,—with some little degree of constraint and involution,—very often characterised by a studied briefness and simplicity of diction, yet relieved by a certain indirect and figurative cast of expression,—and almost always coloured with a modest tinge of ingenuity, and fashioned, rather too visibly, upon a particular model of elegance and purity. In scenes of powerful passion, this sort of artificial prettiness is commonly shaken off; and, in Shakespeare, it disappears under all his forms of animation: But it sticks closer to most of his contemporaries. In Massinger (who has no passion), it is almost always discernible; and, in the author before us, it gives a peculiar tone to almost all the estimable parts of his productions.

17. Hazlitt's *Characters of Shakespeare's Plays*

Edinburgh Review, 28, August 1817; *Contributions*, 2

Hazlitt at this time was himself a contributor to the *Edinburgh*. Like the essayist, Jeffrey particularly admires Shakespeare's 'fine sense' of the 'undefinable relation' between the 'material elements' of poetry and emotion. Hazlitt especially asked Jeffrey to review his book, in order to enhance its sale.

The general introduction to the article is here given.

This is not a book of black-letter learning, or historical elucidation;—neither is it a metaphysical dissertation, full of wise perplexities and elaborate reconcilements. It is, in truth, rather an encomium on Shakespeare, than a commentary or critique on him—and is written, more to show extraordinary love, than extraordinary knowledge of his productions. Nevertheless, it is a very pleasing book— and, we do not hesitate to say, a book of very considerable originality and genius. The author is not merely an admirer of our great dramatist, but an Idolater of him; and openly professes his idolatry. We have ourselves too great a leaning to the same superstition, to blame him very much for his error: and though we think, of course, that our own admiration is, on the whole, more discriminating and judicious, there are not many points on which, especially after reading his eloquent exposition of them, we should be much inclined to disagree with him.

The book, as we have already intimated, is written less to tell the reader what Mr. H. *knows* about Shakespeare or his writings, than to explain to them what he *feels* about them—and *why* he feels so—and thinks that all who profess to love poetry should feel so likewise. What we chiefly look for in such a work, accordingly, is a fine sense of the beauties of the author, and an eloquent exposition of them; and all this, and more, we think, may be found in the volume before us. There is nothing niggardly in Mr. H.'s praises, and nothing affected in his raptures. He seems animated throughout with a full and hearty sympathy with the delight which his author should inspire, and pours himself gladly out in explanation of it, with a fluency and ardour, obviously much more akin to enthusiasm than affectation. He seems pretty generally, indeed, in a state of happy intoxication—and has borrowed from his great original, not indeed the force or brilliancy of his fancy, but something of its playfulness, and a large share of his apparent joyousness and self-indulgence in its exercise. It is evidently a great pleasure to him to be fully possessed with the beauties of his author, and to follow the impulse of his unrestrained eagerness to impress them upon his readers.

When we have said that his observations are generally right, we have said, in substance, that they are not generally original; for the beauties of Shakespeare are not of so dim or equivocal a nature as to be visible only to learned eyes—and undoubtedly his finest passages are those which please all classes of readers, and are admired for the same qualities by judges from every school of criticism. Even with regard to those passages, however, a skilful commentator will find something worth hearing to tell. Many persons are very sensible of the effect of fine poetry on their feelings, who do not well know how to refer these feelings to their causes; and it is always a delightful thing to be made to see clearly the sources from which our delight has proceeded—and to trace back the mingled stream that has flowed upon our hearts, to the remoter fountains from which it has been gathered. And when this is done with warmth as well as precision, and embodied in an eloquent description of the beauty which is explained, it forms one of the most attractive, and not the least instructive, of literary exercises. In all works of merit, however, and especially in all works of original genius, there are a thousand retiring and less obtrusive graces, which escape hasty and superficial observers, and only give out their beauties to fond and patient contemplation;—a thousand slight and harmonising touches, the merit and the effect of which are equally imperceptible to vulgar eyes; and a thousand indications of the continual presence of that poetical spirit, which can only be recognised by those who are in some measure under its influence, or have prepared themselves to receive it, by worshipping meekly at the shrines which it inhabits.

In the exposition of these, there is room enough for originality,— and more room than Mr. H. has yet filled. In many points, however, he has acquitted himself excellently;—partly in the development of the principal characters with which Shakespeare has peopled the fancies of all English readers—but principally, we think, in the delicate sensibility with which he has traced, and the natural eloqu- ence with which he has pointed out that fond familiarity with beautiful forms and images—that eternal recurrence to what is sweet or majestic in the simple aspects of nature—that indestructi- ble love of flowers and odours, and dews and clear waters, and soft airs and sounds, and bright skies, and woodland solitudes, and moonlight bowers, which are the Material elements of Poetry—and that fine sense of their undefinable relation to mental emotion, which is its essence and vivifying Soul—and which, in the midst of Shakespeare's most busy and atrocious scenes, falls like gleams of sunshine on rocks and ruins—contrasting with all that is rugged and repulsive, and reminding us of the existence of purer and brighter elements!—which HE ALONE has poured out from the richness of his own mind, without effort or restraint; and contrived to intermingle with the play of all the passions, and the vulgar course of this world's affairs, without deserting for an instant the proper business of the scene, or appearing to pause or digress, from love of ornament or need of repose!—HE ALONE, who, when the object requires it, is always keen and worldly and practical—and who yet, without changing his hand, or stopping his course, scatters around him, as he goes, all sounds and shapes of sweetness—and conjures up landscapes of immortal fragrance and freshness, and peoples them with Spirits of glorious aspect and attractive grace—and is a thousand times more full of fancy and imagery, and splendour, than those who, in pursuit of such enchantments, have shrunk back from the delineation of character or passion, and declined the discussion of human duties and cares. More full of wisdom and ridicule and sagacity, than all the moralists and satirists that ever existed—he is more wild, airy, and inventive, and more pathetic and fantastic, than all the poets of all regions and ages of the world:—and has all those elements so happily mixed up in him, and bears his high faculties so temperately, that the most severe reader cannot com- plain of him for want of strength or of reason—nor the most sensitive for defect of ornament or ingenuity. Every thing in him is in unmeasured abundance, and unequalled perfection—but every thing so balanced and kept in subordination, as not to jostle or disturb or take the place of another. The most exquisite poetical conceptions, images and descriptions, are given with such brevity, and introduced with such skill, as merely to adorn, without loading the sense they accompany. Although his sails are purple and per-fumed, and his prow of beaten gold, they waft him on his voyage, not less, but more rapidly and directly than if they had been composed of baser materials. All his excellences, like those of Nature herself, are thrown out together; and, instead of interfering with, support and recommend each other. His flowers are not tied up in garlands, nor his fruits crushed into baskets—but spring living from the soil, in all the dew and freshness of youth; while the graceful foliage in which they lurk, and the ample branches, the rough and vigorous stem, and the wide-spreading roots on which they depend, are present along with them, and share, in their places, the equal care of their Creator.

18. Byron's *Tragedies*

Edinburgh Review, 36, February 1822; *Contributions*, 2

Jeffrey regrets, in the words of the running titles of the pages of the *Contributions*, the 'singular decline of our tragic genius, even after our return to its true standards.' The return had been discussed ten years earlier in the article on Ford's plays (no. 16). Byron's 'hard-wrought compositions' betray his un-Shakespearian egotism and dangerous intellectual tendencies. He fails by the highest test, that of morality. How different from the pure example of Scott! Here Jeffrey eloquently expresses a representative contemporary critical reaction to Byron. The general reaction would darken further with the publication of the later cantos of *Don Juan*.

It must be a more difficult thing to write a good play—or even a good dramatic poem—than we had imagined. Not that we should, *a priori*, have imagined it to be very easy: But it is impossible not to be struck with the fact, that, in comparatively rude times, when the resources of the art had been less carefully considered, and Poetry certainly had not collected all her materials, success seems to have been more frequently, and far more easily obtained. From the middle of Elizabeth's reign till the end of James's, the drama formed by far the most brilliant and beautiful part of our poetry,—and indeed of our literature in general. From that period to the Revolution, it lost a part of its splendour and originality; but still continued to occupy the most conspicuous and considerable place in our literary annals. For the last century, it has been quite otherwise.

Our poetry has ceased almost entirely to be dramatic; and, though men of great name and great talent have occasionally adventured into this once fertile field, they have reaped no laurels, and left no trophies behind them. The genius of Dryden appears nowhere to so little advantage as in his tragedies; and the contrast is truly humiliating when, in a presumptuous attempt to heighten the colouring, or enrich the simplicity of Shakespeare, he bedaubs with obscenity, or deforms with rant, the genuine passion and profligacy of Antony and Cleopatra—or intrudes on the enchanted solitude of Prospero and his daughter, with the tones of worldly gallantry, or the caricatures of affected simplicity. Otway, with the sweet and mellow diction of the former age, had none of its force, variety, or invention. Its decaying fires burst forth in some strong and irregular flashes, in the disorderly scenes of Lee; and sunk at last in the ashes, and scarcely glowing embers, of Rowe.

Since his time—till very lately—the school of our ancient dramatists has been deserted: and we can scarcely say that any new one has been established. Instead of the irregular and comprehensive plot—the rich discursive dialogue—the ramblings of fancy—the magic creations of poetry—the rapid succession of incidents and characters—the soft, flexible, and ever-varying diction—and the flowing, continuous, and easy versification, which characterised those masters of the golden time, we have had tame, formal, elaborate, and stately compositions—meagre stories—few personages—characters decorous and consistent, but without nature or spirit—a guarded, timid, classical diction—ingenious and methodical disquisitions—turgid or sententious declamations—and a solemn and monotonous strain of versification. Nor can this be ascribed, even plausibly, to any decay of genius among us; for the most remarkable failures have fallen on the highest talents. We have already hinted at the miscarriages of Dryden. The exquisite taste and fine observation of Addison, produced only the solemn mawkishness of Cato. The beautiful fancy, the gorgeous diction, and generous affections of Thomson, were chilled and withered as soon as he touched the verge of the Drama; where his name is associated with a mass of verbose puerility, which it is difficult to conceive could ever have proceeded from the author of the Seasons and the Castle of Indolence. Even the mighty intellect, the eloquent morality, and lofty style of Johnson, which gave too tragic and magnificent a tone to his ordinary writing, failed altogether to support him in his attempt to write actual tragedy; and Irene is not only unworthy of the imitator of Juvenal and the author of Rasselas and the Lives of the Poets, but is absolutely, and in itself, nothing better than a tissue of wearisome and unimpassioned declamations. We have named the most celebrated names in our literature, since the decline of the drama, almost to our own days; and if *they* have neither lent any new honours to the stage, nor borrowed any from it, it is needless to say, that those who adventured with weaker powers had no better fortune. The Mourning Bride of Congreve, the Revenge of Young, and the Douglas of Home [we cannot add the Mysterious Mother of Walpole—even to please Lord Byron], are almost the only tragedies of the last age that are familiar to the present; and they are evidently the works of a feebler and more effeminate generation— indicating, as much by their exaggerations as by their timidity, their own consciousness of inferiority to their great predecessors—whom they affected, however, not to imitate, but to supplant.

But the native taste of our people was not thus to be seduced and perverted; and when the wits of Queen Anne's time had lost the authority of living authors, it asserted itself by a fond recurrence to its original standards, and a resolute neglect of the more regular and elaborate dramas by which they had been succeeded. Shakespeare, whom it had long been the fashion to decry and even ridicule, as the poet of a rude and barbarous age, was reinstated in his old supremacy: and when his legitimate progeny could no longer be found at home, his spurious issue were hailed with rapture from foreign countries, and invited and welcomed with the most eager enthusiasm on their arrival. The German imitations, of Schiller and Kotzebue, caricatured and distorted as they were by the aberrations of a vulgar and vitiated taste, had still so much of the raciness and vigour of the Old English drama, from which they were avowedly derived, that they instantly become more popular in England than any thing that her own artists had recently produced; and served still more effectually to recall our affections to their native and legitimate rulers. Then followed republications of Massinger, and Beaumont and Fletcher, and Ford, and their contemporaries—and a host of new tragedies, all written in avowed and elaborate imitation of the ancient models. Miss Baillie, we rather think, had the merit of leading the way in this return to our old allegiance—and then came a volume of plays by Mr. Chenevix, and a succession of single plays, all of considerable merit, from Mr. Coleridge, Mr. Maturin, Mr. Wilson, Mr. Barry Cornwall and Mr. Milman. The first and the last of these names are the most likely to be remembered; but none of them, we fear, will ever be ranked with the older worthies; nor is it conceivable that any age should ever class them together.

We do not mean, however, altogether to deny, that there may be some illusion, in our habitual feelings, as to the merits of the great originals—consecrated as they are, in our imaginations, by early admiration, and associated, as all their peculiarities, and the mere accidents and oddities of their diction now are, with the recollection of their intrinsic excellences. It is owing to this, we suppose, that we can scarcely venture to ask ourselves, steadily, and without an inward startling and feeling of alarm, what reception one of Shakespeare's irregular plays—the Tempest for example, or the Midsummer Night's Dream—would be likely to meet with, if it were *now* to appear for the first time, without name, notice, or preparation? Nor can we pursue the hazardous supposition through all the possibilities to which it invites us, without something like a sense of impiety and profanation. Yet, though some little superstition may mingle with our faith, we must still believe it to be the true one. Though time may have hallowed many things that were at first but common, and accidental associations imparted a charm to much that was in itself indifferent, we cannot but believe that there was an original sanctity, which time only matured and extended—and an inherent charm from which the association derived all its power. And when we look candidly and calmly to the works of our early dramatists, it is impossible, we think, to dispute, that after criticism has done its worst on them—after all deductions for impossible plots and fantastical characters, unaccountable forms of speech, and occasional extravagance, indelicacy, and horrors—there is a facility and richness about them, both of thought and of diction—a force of invention, and a depth of sagacity—an originality of conception, and a play of fancy—a nakedness and energy of passion, and, above all, a copiousness of imagery, and a sweetness and flexibility of verse, which is altogether unrivalled, in earlier or in later times;—and places them, in our estimation, in the very highest and foremost place among ancient or modern poets.

It is in these particulars that the inferiority of their recent imitators is most apparent—in the want of ease and variety—originality and grace. There is, in all their attempts, whatever may be their other merits or defects, an air of anxiety and labour—and indications, by far too visible, at once of timidity and ambition. This may arise, in part, from the fact of their being, too obviously and consciously, imitators. They do not aspire so much to rival the genius of their originals, as to copy their manner. They do not write as *they* would have written in the present day, but as they imagine they themselves would have written two hundred years ago. They revive the antique phraseology, repeat the venerable oaths, and emulate the quaint familiarities of that classical period—and wonder that they are not mistaken for new incarnations of its departed poets! One great cause why they are not, is, that they speak an unnatural dialect, and are constrained by a masquerade habit; in neither of which it is possible to display that freedom, and those delicate traits of character, which are the life of the drama, and were among the chief merits of those who once exalted it so highly. Another bad effect of imitation, and especially of the imitation of unequal and irregular models in a critical age, is, that nothing is thought fit to be copied but the exquisite and shining passages;—from which it results, in the *first* place, that all our rivalry is reserved for occasions in which its success is most hopeless; and, in the *second* place, that instances, even of occasional success, want their proper grace and effect, by being deprived of the relief, shading, and preparation, which they would naturally have received in a less fastidious composition; and, instead of the warm and native and ever-varying graces of a spontaneous effusion, the work acquires the false and feeble brilliancy of a prize essay in a foreign tongue—a collection of splendid patches of different texture and pattern.

At the bottom of all this—and perhaps as its most efficient cause—there lurks, we suspect, an unreasonable and undue dread of criticism;—not the deliberate and indulgent criticism which *we* exercise, rather for the encouragement of talent than its warning—but the vigilant and paltry derision which is perpetually stirring in idle societies, and but too continually present to the spirits of all who aspire to their notice. There is nothing so certain, we take it, as that those who are the most alert in discovering the faults of a work of genius, are the least touched with its beauties. Those who admire and enjoy fine poetry, in short, are quite a different class of persons from those who find out its flaws and defects—who are sharp at detecting a plagiarism or a grammatical inaccuracy, and laudably industrious in bringing to light an obscure passage—sneering at an exaggerated one—or wondering at the meaning of some piece of excessive simplicity. It is in vain to expect the praises of such people; for they never praise;—and it is truly very little worth while to disarm their censure. It is only the praises of the real lovers of poetry that ever give it true fame or popularity—and these are little affected by the cavils of the fastidious. Yet the genius of most modern writers seems to be rebuked under that of those pragmatical and insignificant censors. They are so much afraid of faults, that they will scarcely venture upon beauties; and seem more anxious in general to be *safe,* than original. They dare not indulge in a florid and magnificent way of writing, for fear of being charged with bombast by the cold-blooded and malignant. They must not be tender, lest they should be laughed at for puling and whining; nor discursive and fanciful like their great predecessors, under pain of being held out to derision, as ingenious gentlemen who have dreamed that the gods have made them poetical!

Thus, the dread of ridicule, which they have ever before their eyes, represses all the emotions, on the expression of which their success entirely depends; and in order to escape the blame of those to whom they can give no pleasure, and through whom they can gain no fame, they throw away their best chance of pleasing those who are capable of relishing their excellences, and on whose admiration alone their reputation must at all events be founded. There is a great want of magnanimity, we think, as well as of wisdom, in this sensitiveness to blame; and we are convinced that no modern author will ever write with the grace and vigour of the older ones, who does not write with some portion of their fearlessness and indifference to censure. *Courage,* in short, is at least as necessary as genius to the success of a work of imagination; since, without this, it is impossible to attain that freedom and self-possession, without which no talents can ever have fair play, and, far less, that inward confidence and exaltation of spirit which must accompany all the higher acts of the understanding. The earlier writers had probably less occasion for courage to secure them these advantages; as the public was far less critical in their day, and much more prone to admiration than to derision: But we can still trace in their writings the indications both of a proud consciousness of their own powers and privileges, and of a brave contempt for the cavils to which they might expose themselves. In our own times, we know but one writer who is emancipated from this slavish awe of vulgar detraction—this petty timidity about being detected in blunders and faults; and that is the illustrious author of Waverley, and the other novels that have made an era in our literature as remarkable, and as likely to be remembered, as any which can yet be traced in its history. We shall not now say how large a portion of his success we ascribe to this intrepid temper of his genius; but we are confident that no person can read any one of his wonderful works, without feeling that their author was utterly careless of the reproach of small imperfections; disdained the inglorious labour of perpetual correctness, and has *consequently* imparted to his productions that spirit and ease and variety, which reminds us of better times, and gives lustre and effect to those rich and resplendent passages to which it left him free to aspire.

Lord Byron, in some respects, may appear not to have been wanting in intrepidity. He has not certainly been very tractable to advice, nor very patient of blame. But this, in him, we fear, is not superiority to censure, but aversion to it; and, instead of proving that he is indifferent to detraction, shows only, that the dread and dislike of it operate with more than common force on his mind. A critic, whose object was to give pain, would desire no better proof of the efficacy of his inflictions, than the bitter scorn and fierce defiance with which they are encountered; and the more vehemently the noble author protests that he despises the reproaches that have been bestowed on him, the more certain it is that he suffers from their severity, and would be glad to escape, if he cannot overbear, them. But however this may be, we think it is certain that his late dramatic efforts have not been made carelessly, or without anxiety. To us, at least, they seem very elaborate and hard-wrought compositions; and this indeed we take to be their leading characteristic, and the key to most of their peculiarities.

Considered as Poems, we confess they appear to us to be rather heavy, verbose, and inelegant—deficient in the passion and energy which belongs to the other writings of the noble author—and still more in the richness of imagery, the originality of thought, and the sweetness of versification for which he used to be distinguished. They are for the most part solemn, prolix, and ostentatious—lengthened out by large preparations for catastrophes that never arrive, and tantalizing us with slight specimens and glimpses of a higher interest, scattered thinly up and down many weary pages of declamation. Along with the concentrated pathos and homestruck sentiments of his former poetry, the noble author seems also, we cannot imagine why, to have discarded the spirited and melodious versification in which they were embodied, and to have formed to himself a measure equally remote from the spring and vigour of his former compositions, and from the softness and flexibility of the ancient masters of the drama. There are some sweet lines, and many of great weight and energy; but the general march of the verse is cumbrous and unmusical. His lines do not vibrate like polished lances, at once strong and light, in the hands of his persons, but are wielded like clumsy batons in a bloodless affray. Instead of the graceful familiarity and idiomatical melodies of Shakespeare, they are apt, too, to fall into clumsy prose, in their approaches to the easy and colloquial style; and, in the loftier passages, are occasionally deformed by low and common images, that harmonize but ill with the general solemnity of the diction.

As Plays, we are afraid we must also say that the pieces before us are wanting in interest, character, and action:—at least we must say this of the two last of them—for *there is* interest in Sardanapalus—and beauties besides, that make us blind to its other defects. There is, however, throughout, a want of dramatic effect and variety; and we suspect there is something in the character or habit of Lord Byron's genius which will render this unattainable. He has too little sympathy with the ordinary feelings and frailties of humanity, to succeed well in their representation—'His soul is like a star, and dwells apart.' It does not 'hold the mirror up to nature,' nor catch the hues of surrounding objects; but, like a kindled furnace, throws out its intense glare and gloomy grandeur on the narrow scene which it irradiates. He has given us, in his other works, some glorious pictures of nature—some magnificent reflections, and some inimitable delineations of character: But the same feelings prevail in them all; and his portraits in particular, though a little varied in the drapery and attitude, seem all copied from the same original. His Childe Harold, his Giaour, Conrad, Lara, Manfred, Cain, and Lucifer—are all one individual. There is the same varnish of voluptuousness on the surface—the same canker of misanthropy at the core, of all he touches. He cannot draw the changes of many-coloured life, nor transport himself into the condition of the infinitely diversified characters by whom a stage should be peopled. The very intensity of his feelings—the loftiness of his views—the pride of his nature or his genius—withhold him from this identification; so that in personating the heroes of the scene, he does little but repeat himself. It would be better for him, we think, if it were otherwise. We are sure it would be better for his readers. He would get more fame, and things of far more worth than fame, if he would condescend to a more extended and cordial sympathy with his fellow-creatures; and we should have more variety of fine poetry, and, at all events, better tragedies. We have no business to read him a homily on the sinfulness of pride and uncharity; but we have a right to say, that it argues a poorness of genius to keep always to the same topics and persons; and that the world will weary at last of the most energetic pictures of misanthropes and madmen—outlaws and their mistresses!

A man gifted as he is, when he aspires at dramatic fame, should emulate the greatest of dramatists. Let Lord Byron then think of Shakespeare—and consider what a noble range of character, what a freedom from mannerism and egotism, there is in him! How much he seems to have studied nature; how little to have thought about himself; how seldom to have repeated or glanced back at his own most successful inventions! Why indeed should he? Nature was still open before him, and inexhaustible; and the freshness and variety that still delight his readers, must have had constant attractions for himself. Take his Hamlet, for instance. What a character is there!—how full of thought and refinement, and fancy and individuality! 'How infinite in faculties! In form and motion how express and admirable! The beauty of the universe, the paragon of animals!' Yet close the play, and we meet with him no more—neither in the author's other works, nor any where else! A common author, who had hit upon such a character, would have dragged it in at every turn, and worn it to very tatters. Sir John Falstaff, again, is a world of wit and humour in himself. But except in the two parts of Henry IV., there would have been no trace of such a being, had not the author been 'ordered to continue him' in the Merry Wives of Windsor. He is not the least like Benedick, or Mercutio, or Sir Toby Belch, or any of the other witty and jovial personages of the same author—nor are they like each other. Othello is one of the most striking and powerful inventions on the stage. But when the play closes, we hear no more of him! The poet's creation comes no more to life again, under a fictitious name, than the real man would have done. Lord Byron in Shakespeare's place, would have peopled the world with black Othellos! What indications are there of Lear in any of his earlier plays? What traces of it in any that he wrote after-wards? None. It might have been written by any other man, he is so little conscious of it. He never once returns to that huge sea of sorrow; but has left it standing by itself, shoreless and unapproach-able! Who else could have afforded not to have 'drowned the stage with tears' from such a source? But we must break away from Shakespeare, and come at last to the work before us.

[Jeffrey mocks Byron's championship of the dramatic unities, before going on to survey the plays separately, concluding with *Cain*.]

Of 'Cain, a Mystery,' we are constrained to say, that, though it abounds in beautiful passages, and shows more *power* perhaps than any of the author's dramatical compositions, we regret very much that it should ever have been published. It will give great scandal and offence to pious persons in general—and may be the means of suggesting the most painful doubts and distressing perplexities, to hundreds of minds that might never otherwise have been exposed to such dangerous disturbance. It is nothing less than absurd, in such a case, to observe, that Lucifer cannot well be expected to talk like an orthodox divine—and that the conversation of the first Rebel and the first Murderer was not likely to be very unexceptionable—or to plead the authority of Milton, or the authors of the old mysteries, for such offensive colloquies. The fact is, that here *the whole argument*—and a very elaborate and specious argument it is—is directed against the goodness or the power of the Deity, and against the reasonableness of religion in general; and there is no answer so much as attempted to the offensive doctrines that are so strenuously inculcated. The Devil and his pupil have the field entirely to themselves—and are encountered with nothing but feeble obtesta-tions and unreasoning horrors. Nor is this argumentative blasphemy a mere incidental deformity that arises in the course of an action directed to the common sympathies of our nature. It forms, on the contrary, the great staple of the piece—and occupies, we should

think, not less than two thirds of it; so that it is really difficult to
believe that it was written for any other purpose than to inculcate
these doctrines—or at least to discuss the question upon which they
bear. Now, we can certainly have no objection to Lord Byron
writing an Essay on the Origin of Evil—and sifting the whole of that
vast and perplexing subject with the force and the freedom that
would be expected and allowed in a fair philosophical discussion.
But we do not think it fair, thus to argue it partially and *con amore,*
in the name of Lucifer and Cain; without the responsibility or the
liability to answer that would attach to a philosophical disputant—
and in a form which both doubles the danger, if the sentiments are
pernicious, and almost precludes his opponents from the possibility
of a reply.

Philosophy and Poetry are both very good things in their way;
but, in our opinion, they do not go very well together. It is but a
poor and pedantic sort of poetry that seeks chiefly to embody
metaphysical subtilties and abstract deductions of reason—and a
very suspicious philosophy that aims at establishing its doctrines by
appeals to the passions and the fancy. Though such arguments,
however, are worth little in the schools, it does not follow that their
effect is inconsiderable in the world. On the contrary, it is the
mischief of all poetical paradoxes, that, from the very limits and end
of poetry, which deals only in obvious and glancing views, they are
never brought to the fair test of argument. An allusion to a doubtful
topic will often pass for a definitive conclusion on it; and, when
clothed in beautiful language, may leave the most pernicious impressions behind. In the courts of morality, poets are unexceptionable *witnesses*; they may give in the evidence, and depose to facts
whether good or ill; but we demur to their arbitrary and self-
pleasing summings up. They are suspected *judges,* and not very
often safe advocates; where great questions are concerned, and
universal principles brought to issue. But we shall not press this
point farther at present.

[Finally], we have a word or two to say on the griefs of Lord
Byron himself. He complains bitterly of the detraction by which he
has been assailed—and intimates that his works have been received
by the public with far less cordiality and favour than he was entitled
to expect. We are constrained to say that this appears to us a very
extraordinary mistake. In the whole course of our experience, we
cannot recollect a single author who has had so little reason to
complain of his reception—to whose genius the public has been so
early and so constantly just—to whose faults they have been so long
and so signally indulgent. From the very first, he must have been
aware that he offended the principles and shocked the prejudices of

the majority, by his sentiments, as much as he delighted them by his talents. Yet there never was an author so universally and warmly applauded, so gently admonished—so kindly entreated to look more heedfully to his opinions. He took the praise, as usual, and rejected the advice. As he grew in fame and authority, he aggravated all his offences—clung more fondly to all he had been reproached with—and only took leave of Childe Harold to ally himself to Don Juan! That he has since been talked of, in public and in private, with less unmingled admiration—that his name is now mentioned as often for censure as for praise—and that the exultation with which his countrymen once hailed the greatest of our living poets, is now alloyed by the recollection of the tendency of his writings—is matter of notoriety to all the world; but matter of surprise, we should imagine, to nobody but Lord Byron himself.

He would fain persuade himself, indeed, that for this decline of his popularity—or rather this stain upon its lustre—for he is still popular beyond all other example—and it is only because he is so that we feel any interest in this discussion;—he is indebted, not to any actual demerits of his own, but to the jealousy of those he has supplanted, the envy of those he has outshone, or the party rancour of those against whose corruptions he has testified;—while, at other times, he seems inclined to insinuate, that it is chiefly because he is a *Gentleman* and a *Nobleman* that plebeian censors have conspired to bear him down! We scarcely think, however, that these theories will pass with Lord Byron himself—we are sure they will pass with no other person. They are so manifestly inconsistent, as mutually to destroy each other—and so weak, as to be quite insufficient to account for the fact, even if they could be effectually combined for that purpose. *The party* that Lord Byron has chiefly offended, bears no malice to Lords and Gentlemen. Against its rancour, on the contrary, these qualities have undoubtedly been his best protection; and had it not been for them, he may be assured that he would, long ere now, have been shown up in the pages of the Quarterly, with the same candour and liberality that has there been exercised towards his friend Lady Morgan. That the base and the bigotted—those whom he has darkened by his glory, spited by his talent, or mortified by his neglect—have taken advantage of the prevailing disaffection, to vent their puny malice in silly nicknames and vulgar scurrility, is natural and true. But Lord Byron may depend upon it, that the dissatisfaction is not confined to them—and, indeed, that they would never have had the courage to assail one so immeasurably their superior, if he had not at once made himself vulnerable by his errors, and alienated his natural defenders by his obstinate adherence to them. *We* are not bigots or rival poets. We have not been detractors from Lord Byron's fame, nor the friends of his detractors; and *we* tell him—far more in sorrow than in anger—that we verily believe the great body of the English nation—the religious, the moral, and the candid part of it—consider the tendency of his writings to be immoral and pernicious—and look upon his perseverance in that strain of composition with regret and reprehension.

He has no priestlike cant or priestlike reviling to apprehend from us. We do not charge him with being either a disciple or an apostle of Satan; nor do we describe his poetry as a mere compound of blasphemy and obscenity. On the contrary, we are inclined to believe that he wishes well to the happiness of mankind—and are glad to testify, that his poems abound with sentiments of great dignity and tenderness, as well as passages of infinite sublimity and beauty. But their general tendency we believe to be in the highest degree pernicious; and we even think that it is chiefly by means of the fine and lofty sentiments they contain, that they acquire their most fatal power of corruption. This may sound at first, perhaps, like a paradox; but we are mistaken if we shall not make it intelligible enough in the end.

We think there are indecencies and indelicacies, seductive descriptions and profligate representations, which are extremely reprehensible; and also audacious speculations, and erroneous and uncharitable assertions, equally indefensible. But if these had stood alone, and if the whole body of his works had been made up of gaudy ribaldry and flashy scepticism, the mischief, we think, would have been much less than it is. He is not more obscene, perhaps, than Dryden or Prior, and other classical and pardoned writers; nor is there any passage in the history even of Don Juan, so offensively degrading as Tom Jones's affair with Lady Bellaston. It is no doubt a wretched apology for the indecencies of a man of genius, that equal indecencies have been forgiven to his predecessors: But the precedent of lenity might have been followed; and we might have passed both the levity and the voluptuousness—the dangerous warmth of his romantic situations, and the scandal of his cold-blooded dissipation. It might not have been so easy to get over his dogmatic scepticism—his hard-hearted maxims of misanthropy—his cold-blooded and eager expositions of the non-existence of virtue and honour. Even this, however, might have been comparatively harmless, if it had not been accompanied by that which may look, at first sight, as a palliation—the frequent presentment of the most touching pictures of tenderness, generosity, and faith.

The charge we bring against Lord Byron, in short, is, that his writings have a tendency to destroy all belief in the reality of virtue—and to make all enthusiasm and constancy of affection ridiculous; and this, not so much by direct maxims and examples, of an imposing or seducing kind, as by the constant exhibition of the most profligate heartlessness in the persons who had been transiently represented as actuated by the purest and most exalted emotions—and in the lessons of that very teacher who had been, but a moment before, so beautifully pathetic in the expression of the loftiest conceptions. When a gay voluptuary descants, somewhat too freely, on the intoxications of love and wine, we ascribe his excesses to the effervescence of youthful spirits, and do not consider him as seriously impeaching either the value or the reality of the severer virtues; and in the same way, when the satirist deals out his sarcasms against the sincerity of human professions, and unmasks the secret infirmities of our bosoms, we consider this as aimed at hypocrisy, and not at mankind: or, at all events, and in either case, we consider the Sensualist and the Misanthrope as wandering, each in his own delusion—and are contented to pity those who have never known the charms of a tender or generous affection. The true antidote to such seductive or revolting views of human nature, is to turn to the scenes of its nobleness and attraction; and to reconcile ourselves again to our kind, by listening to the accents of pure affection and incorruptible honour. But if those accents have flowed in all their sweetness, from the very lips that instantly open again to mock and blaspheme them, the antidote is mingled with the poison, and the draught is more deadly for the mixture!

The reveller may pursue his orgies, and the wanton display her enchantments, with comparative safety to those around them, as long as they know or believe that there are purer and higher enjoyments, and teachers and followers of a happier way. But if the Priest pass from the altar, with persuasive exhortations to peace and purity still trembling on his tongue, to join familiarly in the grossest and most profane debauchery—if the Matron, who has charmed all hearts by the lovely sanctimonies of her conjugal and maternal endearments, glides out from the circle of her children, and gives bold and shameless way to the most abandoned and degrading vices—our notions of right and wrong are at once confounded—our confidence in virtue shaken to the foundation—and our reliance on truth and fidelity at an end for ever.

This is the charge which we bring against Lord Byron. We say that, under some strange misapprehension as to the truth, and the duty of proclaiming it, he has exerted all the powers of his powerful mind to convince his readers, both directly and indirectly, that all ennobling pursuits, and disinterested virtues, are mere deceits or illusions—hollow and despicable mockeries for the most part, and, at best, but laborious follies. Religion, love, patriotism, valour, devotion, constancy, ambition—all are to be laughed at, disbelieved in, and despised!—and nothing is really good, so far as we can gather, but a succession of dangers to stir the blood, and of banquets and intrigues to sooth it again! If this doctrine stood alone, with its examples, it would revolt, we believe, more than it would seduce:—But the author of it has the unlucky gift of personating all those sweet and lofty illusions, and that with such grace and force, and truth to nature, that is impossible not to suppose, for the time, that he is among the most devoted of their votaries—till he casts off the character with a jerk—and, the moment after he has moved and exalted us to the very height of our conception, resumes his mockery at all things serious or sublime—and lets us down at once on some coarse joke, hard-hearted sarcasm, or fierce and relentless personality—as if on purpose to show

'Whoe'er was edified, himself was not'—

or to demonstrate practically as it were, and by example, how possible it is to have all fine and noble feelings, or their appearance, for a moment, and yet retain no particle of respect for them—or of belief in their intrinsic worth or permanent reality. Thus, we have an indelicate but very clever scene of young Juan's concealment in the bed of an amorous matron, and of the torrent of 'rattling and audacious eloquence' with which she repels the too just suspicions of her jealous lord. All this is merely comic, and a little coarse:— But then the poet chooses to make this shameless and abandoned woman address to her young gallant an epistle breathing the very spirit of warm, devoted, pure, and unalterable love—thus profaning the holiest language of the heart, and indirectly associating it with the most hateful and degrading sensuality. In like manner, the sublime and terrific description of the Shipwreck is strangely and disgustingly broken by traits of low humour and buffoonery;—and we pass immediately from the moans of an agonizing father fainting over his famished son, to facetious stories of Juan's begging a paw of his father's dog—and refusing a slice of his tutor!—as if it were a fine thing to be hard-hearted—and pity and compassion were fit only to be laughed at. In the same spirit, the glorious Ode on the aspirations of Greece after Liberty, is instantly followed up by a strain of dull and cold-blooded ribaldry;—and we are hurried on from the distraction and death of Haidee to merry scenes of intrigue and masquerading in the seraglio. Thus all good feelings are excited only to accustom us to their speedy and complete extinction; and we are brought back, from their transient and theatrical exhibition, to the staple and substantial doctrine of the work—the non-existence of constancy in women or honour in men, and the folly of expecting to meet with any such virtues, or of cultivating them, for an undeserving world;—and all this mixed up with so much wit and cleverness, and knowledge of human nature, as to make it irresistibly pleasant and plausible—while there is not only no antidote supplied, but every thing that might have operated in that way has been anticipated, and presented already in as strong and engaging a form as possible—but under such associations as to rob it of all efficacy, or even turn it into an auxiliary of the poison.

This is our sincere opinion of much of Lord Byron's most splendid poetry—a little exaggerated perhaps in the expression, from a desire to make our exposition clear and impressive—but, in substance, we think merited and correct. We have already said, and we deliberately repeat, that we have no notion that Lord Byron had any mischievous intention in these publications—and readily acquit him of any wish to corrupt the morals, or impair the happiness of his readers. Such a wish, indeed, in in itself altogether inconceivable; but it is our duty, nevertheless, to say, that much of what he has published appears to us to have this tendency—and that we are acquainted with no writings so well calculated to extinguish in young minds all generous enthusiasm and gentle affection—all respect for themselves, and all love for their kind—to make them practise and profess hardily what it teaches them to suspect in others—and actually to persuade them that it is wise and manly and knowing to laugh, not only at self-denial and restraint, but at all aspiring ambition, and all warm and constant affection.

How opposite to this is the system, or the temper, of the great author of Waverley—the only living individual to whom Lord Byron must submit to be ranked as inferior in genius—and still more deplorably inferior in all that makes genius either amiable in itself, or useful to society! With all his unrivalled power of invention and judgment, of pathos and pleasantry, the tenor of his sentiments is uniformly generous, indulgent, and good-humoured; and so remote from the bitterness of misanthropy, that he never indulges in sarcasm, and scarcely, in any case, carries his merriment so far as derision. But the peculiarity by which he stands most broadly and proudly distinguished from Lord Byron is, that, beginning, as he frequently does, with some ludicrous or satirical theme, he never fails to raise out of it some feelings of a generous or gentle kind, and to end by exciting our tender pity, or deep respect, for those very individuals or classes of persons who seemed at first to be brought on the stage for our mere sport and amusement—thus making the ludicrous itself subservient to the cause of benevolence—and inculcating, at every turn, and as the true end and result of all his trials and experiments, the love of our kind, and the duty and delight of a cordial and genuine sympathy with the joys and sorrows of every condition of men. It seems to be Lord Byron's way, on the contrary, never to excite a kind or a noble sentiment, without making haste to obliterate it by a torrent of unfeeling mockery or relentless abuse, and taking pains to show how well those passing fantasies may be reconciled to a system of resolute misanthropy, or so managed as even to enhance its merits, or confirm its truth. With what different sensations, accordingly, do we read the works of those two great writers!—With the one, we seem to share a gay and gorgeous banquet—with the other, a wild and dangerous intoxication. Let Lord Byron bethink him of this contrast—and its causes and effects. Though he scorns the precepts, and defies the censure of ordinary men, he may yet be moved by *the example* of his only superior!—In the mean time, we have endeavoured to point out the canker that stains the splendid flowers of his poetry—or, rather, the serpent that lurks beneath them. If it will not listen to the voice of the charmer, that brilliant garden, gay and glorious as it is, must be deserted, and its existence deplored, as a snare to the unwary.

English Literature—Prose

Jeffrey's interest in prose ranged widely from philosophy through polemics, history and memoirs to the novel. It is represented here by extracts from his reviews indicating his appreciation of the diary of Pepys and the novels of Richardson and Scott. In the article on Swift, Jeffrey draws a dark picture of the man and politician, which makes a fair critical assessment difficult for him.

19. Pepys's *Memoirs*

Edinburgh Review, 43, November 1825; *Contributions,* 1

The early nineteenth century was a golden age for the publication of the memoirs of the last two centuries. Their appearance was relished generally, and their contribution to both literature and history recognized. Such material was creatively used by Jeffrey's later reviewers, Carlyle and Macaulay.

We have a great indulgence, we confess, for the taste, or curiosity, or whatever it may be called, that gives its value to such publications as this; and are inclined to think the desire of knowing, pretty minutely, the manners and habits of former times,—of understanding, in all their details, the character and ordinary way of life and conversation of our forefathers—a very liberal and laudable desire; and by no means to be confounded with that hankering after contemporary slander, with which this age is so miserably infested, and so justly reproached. It is not only curious to see from what beginnings, and by what steps, we have come to be what we are: But it is most important, for the future and for the present, to ascertain what practices, and tastes, and principles, have been commonly found associated or dis-united: And as, in uncultivated lands, we can often judge of their inherent fertility by the quality of the weeds they spontaneously produce—so we may learn, by such an inspection of the moral growths of a country, compared with its subsequent history, what prevailing manners are indicative of vice or of virtue—what existing follies foretell approaching wisdom— what forms of licentiousness give promise of coming purity, and what of deeper degradation—what uncertain lights, in short, announce the *rising*, and what the *setting* sun! While, in like manner, we may trace in the same records the connection of public and private morality, and the mutual action and reaction of government and manners;—and discover what individual corruptions spring from political dishonour—what domestic profligacy leads to the sacrifice of freedom—and what national virtues are most likely to resist the oppressions, or yield to the seductions of courts.

Of all these things History tells us little—and yet they are the most important that she could have been employed in recording. She has been contented, however, for the most part, with detailing merely the broad and apparent results—the great public events and transactions, in which the true working principles of its destiny have their end and consummation; and points only to the wrecks or the triumphs that float down the tide of human affairs, without giving us any light as to those *ground currents* by which its central masses are governed, and of which those superficial appearances are, in most cases, the necessary, though unsuspected effects.

Every one feels, we think, how necessary this information is, if we wish to understand what antiquity really was, and what manner of men existed in former generations. How vague and unsatisfactory, without it, are all public annals and records of dynasties and battles—of how little interest to private individuals—of how little use even to philosophers and statesmen! Before we can apply any example in history, or even comprehend its actual import, we must know something of the character, both of the age and of the persons to which it belongs—and understand a good deal of the temper, tastes, and occupations, both of the actors and the sufferers. Good and evil, in truth, change natures, with a change of those circumstances; and we may be lamenting as the most intolerable of calamities, what was scarcely felt as an infliction, by those on whom it fell. Without this knowledge, therefore, the most striking and important events are mere wonders, to be stared at—altogether barren of instruction—and probably leading us astray, even as occasions of sympathy or moral emotion. Those minute details, in short, which History has so often rejected as below her dignity, are indispensable to give life, certainty, or reality to her delineations; and we should have little hesitation in asserting, that no history is really worth any thing, unless it relate to a people and an age of which we have also those humbler and more private memorials. It is not in the grand tragedy, or rather the epic fictions, of History, that we learn the true condition of former ages—the real character of past generations, or even the actual effects that were produced on society or individuals at the time, by the great events that are there so solemnly recorded.

If we have not some remnants or some infusion of the Comedy of middle life, we neither have any idea of the state and colour of the general existence, nor any just understanding of the transactions about which we are reading.

For what we know of the ancient Greeks for example—for all that enables us to imagine what sort of thing it would have been to have lived among them, or even what effects were produced on the society of Athens or Sparta by the battles of Marathon or Salamis, we are indebted not so much to the histories of Herodotus, Xenophon, or Thucydides, as to the Deipnosophists of Athenæus—the anecdotes of Plutarch—the introductory and incidental passages of the Platonic dialogues—the details of some of the private orations—and parts of the plays of Plautus and Terence, apparently copied from the Greek comedies. For our personal knowledge of the Romans, again, we do not look to Livy, or Dionysius—or even to Cæsar, Sallust, or Tacitus; but to Horace, Petronius, Juvenal, and the other satirists—to incidental notices in the Orations and Dialogues of Cicero—and above all to his invaluable letters,—followed up by those of Pliny,—to intimations in Plutarch, and Seneca, and Lucian—to the books of the Civil law—and the biographies and anecdotes of the Empire, from Suetonius to Procopius. Of the feudal times—the heroic age of modern Europe—we have fortunately more abundant and minute information, both in the Romances of chivalry, which embody all the details of upper life; and in the memoirs and chronicles of such writers as Commines and Froissart, which are filled with so many individual pictures and redundant particularities, as to leave us scarcely any thing more to learn or to wish for, as to the manners and character, the temper and habits, and even the daily life and conversation, of the predominating classes of society, who then stood for every thing in those countries: And, even with regard to their serfs and vassals, we are not without most distinct and intelligible lights—both in scattered passages of the works we have already referred to, in various ancient ballads and legends relating to their condition, and in such invaluable records as the humorous and more familiar tales of our immortal Chaucer. For the character and ordinary life of our more immediate ancestry, we may be said to owe our chief knowledge of it to Shakespeare, and the comic dramatists by whom he was succeeded—reinforced and supported by the infinite quantity of obscure and insignificant matter which the industry of his commentators has brought back to light for his elucidation—and which the matchless charm of his popularity has again rendered both interesting and familiar. The manners and habits of still later times are known to us, not by any means by our public histories, but by the writers of farces and comedies, polite essays, libels and satires—by collections of private letters, like those of Gray, Swift, Arbuthnot, and Lord Orford—by private memoirs or journals, such as those of Mrs. Lucy Hutchinson, Swift's Journal to Stella, and Doddington's Diary—and, in still later times, by the best of our gay and satirical novels—by caricature prints—by the better newspapers and magazines,—and by various minute accounts (in the manner of Boswell's Life of Johnson) of the private life and conversation of distinguished individuals.

The work before us relates to a period of which we have already very considerable memorials. But it is, notwithstanding, of very great interest and curiosity. A good deal of what it contains derives, no doubt, its chief interest from having happened 180 years ago: But there is little of it that does not, for that very reason, throw valuable lights on our intermediate history. It consists, as the title shows, of a very minute and copious Diary, continued from the year 1659 to 1669—and a correspondence, much less perfect and continuous, down nearly to the death of the author in 1703. Fortunately for the public part of the story, the author was, from the very beginning, in immediate contact with persons in high office and about court—and, still more fortunately for the private part, seems to have been possessed of the most extraordinary activity, and the most indiscriminating, insatiable, and miscellaneous curiosity, that ever prompted the researches, or supplied the pen, of a daily chronicler. Although excessively busy and diligent in his attendance at his office, he finds time to go to every play, to every execution, to every procession, fire, concert, riot, trial, review, city feast, public dissection, or picture gallery that he can hear of. Nay, there seems scarcely to have been a school examination, a wedding, christening, charity sermon, bull-baiting, philosophical meeting, or private merry-making in his neighbourhood, at which he was not sure to make his appearance, and mindful to record all the particulars. He is the first to hear all the court scandal, and all the public news—to observe the changes of fashions, and the downfall of parties—to pick up family gossip, and to retail philosophical intelligence—to criticise every new house or carriage that is built—every new book or new beauty that appears—every measure the King adopts, and every mistress he discards.

20. Swift's *Works*, edited by Scott

Edinburgh Review, 27, September 1816; *Contributions*, 1

The publication of Scott's edition gave Jeffrey an opportunity to present a pocket history of English literature, like that in the review of Ford's *Dramatic Works* five years before (no. 16). This discussion is not reprinted here.

In surveying Swift's life, Jeffrey attacks his sexual misconduct and political apostacy in terms worthy of Macaulay and almost of Swift himself. Having given this black portrait of the man, he finds it difficult to assess the qualities of the writing. Moreover, satire is not congenial to him. His judgment of Swift was highly partisan and unfortunately influential.

Of those ingenious writers, whose characteristic certainly was not vigour, any more than tenderness or fancy, SWIFT was indisputably the most vigorous—and perhaps the least tender or fanciful. The greater part of his works being occupied with politics and personalities that have long since lost all interest, can now attract but little attention, except as memorials of the manner in which politics and personalities were then conducted. In other parts, however, there is a vein of peculiar humour and strong satire, which will always be agreeable—and a sort of heartiness of abuse and contempt of mankind, which produces a greater sympathy and animation in the reader than the more elaborate sarcasms that have since come into fashion. Altogether his merits appear to be more *unique* and inimitable than those of any of his contemporaries . . . .

The Life is not every where extremely well written, in a literary point of view; but is drawn up, in substance, with great intelligence, liberality, and good feeling. It is quite fair and moderate in politics; and perhaps rather too indulgent and tender towards individuals of all descriptions,—more full, at least, of kindness and veneration for genius and social virtue, than of indignation at baseness and profligacy. Altogether, it is not much like the production of a mere man of letters, or a fastidious speculator in sentiment and morality; but exhibits throughout, and in a very pleasing form, the good sense and large toleration of a man of the world,—with much of that generous allowance for the

'Fears of the brave, and follies of the wise,'

which genius too often requires, and should therefore always be most forward to show. It is impossible, however, to avoid noticing, that Mr. Scott is by far too favourable to the personal character of his author; whom we think, it would really be injurious to the cause of morality to allow to pass, either as a very dignified or a very amiable person. The truth is, we think, that he was extremely ambitious, arrogant, and selfish; of a morose, vindictive, and haughty temper; and, though capable of a sort of patronizing generosity towards his dependants, and of some attachment towards those who had long known and flattered him, his general demeanour, both in public and private life, appears to have been far from exemplary.

Destitute of temper and magnanimity—and, we will add, of principle, in the former; and, in the latter, of tenderness, fidelity, or
compassion.

[Jeffrey verifies this sketch with reference to the documents in
Scott's edition, then he amplifies it, before turning to the writings.]

With these impressions of his personal character, perhaps it is not
easy for us to judge quite fairly of his works. Yet we are far from
being insensible to their great and very peculiar merits. Their chief
peculiarity is, that they were almost all what may be called occasional productions—not written for fame or for posterity—from the
fulness of the mind, or the desire of instructing mankind—but on
the spur of the occasion—for promoting some temporary and immediate object, and producing a practical effect, in the attainment
of which their whole importance centered. With the exception of the
Tale of a Tub, Gulliver, the Polite Conversation, and about half a
volume of poetry, this description will apply to almost all that is now
before us;—and it is no small proof of the vigour and vivacity of his
genius, that posterity should have been so anxious to preserve these
careless and hasty productions, upon which their author appears to
have set no other value that as means for the attainment of an end.
The truth is, accordingly, that *they are* very extraordinary performances: And, considered with a view to the purposes for which they
were intended, have probably never been equalled in any period of
the world. They are written with great plainness, force, and intrepidity—advance at once to the matter in dispute—give battle to the
strength of the enemy, and never seek any kind of advantage from
darkness or obscurity. Their distinguishing feature, however, is the
force and the vehemence of the invective in which they abound;—
the copiousness, the steadiness, the perseverance, and the dexterity
with which abuse and ridicule are showered upon the adversary.
This, we think, was, beyond all doubt, Swift's great talent, and the
weapon by which he made himself formidable. He was, without
exception, the greatest and most efficient *libeller* that ever exercised
the trade; and possessed, in an eminent degree, all the qualifications
which it requires:—a clear head—a cold heart—a vindictive temper—no admiration of noble qualities—no sympathy with suffering—not much conscience—not much consistency—a ready wit—a
sarcastic humour—a thorough knowledge of the baser parts of
human nature—and a complete familiarity with every thing that is
low, homely, and familiar in language. These were his gifts;—and he
soon felt for what ends they were given. Almost all his works are
libels; generally upon individuals, sometimes upon sects and parties,
sometimes upon human nature. Whatever be his end, however,

personal abuse, direct, vehement, unsparing invective, is his means. It is his sword and his shield, his panoply and his chariot of war. In all his writings, accordingly, there is nothing to raise or exalt our notions of human nature,—but every thing to vilify and degrade. We may learn from them, perhaps, to dread the consequences of base actions, but never to love the feelings that lead to generous ones. There is no spirit, indeed, of love or of honour in any part of them; but an unvaried and harassing display of insolence and animosity in the writer, and villainy and folly in those of whom he is writing. Though a great polemic, he makes no use of general principles, nor ever enlarges his views to a wide or comprehensive conclusion. Every thing is particular with him, and, for the most part, strictly personal. To make amends, however, we do think him quite without a competitor in personalities. With a quick and sagacious spirit, and a bold and popular manner, he joins an exact knowledge of all the strong and the weak parts of every cause he has to manage; and, without the least restraint from delicacy, either of taste or of feeling, he seems always to think the most effectual blows the most advisable, and no advantage unlawful that is likely to be successful for the moment. Disregarding all the laws of polished hostility, he uses, at one and the same moment, his sword and his poisoned dagger—his hands and his teeth, and his envenomed breath,—and does not even scruple, upon occasion, to imitate his own yahoos, by discharging on his unhappy victims a shower of filth, from which neither courage nor dexterity can afford any protection.—Against such an antagonist, it was, of course, at no time very easy to make head; and accordingly his invective seems, for the most part, to have been as much dreaded, and as tremendous as the personal ridicule of Voltaire. Both were inexhaustible, well directed and unsparing; but even when Voltaire drew blood, he did not mangle the victim, and was only mischievous when Swift was brutal. Any one who will compare the epigrams on M. Franc de Pompignan and those on Tighe or Bettesworth, will easily understand the distinction.

[Jeffrey discusses *The Tale of the Tub* and then *Gulliver.*]

The voyages of Captain Lemuel Gulliver is indisputably his greatest work. The idea of making fictitious travels the vehicle of satirc as well as of amusement, is at least as old as Lucian; but has never been carried into execution with such success, spirit, and originality, as in this celebrated performance. The brevity, the minuteness, the homeliness, the unbroken seriousness of the narrative, all give a character of truth and simplicity to the work, which at once palliates the extravagance of the fiction, and enhances the effect of those weighty reflections and cutting severities in which it abounds. Yet though it is probable enough, that without those touches of satire and observation the work would have appeared childish and preposterous, we are persuaded that it pleases chiefly by the novelty and vivacity of the extraordinary pictures it presents, and the entertainment we receive from following the fortunes of the traveller in his several extraordinary adventures. The greater part of the wisdom and satire at least appears to us to be extremely vulgar and common-place; and we have no idea that they could possibly appear either impressive or entertaining, if presented without these accompaniments. A considerable part of the pleasure we derive from the voyages of Gulliver, in short, is of the same description with that which we receive from those of Sinbad the sailor; and is chiefly heightened, we believe, by the greater brevity and minuteness of the story, and the superior art that is employed to give it an appearance of truth and probability, in the very midst of its wonders . . . .

That the interest does not arise from the satire but from the plausible description of physical wonders, seems to be farther proved by the fact, that the parts which please the least are those in which there is most satire and least of those wonders. In the voyage to Laputa, after the first description of the flying island, the attention is almost exclusively directed to intellectual absurdities; and every one is aware of the dulness that is the result. Even as a satire, indeed, this part is extremely poor and defective; nor can any thing show more clearly the author's incapacity for large and comprehensive views than his signal failure in all those parts which invited him to such contemplations. In the multitude of his vulgar and farcical representations of particular errors in philosophy, he nowhere appears to have any sense of its true value or principles; but satisfies himself with collecting or imagining a number of fantastical quackeries, which tend to illustrate nothing but his contempt for human understanding. Even where his subject seems to invite him to something of a higher flight, he uniformly shrinks back from it, and takes shelter in common-place derision. What, for instance, can be poorer than the use he makes of the evocation of the illustrious dead—in which Hannibal is conjured up, just to say that he had not a drop of vinegar in his camp; and Aristotle, to ask two of his commentators, 'whether the rest of the tribe were as great dunces as themselves?' The voyage to the Houyhnhmns is commonly supposed to displease by its vile and degrading representations of human nature; but, if we do not strangely mistake our own feelings on the subject, the impression it produces is not so much that of disgust as of dulness. The picture is not only extravagant, but bald and tame in the highest degree; while the story is not enlivened by any of those numerous and uncommon incidents which are detailed in the two first parts, with such an inimitable air of probability as almost to persuade us of their reality. For the rest, we have observed already, that the scope of the whole work, and indeed of all his writings, is to degrade and vilify human nature; and though some of the images which occur in this part may be rather coarser than the others, we do not think the difference so considerable as to account for its admitted inferiority in the power of pleasing.

His only other considerable works in prose, are the 'Polite Conversation,' which we think admirable in its sort, and excessively entertaining; and the 'Directions to Servants,' which, though of a lower pitch, contains as much perhaps of his peculiar, vigorous and racy humour, as any one of his productions. The Journal to Stella, which was certainly never intended for publication, is not to be judged of as a literary work at all—but to us it is the most interesting of all his productions—exhibiting not only a minute and masterly view of a very extraordinary political crisis, but a truer, and, upon the whole, a more favourable picture of his own mind, than can be gathered from all the rest of his writings—together with innumerable anecdotes characteristic not only of various eminent individuals, but of the private manners and public taste and morality of the times, more nakedly and surely authentic than any thing that can be derived from contemporary publications.

[Jeffrey dismisses Swift as a poet before reaching a general conclusion.]

We have not left ourselves room now to say much of Swift's style, or of the general character of his literary genius:—But our opinion may be collected from the remarks we have made on particular passages, and from our introductory observations on the school or class of authors, with whom he must undoubtedly be rated. On the subjects to which he confines himself, he is unquestionably a strong, masculine, and perspicuous writer. He is never finical, fantastic, or absurd—takes advantage of no equivocations in argument—and puts on no tawdriness for ornament. Dealing always with particulars, he is safe from all great and systematic mistakes; and, in fact, reasons mostly in a series of small and minute propositions, in the handling of which, dexterity is more requisite than genius; and practical good sense, with an exact knowledge of transactions, of far more importance than profound and high-reaching judgment. He did not write history or philosophy, but party pamphlets and journals;—not satire, but particular lampoons;—not pleasantries for all mankind, but jokes for a particular circle. Even in his pamphlets, the broader questions of party are always waved, to make way for discussions of personal or immediate interest. His object is not to show that the Tories have better principles of government than the Whigs,—but to prove Lord Oxford an angel, and Lord Somers a fiend, to convict the Duke of Marlborough of avarice or Sir Richard Steele of insolvency;—not to point out the wrongs of Ireland, in the depression of her Catholic population, her want of education, or the discouragement of her industry; but to raise an outcry against an amendment of the copper or the gold coin, or against a parliamentary proposition for remitting the tithe of *agistment.* For those ends, it cannot be denied, that he chose his means judiciously, and used them with incomparable skill and spirit. But to choose such ends, we humble conceive, was not the part either of a high intellect or a high character; and his genius must share in the disparagement which ought perhaps to be confined to the impetuosity and vindictiveness of his temper.

Of his style, it has been usual to speak with great, and, we think, exaggerated praise. It is less mellow than Dryden's—less elegant than Pope's or Addison's—less free and noble than Lord Bolingbroke's—and utterly without the glow and loftiness which belonged to our earlier masters. It is radically a low and homely style— without grace and without affectation; and chiefly remarkable for a great choice and profusion of *common* words and expressions. Other writers, who have used a plain and direct style, have been for the most part jejune and limited in their diction, and generally give us an impression of the poverty as well as the tameness of their language; but Swift, without ever trespassing into figured or poetical expressions, or ever employing a word that can be called fine, or pedantic, has a prodigious variety of good set phrases always at his command, and displays a sort of homely richness, like the plenty of an old English dinner, or the wardrobe of a wealthy burgess. This taste for the plain and substantial was fatal to his poetry, which subsists not on such elements; but was in the highest degree favourable to the effect of his humour, very much of which depends on the imposing gravity with which it is delivered, and on the various turns and heightenings it may receive from a rapidly shifting and always appropriate expression. Almost all his works, after the Tale of a Tub, seem to have been written very fast, and with very little minute care of the diction. For his own ease, therefore, it is probable they were all pitched on a low key, and set about on the ordinary tone of a familiar letter or conversation; as that from which there was little hazard of falling, even in moments of negligence, and from which any rise that could be effected, must always be easy and conspicuous. A man fully possessed of his subject, indeed, and confident of his cause, may almost always write with vigour and effect, if he can get over the temptation of writing finely, and really confine himself to the strong and clear exposition of the matter he has to bring forward. Half of the affectation and offensive pretension we meet with in authors, arises from a want of matter,—and the other half, from a paltry ambition of being eloquent and ingenious out of place. Swift had complete confidence in himself; and had too much real business on his hands, to be at leisure to intrigue for the fame of a fine writer;—in consequence of which, his writings are more admired by the judicious than if he had bestowed all his attention on their style. He was so much a man of business, indeed, and so much accustomed to consider his writings merely as means for the attainment of a practical end—whether that end was the strengthening of a party, or the wounding a foe—that he not only disdained the reputation of a composer of pretty sentences, but seems to have been thoroughly indifferent to all sorts of literary fame. He enjoyed the notoriety and influence which he had procured by his writings; but it was the glory of having carried his point, and not of having written well, that he valued. As soon as his publications had served their turn, they seem to have been entirely forgotten by their author;—and, desirous as he was of being richer, appears to have thought as little of making money as immortality by means of them. He mentions somewhere, that except 300*l.* which he got for Gulliver, he never made a farthing by any of his writings . . . .

In humour and in irony, and in the talent of debasing and defiling what he hated, we join with all the world in thinking the Dean of St. Patrick's without a rival. His humour, though sufficiently marked and peculiar, is not to be easily defined. The nearest description we can give of it, would make it consist in expressing sentiments the most absurd and ridiculous—the most shocking and atrocious—or sometimes the most energetic and original—in a sort of composed, calm, and unconscious way, as if they were plain, undeniable, commonplace truths, which no person could dispute, or expect to gain credit by announcing—and in maintaining them, always in the gravest and most familiar language, with a consistency which somewhat palliates their extravagance, and a kind of perverted ingenuity, which seems to give pledge for their sincerity. The secret, in short, seems to consist in employing the language of humble good sense, and simple undoubting conviction, to express, in their honest nakedness, sentiments which it is usually thought necessary to disguise under a thousand pretences—or truths which are usually introduced with a thousand apologies. The basis of the art is the personating a character of great simplicity and openness, for whom the conventional or artificial distinctions of society are supposed to have no existence; and making use of this character as an instrument to strip vice and folly of their disguises, and expose guilt in all its deformity, and truth in all its terrors. Independent of the moral or satire, of which they may thus be the vehicle, a great part of the entertainment to be derived from works of humour, arises from the contrast between the grave, unsuspecting indifference of the character personated, and the ordinary feelings of the world on the subjects which he discusses. The contrast it is easy to heighten, by all sorts of imputed absurdities: in which case, the humour degenerates into mere farce and buffoonery. Swift has yielded a little to this temptation in the Tale of a Tub; but scarcely at all in Gulliver, or any of his later writings in the same style. Of his talent for reviling, we have already said at least enough, in some of the preceding pages.

21. Richardson's *Correspondence*

Edinburgh Review, 5, October 1804; *Contributions,* 1

The conclusion of the review is given. It is favourable to the novelist, though not to his letters.

The great excellence of Richardson's novels consists, we think, in the unparalleled minuteness and copiousness of his descriptions, and in the pains he takes to make us thoroughly and intimately acquainted with every particular in the character and situation of the personages with whom we are occupied. It has been the policy of other writers to avoid all details that are not necessary or impressive, to hurry over all the preparatory scenes, and to reserve the whole of the reader's attention for those momentous passages in which some decisive measure is adopted, or some great passion brought into action. The consequence is, that we are only acquainted with their characters in their dress of ceremony, and that, as we never see them except in those critical circumstances, and those moments of strong emotion, which are but of rare occurrence in real life, we are never deceived into any belief of their reality, and contemplate the whole as an exaggerated and dazzling illusion. With such authors we merely make a visit by appointment, and see and hear only what we know has been prepared for our reception. With Richardson, we slip, invisible, into the domestic privacy of his characters, and hear and see every thing that is said and done among them, whether it be interesting or otherwise, and whether it gratify our curiosity or disappoint it. We sympathise with the former, therefore, only as we sympathise with the monarchs and statesmen of history, of whose condition as individuals we have but a very imperfect conception. We feel for the latter, as for our private friends and acquaintance, with whose whole situation we are familiar, and as to whom we can conceive exactly the effects that will be produced by every thing that may befall them. In this art Richardson is undoubtedly without an equal, and, if we except De Foe, without a competitor, we believe, in the whole history of literature. We are often fatigued, as we listen to his prolix descriptions, and the repetitions of those rambling and inconclusive conversations, in which so many pages are consumed, without any apparent progress in the story; but, by means of all this, we get so intimately acquainted with the characters, and so impressed with a persuasion of their reality, that when any thing really disastrous or important occurs to them, we feel as for old friends and companions, and are irresistibly led to as lively a conception of their sensations, as if we had been spectators of a real transaction. This we certainly think the chief merit of Richardson's productions: For, great as his knowledge of the human heart, and his powers of pathetic description, must be admitted to be, we are of opinion that he might have been equalled in those particulars by many, whose productions are infinitely less interesting.

That his pieces were all intended to be strictly moral, is indisputable; but it is not quite so clear, that they will uniformly be found to have this tendency. We have already quoted some observations of Mrs. Barbauld's on this subject, and shall only add, in general, that there is a certain air of irksome regularity, gloominess, and pedantry, attached to most of his virtuous characters, which is apt to encourage more unfortunate associations than the engaging qualities with which he has invested some of his vicious ones. The mansion of the Harlowes, which, before the appearance of Lovelace, is represented as the abode of domestic felicity, is a place in which daylight can scarcely be supposed to shine; and Clarissa, with her formal devotions, her intolerably early rising, her day divided into tasks, and her quantities of needle-work and discretion, has something in her much less winning and attractive than inferior artists have often communicated to an innocent beauty of seventeen. The solemnity and moral discourses of Sir Charles, his bows, minuets, compliments and immoveable tranquillity, are much more likely to excite the derision than the admiration of a modern reader. Richardson's good people, in short, are too wise and too formal, ever to appear in the light of desirable companions, or to excite in a youthful mind any wish to resemble them. The gaiety of all his characters, too, is extremely girlish and silly, and is much more like the prattle of spoiled children, than the wit and pleasantry of persons acquainted with the world. The diction throughout is heavy, vulgar, and embarrassed; though the interest of the tragical scenes is too powerful to

allow us to attend to any inferior consideration. The novels of
Richardson, in short, though praised perhaps somewhat beyond
their merits, will always be read with admiration; and certainly can
never appear to greater advantage than when contrasted with the
melancholy farrago which is here entitled his Correspondence.

22. Scott's *Waverley*

Edinburgh Review, 24, November 1814; *Contributions*, 3

Scott's poetry and novels were so popular that he did not need the
support of Jeffrey's critical enthusiasm. Though Jeffrey admires his
compatriot as a national writer, capable of something of the fidelity
to nature of Shakespeare himself, his immediate reaction is generally cool. He wants to temper the popular reaction to the works of a
writer who, though a friend, was also a prominent and influential
Tory.

Later, in the *Contributions*,[45] Jeffrey called Scott's novels 'the
most remarkable productions of the age,' and their author inferior
only to Shakespeare.

It is wonderful what genius and adherence to nature will do, in spite
of all disadvantages. Here is a thing obviously very hastily, and, in
many places, somewhat unskilfully written—composed, one half of
it, in a dialect unintelligible to four-fifths of the reading population
of the country—relating to a period too recent to be romantic, and
too far gone by to be familiar—and published, moreover, in a
quarter of the island where materials and talents for novel-writing
have been supposed to be equally wanting: And yet, by the mere
force and truth and vivacity of its colouring, already casting the
whole tribe of ordinary novels into the shade, and taking its place
rather with the most popular of our modern poems, than with the
rubbish of provincial romances.

The secret of this success, we take it, is merely that the author is a
man of Genius; and that he has, notwithstanding, had virtue enough
to be true to Nature throughout; and to content himself, even in the
marvellous parts of his story, with copying from actual existences,
rather than from the phantasms of his own imagination. The charm
which this communicates to all works that deal in the representation
of human actions and character, is more readily felt than understood; and operates with unfailing efficacy even upon those who
have no acquaintance with the originals from which the picture has
been borrowed. It requires no ordinary talent, indeed, to choose
such realities as may outshine the bright imaginations of the inven-

tive, and so to combine them as to produce the most advantageous effect; but when this is once accomplished, the result is sure to be something more firm, impressive, and engaging, than can ever be produced by mere fiction.

The object of the work before us, was evidently to present a faithful and animated picture of the manners and state of society that prevailed in this northern part of the island, in the earlier part of last century; and the author has judiciously fixed upon the era of the Rebellion in 1745, not only as enriching his pages with the interest inseparably attached to the narration of such occurrences, but as affording a fair opportunity for bringing out all the contrasted principles and habits which distinguished the different classes of persons who then divided the country, and formed among them the basis of almost all that was peculiar in the national character. That unfortunate contention brought conspicuously to light, and, for the last time, the fading image of feudal chivalry in the mountains, and vulgar fanaticism in the plains; and startled the more polished parts of the land with the wild but brilliant picture of the devoted valour, incorruptible fidelity, patriarchal brotherhood, and savage habits, of the Celtic Clans, on the one hand,—and the dark, intractable, and domineering bigotry of the Covenanters on the other. Both aspects of society had indeed been formerly prevalent in other parts of the country,—but had there been so long superseded by more peaceable habits, and milder manners, that their vestiges were almost effaced, and their very memory nearly extinguished. The feudal principalities had been destroyed in the South, for near 300 years,—and the dominion of the Puritans from the time of the Restoration. When the glens, and banded clans, of the central Highlands, therefore, were opened up to the gaze of the English, in the course of that insurrection, it seemed as if they were carried back to the days of the Heptarchy;—and when they saw the array of the West country Whigs, they might imagine themselves transported to the age of Cromwell. The effect, indeed, is almost as startling at the present moment; and one great source of the interest which the volumes before us undoubtedly possess, is to be sought in the surprise that is excited by discovering, that in our own country, and almost in our own age, manners and characters existed, and were conspicuous, which we had been accustomed to consider as belonging to remote antiquity, or extravagant romance.

The way in which they are here represented must satisfy every reader, we think, by an inward *tact* and conviction, that the delineation has been made from actual experience and observation;— experience and observation employed perhaps only on a few surviving relics and specimens of what was familiar a little earlier—but generalised from instances sufficiently numerous and complete, to warrant all that may have been added to the portrait:—And, indeed, the existing records and vestiges of the more extraordinary parts of the representation are still sufficiently abundant, to satisfy all who have the means of consulting them, as to the perfect accuracy of the picture. The great traits of Clannish dependence, pride and fidelity, may still be detected in many districts of the Highlands, though they do not now adhere to the chieftains when they mingle in general society; and the existing contentions of Burghers and Antiburghers, and Cameronians, though shrunk into comparative insignificance, and left, indeed, without protection to the ridicule of the profane, may still be referred to, as complete verifications of all that is here stated about Gifted Gilfillan, or Ebenezer Cruickshank. The traits of Scottish national character in the lower ranks, can still less be regarded as antiquated or traditional; nor is there any thing in the whole compass of the work which gives us a stronger impression of the nice observation and graphical talent of the author, than the extraordinary fidelity and felicity with which all the inferior agents in the story are represented. No one who has not lived extensively among the lower orders of all descriptions, and made himself familiar with their various tempers and dialects, can perceive the full merit of those rapid and characteristic sketches; but it requires only a general knowledge of human nature, to feel that they must be faithful copies from known originals; and to be aware of the extraordinary facility and flexibility of hand which has touched, for instance, with such discriminating shades, the various gradations of the Celtic character, from the savage imperturbability of Dugald Mahony, who stalks grimly about with his battle-axe on his shoulder, without speaking a word to any one,—to the lively unprincipled activity of Callum Beg,—the coarse unreflecting hardihood and heroism of Evan Maccombich,—and the pride, gallantry, elegance, and ambition of Fergus himself. In the lower class of the Lowland characters, again, the vulgarity of Mrs. Flockhart and of Lieutenant Jinker is perfectly distinct and original;—as well as the puritanism of Gilfillan and Cruickshank—the atrocity of Mrs. Mucklewrath—and the slow solemnity of Alexander Saunderson. The Baron of Bradwardine, and Baillie Macwheeble, are caricatures no doubt, after the fashion of the caricatures in the novels of Smollet,—or pictures, at the best, of individuals who must always have been unique and extraordinary: but almost all the other personages in the history are fair representatives of classes that are still existing, or may be remembered at least to have existed, by many whose recollections do not extend quite so far back as to the year 1745.

[Jeffrey gives an outline of the story, with long extracts. He continues:]

The gay scenes of the Adventurer's court—the breaking up of his army from Edinburgh—the battle of Preston—and the whole process of his disastrous advance and retreat from the English provinces, are given with the greatest brilliancy and effect—as well as the scenes of internal disorder and rising disunion that prevail in his scanty army—the quarrel with Fergus—and the mystical visions by which that devoted chieftain foresees his disastrous fate. The lower scenes again with Mrs. Flockhart, Mrs. Nosebag, Callum-Beg, and the Cumberland peasants, though to some fastidious readers they may appear coarse and disgusting, are painted with a force and a truth to nature, which equally bespeak the powers of the artist, and are incomparably superior to any thing of the sort which has been offered to the public for the last 'sixty years.' There are also various copies of verses scattered through the work, which indicate poetical talents of no ordinary description—though bearing, perhaps still more distinctly that the prose, the traces of considerable carelessness and haste.

The worst part of the book by far is that portion of the first volume which contains the history of the hero's residence in England—and next to it is the laborious, tardy, and obscure explanation of some puzzling occurrences in the story, which the reader would, in general, be much better pleased to be permitted to forget—and which are neither well explained after all, nor at all worth explaining.

There has been much speculation, at least in this quarter of the island, about the authorship of this singular performance—and certainly it is not easy to conjecture why it is still anonymous.— Judging by internal evidence, to which alone we pretend to have access, we should not scruple to ascribe it to the highest of those authors to whom it has been assigned by the sagacious conjectures of the public;—and this at least we will venture to say, that if it be indeed the work of an author hitherto unknown, Mr. Scott would do well to look to his laurels, and to rouse himself for a sturdier competition than any he has yet had to encounter!

Foreign Literature

Jeffrey considered genius universal, but, in accordance with the associationist theory of Alison, he allowed for the variety of national taste. In his criticism he paid some attention, not only to the literature of England and Scotland, but also that of ancient Greece and Rome, and of modern France, Italy and Germany. He gave less consideration than he might have otherwise done to the classics, partly because of his Scottish education. In Scotland the emphasis was more on philosophical theory. Jeffrey did comment on Greek literature, particularly drama and poetry, in his article on Mme. de Staël's *De la Littérature* (no. 23). Amongst the writings of modern France, he was attracted to the aristocratic memoirs of the pre-Revolutionary court; he was stimulated by the intellectual contributions of Mme. de Staël to cultural history. Of the Italians he appreciated Alfieri and Foscolo. He showed little sympathy for Goethe (no. 24). He welcomed, though not uncritically, developments in American English, for example in the work of Franklin and Washington Irving.

23. Mme. de Staël's De la Littérature considérée dans ses Rapports avec les Institutions Sociales

Edinburgh Review, 21, February 1813; *Contributions*, 1

Jeffrey provides another appraisal of this author in the *Edinburgh Review* five years later.[46] He is especially impressed with the connection that Mme. de Staël makes between literature and society in their historical development. Her view probably influenced the growth of his own critical thought. He presents an elaborate critique of her theory of human perfectibility from the standpoint of British, Whig empiricism.

Jeffrey's critique of Mme. de Staël's theory of perfectibility is represented here by its conclusion, a discussion of the pressing problem of the growing accumulation of knowledge. His views on this topic have been expounded most fully by Walter Jackson Bate.[47] Jeffrey's critique shows his very cool response to the enlightenment notion of progress.

The real and radical difficulty is to find some laudable pursuit that will permanently interest,—some worthy object that will continue to captivate and engross the faculties: and this, instead of becoming easier in proportion as our intelligence increases, obviously becomes more difficult. It is knowledge that destroys enthusiasm, and dispels all those prejudices of admiration which people simpler minds with so many idols of enchantment. It is knowledge that distracts by its variety, and satiates by its abundance, and generates, by its communication, that dark and cold spirit of fastidiousness and derision which revenges on those whom it possesses, the pangs which it inflicts on those on whom it is exerted. Yet it is to the increase of knowledge and talents alone, that the prophets of perfectibility look forward for the cure of all our vices and all our unhappiness!

Even as to intellect, and the pleasures that are to be derived from the exercise of a vigorous understanding, we doubt greatly whether we ought to look forward to posterity with any very lively feelings of envy or humiliation. More knowledge they probably will have,—as we have undoubtedly more knowledge than our ancestors had two hundred years ago; but for vigour of understanding, or pleasure in the exercise of it, we must beg leave to demur. The more there is already known, the less there remains to be discovered; and the more time a man is obliged to spend in ascertaining what his predecessors have already established, the less he will have to bestow in adding to its amount. The time, however, is of less consequence; but the habits of mind that are formed by walking patiently, humbly, and passively in the paths that have been traced by others, are the very habits that disqualify us for vigorous and independent excursions of our own. There is a certain degree of knowledge to be sure, that is but wholesome aliment to the understanding—materials for it to work upon—or instruments to facilitate its labours:—but a larger quantity is apt to oppress and incumber it; and as industry, which is excited by the importation of the raw material, may be superseded and extinguished by the introduction of the finished manufacture, so the minds which are stimulated to activity by a certain measure of instruction may, unquestionably, be reduced to a state of passive and languid acquiescence, by a more profuse and redundant supply.

Madame de Staël, and the other advocates of her system, talk a great deal of the prodigious advantage of having the results of the laborious discoveries of one generation made matters of familiar and elementary knowledge in another; and for practical utility, it may be so: but nothing, we conceive, can be so completely destructive of all intellectual enterprise, and all force and originality of thinking, as this very process, of the reduction of knowledge to its results, or the multiplication of those summary and accessible pieces of information in which the student is saved the whole trouble of investigation, and put in possession of the prize, without either the toils or the excitement of the contest. This, in the first place, necessarily makes the prize much less a subject of exultation or delight to him; for the chief pleasure is in the chase itself, and not in the object which it pursues: and he who sits at home, and has the dead game brought to the side of his chair, will be very apt, we believe, to regard it as nothing better than an unfragrant vermin. But, in the next place, it does him no good; for he misses altogether the invigorating exercise, and the invaluable training to habits of emulation and sagacity and courage, for the sake of which alone the pursuit is deserving of applause. And, in the last place, he not only fails in this way to acquire the qualities that may enable him to run down knowledge for himself, but necessarily finds himself without taste or inducement for such exertions. He thinks, and in one sense he thinks justly, that if the proper object of study be to acquire knowledge, he can employ his time much more profitably in implicitly listening to the discoveries of others, than in a laborious attempt to discover something for himself. It is infinitely more fatiguing to think, than to remember; and incomparably shorter to be led to an object, than to explore our own way to it. It is inconceivable what an obstruction this furnishes to the original exercise of the understanding in a certain state of information; and how effectually the general diffusion of easily accessible knowledge operates as a bounty upon indolence and mental imbecility. Where the quantity of approved and collected knowledge is already very great in any country, it is naturally required of all well educated persons to possess a considerable share of it; and where it has also been made very accessible, by being reduced to its summary and ultimate results, an astonishing variety of those abstracts may be stowed away in the memory, with scarcely any fatigue or exercise to the other faculties. The whole mass of attainable intelligence, however, must still be beyond the reach of any individual; and he may go on, therefore, to the end of a long and industrious life, constantly acquiring knowledge in this cheap and expeditious manner. But if, in the course of these passive and humble researches, he should be tempted to inquire a little for himself, he cannot fail to be struck with the prodigious waste of time, and of labour, that is necessary for the attainment of a very inconsiderable portion of original knowledge. His progress is as slow as that of a man who is making a road, compared with that of those who afterwards travel over it; and he feels, that in order to make a very small advance in one department of study, he must consent to sacrifice very great attainments in others. He is disheartened, too, by the extreme insignificance of any thing that he can expect to contribute, when compared with the great store that is already in possession of the public; and is extremely apt to conclude, that it is not only safer, but more profitable to follow, than to lead; and that it is fortunate for the lovers of wisdom, that our ancestors have accumulated enough of it for our use, as well as for their own.

But while the general diffusion of knowledge tends thus powerfully to repress all original and independent speculation in individuals, it operates still more powerfully in rendering the public indifferent and unjust to their exertions. The treasures they have inherited from their predecessors are so ample, as not only to take away all disposition to labour for their farther increase, but to lead them to undervalue and overlook any little addition that may be made to them by the voluntary offerings of individuals. The works of the best models are perpetually before their eyes, and their accumulated glory in their remembrance; the very variety of the sorts of excellence which are constantly obtruded on their notice, renders excellence itself cheap and vulgar in their estimation. As the mere possessors or judges of such things, they are apt to ascribe to themselves a character of superiority, which renders any moderate performance unworthy of their regard; and their cold and languid familiarity with what is best, ultimately produces no other effect than to render them insensible to its beauties, and at the same time intolerant of all that appears to fall short of it.

In such a condition of society, it is obvious that men must be peculiarly disinclined from indulging in those bold and original speculations, for which their whole training had previously disqualified them; and we appeal to our readers, whether there are not, at this day, apparent symptoms of such a condition of society. A childish love of novelty may indeed give a transient popularity to works of mere amusement; but the age of original genius, and of comprehensive and independent reasoning, seems to be over. Instead of such works as those of Bacon, and Shakespeare, and Taylor, and Hooker, we have Encyclopædias, and geographical compilations, and county histories, and new editions of black letter authors—and trashy biographies and posthumous letters—and disputations upon prosody—and ravings about orthodoxy and methodism. Men of general information and curiosity seldom think of adding to the knowledge that is already in the world; and the inferior persons upon whom that task is consequently devolved, carry it on, for the most part, by means of that minute subdivision of labour which is the great secret of the mechanical arts, but can never be introduced into literature without depriving its higher branches of all force, dignity, or importance. One man spends his life in improving a method of dyeing cotton red;—another in adding a few insects to a catalogue which nobody reads;—a third in settling the metres of a few Greek Choruses;—a fourth in decyphering illegible romances, or old grants of farms;—a fifth in picking rotten bones out of the earth;—a sixth in describing all the old walls and hillocks in his parish;—and five hundred others in occupations equally liberal and important: each of them being, for the most part, profoundly ignorant of every thing out of his own narrow department, and very generally and deservedly despised, by his competitors for the favour of that public—which despises and supports them all.

Such, however, it appears to us, is the state of mind that is naturally produced by the great accumulation and general diffusion of various sorts of knowledge. Men learn, instead of reasoning. Instead of meditating, they remember; and, in place of the glow of inventive genius, or the warmth of a generous admiration, nothing is to be met with, in society, but timidity on the one hand, and fastidiousness on the other—a paltry accuracy, and a more paltry derision—a sensibility to small faults, and an incapacity of great merits—a disposition to exaggerate the value of knowledge that is not to be used, and to underrate the importance of powers which have ceased to exist.

24. Goethe's *Wilhelm Meister's Apprenticeship*, translated anonymously by Carlyle

Edinburgh Review, 42, August 1825, *Contributions*, 1

As Rosemary Ashton notes,[48] Jeffrey had been critical years before of Lessing's *Nathan the Wise*;[49] and his similarly negative critique of *Wilhelm Meister* followed De Quincey's in the *London Magazine*, August and September 1824.

Jeffrey devotes a large part of his article to an account of the differences in national taste. These had been allowed for in Alison's aesthetic theory (no. 25), and they doubtless constitute the basis for Jeffrey's antipathy towards Goethe's book.

The review shows Jeffrey's broad approach, but also the difficulty which a great German contemporary encountered in gaining access to the British mind of the early nineteenth century. Carlyle's ambition was to overcome such obstacles as Jeffrey threw up, and he succeeded through articles in the *Edinburgh Review* itself, as well as elsewhere.

This is allowed, by the general consent of all Germany, to be the very greatest work of their very greatest writer. The most original, the most varied and inventive,—the most characteristic, in short, of the author, and of his country. We receive it as such accordingly, with implicit faith and suitable respect; and have perused it in consequence with very great attention and no common curiosity. We have perused it, indeed, only in the translation of which we have prefixed the title: But it is a translation by a professed admirer; and by one who is proved by his Preface to be a person of talents, and by every part of the work to be no ordinary master, at least of one of the languages with which he has to deal. We need scarcely say, that we profess to judge of the work only according to our own principles of judgment and habits of feeling; and, meaning nothing less than to dictate to the readers or the critics of Germany what they should think of their favourite authors, propose only to let them know, in all plainness and modesty, what we, and we really believe most of our countrymen, actually think of this *chef-d'œuvre* of Teutonic genius.

We must say, then, at once, that we cannot enter into the spirit of this German idolatry; nor at all comprehend upon what grounds the work before us could ever be considered as an admirable, or even a commendable performance. To us it certainly appears, after the most deliberate consideration, to be eminently absurd, puerile, incongruous, vulgar, and affected;—and, though redeemed by considerable powers of invention, and some traits of vivacity, to be so far from perfection, as to be, almost from beginning to end, one flagrant offence against every principle of taste, and every just rule of composition. Though indicating, in many places, a mind capable both of acute and profound reflection, it is full of mere silliness and childish affectation;—and though evidently the work of one who had seen and observed much, it is throughout altogether unnatural, and not so properly improbable, as affectedly fantastic and absurd— kept, as it were, studiously aloof from general or ordinary nature— never once bringing us into contact with real life or genuine character—and, where not occupied with the professional squabbles, paltry jargon, and scenical profligacy of strolling players, tumblers, and mummers (which may be said to form its staple), is conversant only with incomprehensible mystics and vulgar men of whim, with whom, if it were at all possible to understand them, it would be a baseness to be acquainted. Every thing, and every body we meet with, is a riddle and an oddity; and though the tissue of the story is sufficiently coarse, and the manners and sentiments infected with a strong tinge of vulgarity, it is all kept in the air, like a piece of machinery at the minor theatres, and never allowed to touch the solid ground, or to give an impression of reality, by the disclosure of known or living features. In the midst of all this, however, there are, every now and then, outbreakings of a fine speculation, and gleams of a warm and sprightly imagination—an occasional wild and exotic glow of fancy and poetry—a vigorous heaping up of incidents, and touches of bright and powerful description.

It is not very easy certainly to account for these incongruities, or to suggest an intelligible theory for so strange a practice. But in so far as we can guess, these peculiarities of German taste are to be referred, in part, to the comparative newness of original composition among that ingenious people, and to the state of European literature when they first ventured on the experiment—and in part to the state of society in that great country itself, and the comparatively humble condition of the greater part of those who write, or to whom writing is there addressed.

The Germans, though undoubtedly an imaginative and even enthusiastic race, had neglected their native literature for two hundred years—and were chiefly known for their learning and industry. They wrote huge Latin treatises on Law and Theology—and put forth bulky editions and great tomes of annotations on the classics. At last, however, they grew tired of being respected as the learned drudges of Europe, and reproached with their consonants and commentators; and determined, about fifty years ago, to show what metal they were made of, and to give the world a taste of their quality, as men of genius and invention. In this attempt the first thing to be effected was at all events to avoid the imputation of being scholastic imitators of the classics. *That* would have smelt too much, they thought, of the old shop; and in order to prove their claims to originality, it was necessary to go a little into the opposite extreme,—to venture on something decidedly modern, and to show at once their independence of their old masters, and their superiority to the pedantic rules of antiquity. With this view some of them betook themselves to the French models—set seriously to study how to be gay—*apprendre à être vif*—and composed a variety of petites pieces, and novels of polite gallantry, in a style—of which we shall at present say nothing. This manner, however, ran too much counter to the general character of the nation to be very much followed—and undoubtedly the greater and better part of their writers turned rather to us, for hints and lessons to guide them in their ambitious career. There was a greater original affinity in the temper and genius of the two nations—and, in addition to that consideration, our great authors were indisputably at once more original and less classical than those of France. England, however, we are sorry to say, could furnish abundance of bad as well as of good models—and even the best were perilous enough for rash imitators. As it happened, however, the worst were most generally selected—and the worst parts of the good. Shakespeare was admired—but more for his flights of fancy, his daring improprieties, his trespasses on the borders of absurdity, than for the infinite sagacity and rectifying good sense by which he redeemed those extravagancies, or even the profound tenderness and simple pathos which alternated with the lofty soaring or dazzling imagery of his style. Altogether, however, Shakespeare was beyond their rivalry; and although Schiller has dared, and not ingloriously, to emulate his miracles, it was plainly to other merits and other rivalries that the body of his ingenious countrymen aspired. The ostentatious absurdi-ty—the affected oddity—the pert familiarity—the broken style, and exaggerated sentiment of Tristram Shandy—the mawkish morality, dawdling details and interminable agonies of Richardson—the vul-gar adventures, and homely, though, at the same time, fantastical speculations of John Buncle and others of his forgotten class, found far more favour in their eyes. They were original, startling, unclas-sical, and puzzling. They excited curiosity by not being altogether intelligible—effectually excluded monotony by the rapidity and vio-lence of their transitions, and promised to rouse the most torpid sensibility, by the violence and perseverance with which they thun-dered at the heart. They were the very things, in short, which the German originals were in search of;—and they were not slow, therefore, in adopting and improving on them. In order to make them thoroughly their own, they had only to exaggerate their peculiarities—to mix up with them a certain allowance of their old visionary philosophy, misty metaphysics, and superstitious visions—and to introduce a few crazy sententious theorists, to sprinkle over the whole a seasoning of rash speculation on morality and the fine arts.

The style was also to be relieved by a variety of odd comparisons and unaccountable similes—borrowed, for the most part, from low and revolting objects, and all the better if they did not exactly fit the subject, or even introduced new perplexity into that which they professed to illustrate.

This goes far, we think, to explain the absurdity, incongruity, and affectation of the works of which we are speaking. But there is yet another distinguishing quality for which we have not accounted—and that is a peculiar kind of vulgarity which pervades all their varieties, and constitutes, perhaps, their most repulsive characteris-tic. We do not know very well how to describe this unfortunate peculiarity, except by saying that it is the vulgarity of pacific, comfortable burghers, occupied with stuffing, cooking, and providing for their coarse personal accommodations. There certainly never were any men of genius who condescended to attend so minutely to the *non-naturals* of their heroes and heroines as the novelists of modern Germany. Their works smell, as it were, of groceries—of brown papers filled with greasy cakes and slices of bacon,—and fryings in frowsy back parlours. All the interesting recollections of childhood turn on remembered tidbits and plunderings of savoury store-rooms. In the midst of their most passionate scenes there is always a serious and affectionate notice of the substantial pleasures of eating and drinking. The raptures of a tête-a-tête are not complete without a bottle of nice wine and a 'trim collation.' Their very sages deliver their oracles over a glass of punch; and the enchanted lover finds new apologies for his idolatry in taking a survey of his mistress's 'combs, soap, and towels, with the traces of their use.' These baser necessities of our nature, in short, which all other writers who have aimed at raising the imagination or touching the heart have kept studiously out of view, are ostentatiously brought forward, and fondly dwelt on by the pathetic authors of Germany.

We really cannot well account for this extraordinary taste. But we suspect it is owing to the importance that is really attached to those solid comforts and supplies of necessaries, by the greater part of the readers and writers of that country. Though there is a great deal of freedom in Germany, it operates less by raising the mass of the people to a potential equality with the nobles, than by securing to them their inferior and plebeian privileges; and consists rather in the immunities of their incorporated tradesmen, which may enable them to become rich as such, than in any general participation of national rights, by which they may aspire to dignity and elegance, as well as opulence and comfort. Now, the writers, as well as the readers in that country, belong almost entirely to the plebeian and vulgar class. Their learned men are almost all wofully poor and dependent; and the comfortable burghers, who buy entertaining books by the thousand at the Frankfort fair, probably agree with their authors in nothing so much as the value they set on those homely comforts to which their ambition is mutually limited by their condition; and enter into no part of them so heartily as those which set forth their paramount and continual importance.

It is time, however, that we should proceed to give some more particular account of the work which has given occasion to all these observations. Nor indeed have we anything more of a general nature to premise, except that we really cannot join in the censure which we have found so generally bestowed on it for its alleged grossness and immorality. It is coarse, certainly, in its examples, and by no means very rigorous in its ethical precepts. But it is not worse in those respects than many works on which we pride ourselves at home—Tom Jones, for example, or Roderick Random. There are passages, no doubt, that would shock a delicate young lady; but to the bulk of male readers, for whom we suppose it was chiefly intended, we do not apprehend that it will either do any great harm, or give any great offence.

[An abstract of the novel follows, with full quotations. Jeffrey concludes with an attempt at mollification.]

Many of the passages to which we have now alluded are executed with great talent; and we are very sensible are better worth extracting than many of those we have cited. But it is too late now to change our selections—and we can still less afford to add to them. On the whole, we close the book with some feelings of mollification towards its faults, and a disposition to abate, if possible, some part of the censure we were impelled to bestow on it at the beginning. It improves certainly as it advances—and though nowhere probable, or conversant indeed either with natural or conceivable characters, the inventive powers of the author seem to strengthen by exercise, and come gradually to be less frequently employed on childish or revolting subjects. While we hold out the work therefore as a curious and striking instance of that diversity of national tastes, which makes a writer idolized in one part of polished Europe, who could not be tolerated in another, we would be understood as holding it out as an object rather of wonder than of contempt; and though the greater part certainly could not be endured, and indeed could not have been written in England, there are many passages of which any country might reasonably be proud, and which demonstrate, that if taste be local and variable, genius is permanent and universal.

Aesthetic theory

Large extracts from Jeffrey's review of Alison's *Essays on Taste* are given here, since they indicate his ability at theoretical exposition and criticism. They also show a basis for his critical views in eighteenth-century aesthetic and associationist theory.

25. Alison's *Essays on Taste*

Edinburgh Review, 18, May 1811; *Contributions*, 1

Alison was educated at Glasgow University and Oxford, and he took orders in the Church of England. In 1790 he published *Essays on the Nature and Principles of Taste*. After a correspondence with Jeffrey, he published a second edition of the work, here reviewed. He also published *Sermons,* which in their turn were favourably noticed by the critic.

Alison's work has been regarded as the climax of the aesthetic and associationist theorizing of the eighteenth century. Martin Kallich goes further when he describes it as an 'almost perfect link between the eighteenth and the nineteenth century.'[50] It appeared in several editions until 1879. In his review Jeffrey acted as a publicist for Alison, as well as providing his own elaboration of the theory. He revised the review for publication in the Supplement to the *Encyclopaedia Britannica,* 1824.

Following Alison, Jeffrey declares that 'beauty is not an inherent property' of objects, but it depends upon association. 'The beauty which we impute to outward objects, is nothing more than the reflection of our own inward emotions, and is made up entirely of certain little portions of love, pity, or other affections, which have been connected with these objects, and still adhere as it were to them, and move us anew whenever they are presented to our observation.' Jeffrey illustrates his case interestingly and eloquently with reference to different landscapes, the spring and childhood. This passage of illustration is given here.

Take . . . the case of a common English landscape—green meadows with grazing and ruminating cattle—canals or navigable rivers—well

fenced, well cultivated fields—neat, clean, scattered cottages,—
humble antique churches, with church-yard elms, and crossing
hedgerows—all seen under bright skies, and in good weather:—
There is much beauty, as every one will acknowledge, in such a
scene. But in what does the beauty consist? Not certainly in the
mere mixture of colours and forms; for colours more pleasing, and
lines more graceful (according to any theory of grace that may be
preferred), might be spread upon a board, or a painter's pallet,
without engaging the eye to a second glance, or raising the least
emotion in the mind;—but in the picture of human happiness that is
presented to our imaginations and affections,—in the visible and
unequivocal signs of comfort, and cheerful and peaceful enjoyment,—and of that secure and successful industry that ensures its
continuance,—and of the piety by which it is exalted,—and of the
simplicity by which it is contrasted with the guilt and the fever of a
city life;—in the images of health and temperance and plenty which
it exhibits to every eye—and in the glimpses which it affords to
warmer imaginations, of those primitive or fabulous times, when
man was uncorrupted by luxury and ambition, and of those humble
retreats in which we still delight to imagine that love and philosophy
may find an unpolluted asylum. At all events, however, it is human
feeling that excites our sympathy, and forms the true object of our
emotions. It is man, and man alone, that we see in the beauties of
the earth which he inhabits;—or, if a more sensitive and extended
sympathy connect us with the lower families of animated nature,
and make us rejoice with the lambs that bleat on the uplands, or the
cattle that repose in the valley, or even with the *living* plants that
drink the bright sun and the balmy air beside them, it is still the idea
of enjoyment—of feelings that animate the existence of sentient
beings—that calls forth all our emotions, and is the parent of all the
beauty with which we proceed to invest the inanimate creation
around us.

Instead of this quiet and tame *English* landscape, let us now take
a Welch or a Highland scene; and see whether its beauties will
admit of being explained on the same principle. Here, we shall have
lofty mountains, and rocky and lonely recesses,—tufted woods hung
over precipices,—lakes intersected with castled promontories,—
ample solitudes of unploughed and untrodden valleys,—nameless
and gigantic ruins,—and mountain echoes repeating the scream of
the eagle and the roar of the cataract. This, too, is beautiful;—and,
to those who can interpret the language it speaks, far more beautiful
than the prosperous scene with which we have contrasted it. Yet,
lonely as it is, it is to the recollection of man and the suggestion of
human feelings that its beauty also is owing. The mere forms and

colours that compose its visible appearance, are no more capable of exciting any emotion in the mind, than the forms and colours of a Turkey carpet. It is sympathy with the present or the past, or the imaginary *inhabitants* of such a region, that alone gives it either interest or beauty; and the delight of those who behold it, will always be found to be in exact proportion to the force of their imaginations, and the warmth of their social affections. The leading impressions, here, are those of romantic seclusion, and primeval simplicity; lovers sequestered in these blissful solitudes, 'from towns and toils remote,'—and rustic poets and philosophers communing with nature, and at a distance from the low pursuits and selfish malignity of ordinary mortals;—then there is the sublime impression of the Mighty Power which piled the massive cliffs upon each other, and rent the mountains asunder, and scattered their giant fragments at their base;—and all the images connected with the monuments of ancient magnificence and extinguished hostility,—the feuds, and the combats, and the triumphs of its wild and primitive inhabitants, contrasted with the stillness and desolation of the scenes where they lie interred;—and the romantic ideas attached to their ancient traditions, and the peculiarities of the actual life of their descendants,—their wild and enthusiastic poetry,—their gloomy superstitions,—their attachment to their chiefs,—the dangers, and the hardships and enjoyments of their lonely huntings and fishings,—their pastoral shielings on the mountains in summer,—and the tales and the sports that amuse the little groups that are frozen into their vast and trackless valleys in the winter. Add to all this, the traces of vast and obscure antiquity that are impressed on the language and the habits of the people, and on the cliffs, and caves, and gulfy torrents of the land; and the solemn and touching reflection, perpetually recurring, of the weakness and insignificance of perishable man, whose generations thus pass away into oblivion, with all their toils and ambition; while nature holds on her unvarying course, and pours out her streams, and renews her forests, with undecaying activity, regardless of the fate of her proud and perishable sovereign.

We have said enough, we believe, to let our readers understand what we mean by external objects being the natural signs or concomitants of human sympathies or emotions. Yet we cannot refrain from adding one other illustration, and asking on what other principle we can account for the beauty of Spring? Winter has shades as deep, and colours as brilliant; and the great forms of nature are substantially the same through all the revolutions of the year. We shall seek in vain, therefore, in the accidents of mere organic matter, for the sources of that 'vernal delight and joy,' which subject all finer spirits to an annual intoxication, and strike home the sense of beauty even to hearts that seem proof against it under all other aspects. And it is not among the Dead but among the Living, that this beauty originates. It is the renovation of life and of joy to all animated beings, that constitutes this great jubilee of nature;—the young of animals bursting into existence,—the simple and universal pleasures which are diffused by the mere temperature of the air, and the profusion of sustenance,—the pairing of birds,—the cheerful resumption of rustic toils,—the great alleviation of all the miseries of poverty and sickness,—our sympathy with the young life, and the promise and the hazards of the vegetable creation,—the solemn, yet cheering, impression of the constancy of nature to her great periods of renovation,—and the hopes that dart spontaneously forward into the new circle of exertions and enjoyments that is opened up by her hand and her example. Such are some of the conceptions that are forced upon us by the appearances of returning spring; and that seem to account for the emotions of delight with which these appearances are hailed, by every mind endowed with any degree of sensibility, somewhat better than the brightness of the colours, or the agreeableness of the smells that are then presented to our senses.

They are kindred conceptions that constitute all the beauty of childhood. The forms and colours that are peculiar to that age, are not necessarily or absolutely beautiful in themselves; for, in a grown person, the same forms and colours would be either ludicrous or disgusting. It is their indestructible connection with the engaging ideas of innocence,—of careless gaiety,—of unsuspecting confidence;—made still more tender and attractive by the recollection of helplessness, and blameless and happy ignorance,—of the anxious affection that watches over all their ways,—and of the hopes and fears that seek to pierce futurity, for those who have neither fears nor cares nor anxieties for themselves.

These few illustrations will probably be sufficient to give our readers a general conception of the character and the grounds of that theory of beauty which we think affords the only true or consistent account of its nature. They are all examples, it will be observed, of the *First* and most important connection which we think may be shown to exist between external objects and the sentiments or emotions of the mind; or cases, in which the visible phenomena are the natural and universal accompaniments of the emotion . . . .

[Jeffrey goes on to distinguish between universal and accidental associations. The latter account for the differences in national taste, as well as between the taste of the educated and the lack of it in the uneducated. Later, Jeffrey relates his theory to language, especially to the language of poetry. He then justifies the use for reflected emotion of the name 'beauty.' He concludes that the controversial standard of taste does not exist. Each man properly has his own, but the artist has a special responsibility to concern himself with universal associations. This distinction, elaborated at the conclusion of Jeffrey's essay, provides a justification for his own criticism of Wordsworth. He ends with a championship of the double standard so evident in later English criticism and life. This whole important section of the essay is given here.]

In all the cases we have hitherto considered, the external object is supposed to have acquired its beauty by being actually connected with the causes of our natural emotions, either as a constant sign of their existence, or as being casually present on the ordinary occasions of their excitement. There is a relation, however, of another kind, to which also it is necessary to attend, both to elucidate the general grounds of the theory, and to explain several appearances that might otherwise expose it to objections. This is the relation which external objects may bear to our internal feelings, and the power they may consequently acquire of suggesting them, in consequence of a sort of resemblance or analogy which they seem to have to their natural and appropriate objects. The language of Poetry is founded, in a great degree, upon this analogy; and *all language,* indeed, is full of it; and attests, by its structure, both the extent to which it is spontaneously pursued, and the effects that are produced by its suggestion . . . .
A thousand such analogies, indeed, are suggested to us by the most familiar aspects of nature. The morning and the evening present the same ready picture of youth and of closing life, as the various vicissitudes of the year. The withering of flowers images out to us the languor of beauty, or the sickness of childhood. The loud roar of troubled waters seems to bear some resemblance to the voice of lamentation or violence; and the softer murmur of brighter streams, to be expressive of cheerfulness and innocence. The purity and transparency of water or of air, indeed, is universally itself felt to be expressive of mental purity and gaiety; and their darkness or turbulence, of mental gloom and dejection. The genial warmth of autumn suggests to us the feeling of mild benevolence;—the sunny gleams and fitful showers of early spring, remind us of the waywardness of infancy;—flowers waving on their slender stems, impress us with the notion of flexibility and lightness of temper. All fine and delicate forms are typical of delicacy and gentleness of character;

and almost all forms, bounded by waving or flowing lines. suggest
ideas of easy movement, social pliability, and elegance. Rapid and
impetuous motion seems to be emblematical of violence and passion;—slow and steady motion, of deliberation, dignity, and resolution;—fluttering motion, of inconstancy or terror;—and waving
motion, according as it is slow or swift, of sadness or playfulness. A
lofty tower, or a massive building, gives us at once the idea of
firmness and elevation of character;—a rock battered by the waves,
of fortitude in adversity. Stillness and calmness, in the water or the
air, seem to shadow out tenderness, indolence, and placidity;—
moonlight we call pensive and gentle;—and the unclouded sun gives
us an impression of exulting vigour, and domineering ambition and
glory.

It is not difficult, with the assistance which language affords us, to
trace the origin of all these, and a thousand other associations. In
many instances, the qualities which thus suggest mental emotions,
do actually resemble their constant concomitants in human nature;
as is obviously the case with the forms and motions which are
sublime and beautiful: and, in some, their effects and relations bear
so obvious an analogy to those of human conduct or feeling, as to
force itself upon the notice of the most careless beholder. But,
whatever may have been their original, the very structure of language attests the vast extent to which they have been carried, and
the nature of the suggestions to which they are indebted for their
interest or beauty. Since we all speak familiarly of the sparkling of
wit—and the darkness of melancholy—can it be any way difficult to
conceive that bright light may be agreeable, because it reminds us of
gaiety,—and darkness oppressive, because it is felt to be emblematical of sorrow? It is very remarkable, indeed, that, while almost all
the words by which the affections of the mind are expressed, seem
to have been borrowed originally from the qualities of matter, the
epithets by which we learn afterwards to distinguish such material
objects as are felt to be sublime or beautiful, are all of them epithets
that had been previously appropriated to express some quality or
emotion of mind. Colours are thus familiarly said to be gay or
grave—motions to be lively, or deliberate, or capricious—forms to
be delicate or modest—sounds to be animated or mournful—pros-
pects to be cheerful or melancholy—rocks to be bold—waters to be
tranquil—and a thousand other phrases of the same import; all
indicating, most unequivocally, the sources from which our interest
in matter is derived, and proving, that it is necessary, in all cases, to
confer mind and feeling upon it, before it can be conceived as either
sublime or beautiful. The great charm, indeed, and the great secret
of poetical diction, consists in thus lending life and emotion to all
the objects it embraces; and the enchanting beauty which we

sometimes recognise in descriptions of very ordinary phenomena, will be found to arise from the force of imagination, by which the poet has connected with human emotions, a variety of objects, to which common minds could not discover such a relation. What the poet does for his readers, however, by his original similes and metaphors, in these higher cases, even the dullest of those readers do, in some degree, every day, for themselves; and the beauty which is perceived, when natural objects are unexpectedly vivified by the glowing fancy of the former, is precisely of the same kind that is felt when the closeness of the analogy enables them to force human feelings upon the recollection of all mankind. As the poet sees more of beauty in nature than ordinary mortals, just because he perceives more of these analogies and relations to social emotion, in which all beauty consists; so other men see more or less of this beauty, exactly as they happen to possess that fancy, or those habits, which enable them readily to trace out these relations.

From all these sources of evidence, then, we think it is pretty well made out, that the beauty or sublimity of external objects is nothing but the reflection of emotions excited by the feelings or condition of sentient beings; and is produced altogether by certain little portions, as it were, of love, joy, pity, veneration, or terror, that adhere to the objects that were present on the occasions of such emotions.—Nor, after what we have already said, does it seem necessary to reply to more than one of the objections to which we are aware that this theory is liable.—If beauty be nothing more than a reflection of love, pity, or veneration, how comes it, it may be asked, to be distinguished from these sentiments? They are never confounded with each other, either in our feelings or our language:—Why, then, should they all be confounded under the common name of beauty? and why should beauty, in all cases, affect us in a way so different from the love or compassion of which it is said to be merely the reflection?

Now, to these questions, we are somewhat tempted to answer, after the manner of our country, by asking, in our turn, whether it be really true, that beauty always affects us in one and the same manner, and always in a different manner from the simple and elementary affections which it is its office to recall to us? In very many cases, it appears to us, that the sensations which we receive from objects that are felt to be beautiful, and that in the highest degree, do not differ at all from the direct movements of tenderness or pity towards sentient beings. If the epithet of beauty be correctly (as it is universally) applied to many of the most admired and enchanting passages in poetry, which consist entirely in the expression of affecting sentiments, the question would be speedily decided; and it is a fact, at all events, too remarkable to be omitted, that

some of the most powerful and delightful emotions that are uniformly classed under this name, arise altogether from the direct
influence of such pathetic emotions, without the intervention of any
material imagery. We do not wish, however, to dwell upon an
argument, which certainly is not applicable to all parts of the
question; and, admitting that, on many occasions, the feelings which
we experience from beauty, are sensibly different from the primary
emotions in which we think they originate, we shall endeavour in a
very few words, to give an explanation of this difference, which
seems to be perfectly consistent with the theory we have undertaken
to illustrate.

In the first place, it should make some difference on the primary
affections to which we have alluded, that, in the cases alluded to,
they are *reflected* from material objects, and not directly excited by
their natural causes. The light of the moon has a very different
complexion from that of the sun;—though it is in substance the sun's
light: and glimpses of interesting, or even of familiar objects, caught
unexpectedly from a mirror placed at a distance from these objects,
will affect us, like sudden allusions in poetry, very differently from
the natural perception of those objects in their ordinary relations. In
the next place, the emotion, when suggested in the shape of beauty,
comes upon us, for the most part, disencumbered of all those
accompaniments which frequently give it a peculiar and less satisfactory character, when it arises from direct intercourse with its living
objects. The compassion, for example, that is suggested by beauty
of a gentle and winning description, is not attended with any of that
disgust and uneasiness which frequently accompany the spectacle of
real distress; nor with that importunate suggestion of the duty of
relieving it, from which it is almost inseparable. Nor does the
temporary delight which we receive from beauty of a gay and
animating character, call upon us for any such expenditure of spirits,
or active demonstrations of sympathy, as are sometimes demanded
by the turbulence of real joy. In the third place, the emotion of
beauty, being partly founded upon illusion, is far more transitory in
its own nature, and is both more apt to fluctuate and vary in its
character, and more capable of being dismissed at pleasure, than
any of the primary affections, whose shadow and representative it
is. In the fourth place, the perception of beauty implies a certain
exercise of the imagination that is not required in the case of direct
emotion, and is sufficient, of itself, both to give a new character to
every emotion that is suggested by the intervention of such an
exercise, and to account for our classing all the various emotions
that are so suggested under the same denomination of beauty.
When we are injured, we feel indignation,—when we are wounded,
we feel pain,—when we see suffering, we feel compassion,—and

when we witness any splendid act of heroism or generosity, we feel admiration—without any effort of the imagination, or the intervention of any picture or vision in the mind. But when we feel indignation or pity, or admiration, in consequence of seeing some piece of inanimate matter that merely suggests or recalls to us the ordinary causes or proper objects of these emotions, it is evident that our fancy is kindled by a sudden flash of recollection; and that the effect is produced by means of a certain poetical creation that is instantly conjured up in the mind. It is this active and heated state of the imagination, and this divided and busy occupation of the mind, that constitute the great peculiarity of the emotions we experience from the perception of beauty.

Finally, and this is perhaps the most important consideration of the whole, it should be recollected, that, along with the shadow or suggestion of associated emotions, there is always present a real and direct perception, which not only gives a force and liveliness to all the images which it suggests, but seems to impart to them some share of its own reality. That there is an illusion of this kind in the case, is sufficiently demonstrated by the fact, that we invariably ascribe the interest, which we think has been proved to arise wholly from these associations, to the object itself, as one of its actual and inherent qualities; and consider *its* beauty as no less a property belonging to it, than any of its physical attributes. The associated interest, therefore, is beyond all doubt confounded with the present perception of the object itself; and a livelier and more instant impression is accordingly made upon the mind, than if the interesting conceptions had been merely excited in the memory by the usual operation of reflection or voluntary meditation. Something analogous to this is familiarly known to occur in other cases. When we merely think of an absent friend, our emotions are incomparably less lively than when the recollection of him is suddenly suggested by the unexpected sight of his picture, of the house where he dwelt, or the spot on which we last parted from him,—and all these objects seem for the moment to wear the colours of our own associated affections. When Captain Cook's companions found, in the remotest corner of the habitable globe, a broken spoon with the word *London* stamped upon it—and burst into tears at the sight!—they proved how differently we may be moved by emotions thus connected with the real presence of an actual perception, than by the mere recollection of the objects on which those emotions depend. Every one of them had probably thought of London every day since he left it; and many of them might have been talking of it with tranquillity, but a moment before this more effectual appeal was made to their sensibility.

If we add to all this, that there is necessarily something of vagueness and variableness in the emotions most generally excited by the perception of beauty, and that the mind wanders with the eye, over the different objects which may supply these emotions, with a degree of unsteadiness, and half voluntary half involuntary fluctuation, we may come to understand how the effect not only should be essentially different from that of the simple presentment of any one interesting conception, but should acquire a peculiarity which entitles it to a different denomination. Most of the associations of which we have been last speaking, as being founded on the analogies or fanciful resemblances that are felt to exist between physical objects and qualities, and the interesting affections of mind, are intrinsically of this vague and wavering description,—and when we look at a fine landscape, or any other scene of complicated beauty, a great variety of such images are suddenly presented to the fancy, and as suddenly succeeded by others, as the eye ranges over the different features of which it is composed, and feeds upon the charms which it discloses. Now, the direct perception, in all such cases, not only perpetually accompanies the associated emotions, but is inextricably confounded with them in our feelings, and is even recognised upon reflection as the cause, not merely of their unusual strength, but of the several peculiarities by which we have shown that they are distinguished. It is not wonderful, therefore, either that emotions so circumstanced should not be classed along with similar affections, excited under different circumstances, or that the perception of present existence, thus mixed up, and indissolubly confounded with interesting conceptions, should between them produce a sensation of so distinct a nature as naturally to be distinguished by a peculiar name,—or that the *beauty* which results from this combination should, in ordinary language, be ascribed to the objects themselves,—the presence and perception of which is a necessary condition of its existence.

What we have now said is enough, we believe, to give an attentive reader that general conception of the theory before us, which is all that we can hope to give in the narrow limits to which we are confined. It may be observed, however, that we have spoken only of those sorts of beauty which we think capable of being resolved into some passion, or emotion, or pretty lively sentiment of our nature; and though these are undoubtedly the highest and most decided kinds of beauty, it is certain that there are many things called beautiful which cannot claim so lofty a connection. It is necessary, therefore, to observe, that, though every thing that excites any feeling worthy to be called an *emotion*, by its beauty or sublimity, will be found to be related to the natural objects of human passions or affections, there are many things which are pleasing or agreeable enough to be called beautiful, in consequence of their relation merely to human convenience and comfort;—many others that please by suggesting ideas of human skill and ingenuity;—and many that obtain the name of beautiful, by being associated with human fortune, vanity, or splendour. After what has been already said, it will not be necessary either to exemplify or explain these subordinate phenomena. It is enough merely to suggest, that they all please upon the same great principle of *sympathy with human feelings;* and are explained by the simple and indisputable fact, that we are pleased with the direct contemplation of human comfort, ingenuity, and fortune. All these, indeed, obviously resolve themselves into the great object of sympathy—human enjoyment. Convenience and comfort is but another name for a lower, but very indispensable ingredient of that emotion. Skill and ingenuity readily present themselves as means by which enjoyment may be promoted; and high fortune, and opulence, and splendour, pass, at least at a distance, for its certain causes and attendants. The beauty of fitness and adaptation of parts, even in the works of nature, is derived from the same fountain,—partly by means of its obvious analogy to works of human skill, and partly by suggestions of that Creative power and wisdom, to which all human destiny is subjected. The feelings, therefore, associated with all those qualities, though scarcely rising to the height of emotion, are obviously in a certain degree pleasing or interesting; and when several of them happen to be united in one object, may accumulate to a very great degree of beauty.

[Jeffrey finally discusses the question of the standard of taste, concluding that there is none.]

The only other advantage which we shall specify as likely to result from the general adoption of the theory we have been endeavouring to illustrate is, that it seems calculated to put an end to all these perplexing and vexatious questions about the standard of taste, which have given occasion to so much impertinent and so much elaborate discussion. If things are not beautiful in themselves, but only as they serve to suggest interesting conceptions to the mind, then every thing which does in point of fact suggest such a conception to any individual, *is beautiful* to that individual; and it is not only quite true that there is no room for disputing about tastes, but that all tastes are equally just and correct, in so far as each individual speaks only of his own emotions. When a man calls a thing beautiful, however, he may indeed mean to make two very different assertions;—he may mean that it gives *him* pleasure by suggesting to him some interesting emotion; and, in this sense, there can be no doubt that, if he merely speak truth, the thing is beautiful; and that it pleases him precisely in the same way that all other things please those to whom they appear beautiful. But if he mean farther to say that the thing possesses some quality which should make it appear beautiful to every other person, and that it is owing to some prejudice or defect in them if it appears otherwise, then he is as unreasonable and absurd as he would think those who should attempt to convince him that he felt no emotion of beauty.

All tastes, then, are equally just and true, in so far as concerns the individual whose taste is in question; and what a man feels distinctly to be beautiful, *is beautiful* to him, whatever other people may think of it. All this follows clearly from the theory now in question: but it does not follow, from it, that all tastes are equally good or desirable, or that there is any difficulty in describing that which is really the best, and the most to be envied. The only use of the faculty of taste, is to afford an innocent delight, and to assist in the cultivation of a finer morality; and that man certainly will have the most delight from this faculty, who has the most numerous and the most powerful perceptions of beauty. But, if beauty consist in the reflection of our affections and sympathies, it is plain that *he* will always see the most beauty whose affections are the warmest and most exercised,—whose imagination is the most powerful, and who has most accustomed himself to attend to the objects by which he is surrounded. In so far as mere feeling and enjoyment are concerned, therefore, it seems evident, that the best taste must be that which belongs to the best affections, the most active fancy, and the most attentive habits of observation. It will follow pretty exactly too, that all men's perceptions of beauty will be nearly in proportion to the degree of their sensibility and social sympathies; and that those who have no affections towards sentient beings, will be as certainly insensible to beauty in external objects, as he, who cannot hear the sound of his friend's voice, must be deaf to its echo.

In so far as the sense of beauty is regarded as a mere source of enjoyment, this seems to be the only distinction that deserves to be attended to; and the only cultivation that taste should ever receive, with a view to the gratification of the individual, should be through the indirect channel of cultivating the affections and powers of observation. If we aspire, however, to be *creators,* as well as observers of beauty, and place any part of our happiness in ministering to the gratification of others—as artists, or poets, or authors of any sort—then, indeed, a new distinction of tastes, and a far more laborious system of cultivation, will be necessary. A man who pursues only his own delight, will be as much charmed with objects that suggest powerful emotions in consequence of personal and accidental associations, as with those that introduce similar emotions by means of associations that are universal and indestructible. To him, all objects of the former class are really as beautiful as those of the latter—and for his own gratification, the creation of that sort of beauty is just as important an occupation: but if he conceive the ambition of creating beauties for the admiration of others, he must be cautious to employ only such objects as are the *natural* signs, or the *inseparable* concomitants of emotions, of which the greater part of mankind are susceptible; and his taste will *then* deserve to be called bad and false, if he obtrude upon the public, as beautiful, objects that are not likely to be associated in common minds with any interesting impressions.

For a man himself, then, there is no taste that is either bad or false; and the only difference worthy of being attended to, is that between a great deal and a very little. Some who have cold affections, sluggish imaginations, and no habits of observation, can with difficulty discern beauty in anything; while others, who are full of kindness and sensibility, and who have been accustomed to attend to all the objects around them, feel it almost in everything. It is no matter what other people may think of the objects of their admiration; nor ought it to be any concern of theirs that the public would be astonished or offended, if they were called upon to join in that admiration. So long as no such call is made, this anticipated discrepancy of feeling need give *them* no uneasiness; and the suspicion of it should produce no contempt in any other persons. It is a strange aberration indeed of vanity that makes us despise persons for being happy—for having sources of enjoyment in which we cannot share:—and yet this is the true source of the ridicule, which is so generally poured upon individuals who seek only to enjoy their peculiar tastes unmolested:—for, if there be any truth in the theory we have been expounding, no taste is bad for any other reason than because it is peculiar—as the objects in which it delights must actually serve to suggest to the individual those common emotions and universal affections upon which the sense of beauty is everywhere founded. The misfortune is, however, that we are apt to consider all persons who make known their peculiar relishes, and especially all who create any objects for their gratification, as in some measure dictating to the public, and setting up an idol for general adoration; and hence this intolerant interference with almost all peculiar perceptions of beauty, and the unsparing derision that pursues all deviations from acknowledged standards. This intolerance, we admit, is often provoked by something of a spirit of *proselytism* and arrogance, in those who mistake their own casual associations for natural or universal relations; and the consequence is, that mortified vanity ultimately dries up, even for them, the fountain of their peculiar enjoyment; and disenchants, by a new association of general contempt or ridicule, the scenes that had been consecrated by some innocent but accidental emotion.

As all men must have some peculiar associations, all men must have some peculiar notions of beauty, and, of course, to a certain extent, a taste that the public would be entitled to consider as false or vitiated. For those who make no demands on public admiration, however, it is hard to be obliged to sacrifice this source of enjoyment; and, even for those who labour for applause, the wisest course, perhaps, if it were only practicable, would be, to have *two* tastes,—one to enjoy, and one to work by—one founded upon universal associations, according to which they finished those performances for which they challenged universal praise—and another guided by all casual and individual associations, through which they might still look fondly upon nature, and upon the objects of their secret admiration.

Notes

Bibliographical Note

The main bibliographical guide to Jeffrey's writings is the *New Cambridge Bibliography of English Literature,* ed. George Watson, vol. 3, Cambridge, 1969. The greatest part of Jeffrey's critical work was done for the *Edinburgh Review:* his contributions are listed in the *Wellesley Index to Victorian Periodicals,* ed. W. E. Houghton, vol. 1, 1966. The main collections of Jeffrey MSS are in the National Library of Scotland and the British Museum.

In my discussion in the Introduction of Jeffrey and Carlyle I have been especially indebted to Maxwell H. Goldberg, *Thomas Carlyle's Relations with the Edinburgh Review,* unpublished Ph.D. thesis of Yale University, 1933, not included in the *New Cambridge Bibliography.* Ronald B. Hatch in *RES,* N.S. 21, 1970, 56–62, points out the revisions, mainly of detail, which Jeffrey made when he included *Edinburgh Review* articles in his collection of *Contributions.* The interest of the *Review* format is that this is what contemporaries immediately read. However, whenever possible, I have used the *Contributions* text, as embodying Jeffrey's own considered last words.

Notes to the Text

All books cited in the notes are published in London unless otherwise stated.

1. Walter Jackson Bate, *From Sensibility to Romanticism,* Cambridge, Mass., 1946, 59.
2. See Charles A. Knight, 'The Created World of the Edinburgh Periodicals' (of the late eighteenth century), *Scottish Literary Journal,* vi, 1979, 20–36.
3. Philip Flynn presents Jeffrey as 'a product' of his 'immediate cultural past' in Scotland, see *English Miscellany,* xxv, 1976, 245–87. See also Flynn's *Francis Jeffrey,* 1978.
4. *Selections from the Essays of Francis Jeffrey,* ed. Lewis E. Gates, Boston, 1894, xix.

5. Jeffrey's change of view is credited by Wordsworth to a letter from Coleridge (Wordsworth quoted by Emerson, *Journals*, x, Cambridge, Mass., 1973, 558). This attitude is followed by David V. Erdman, 'Coleridge and the "Review Business",' *Wordsworth Circle*, 6, winter 1975, 18. Unfortunately, Coleridge's letter does not appear to have survived.

6. *Selections*, xli.

7. See Walter E. Houghton, 'Victorian Periodical Literature and the Articulate Classes,' *Victorian Studies*, xxii, 1979, 389–412.

8. F. R. Leavis, *Letters in Criticism*, ed. J. Tasker, 1974, 74.

9. *Edinburgh Review*, 3, October 1803, 156.

10. James McCosh, *Scottish Philosophy*, New York, 1874, 338.

11. *Selections*, xiii.

12. William Cullen Bryant, writing in 1849 after a visit, described Craigcrook as commanding 'fine views of Edinburgh with its hills and crags and old castle, and of the Firth and its shores, and of the Pentland hills.' MS., William Allen Bryant Collection (#6244-a), Clifton Walter Barrett Library, University of Virginia Library.

13. Sydney Smith, *Works*, i, 1839, v.

14. Jeffrey's parliamentary career is summarized by Iain F. Maciver, 'Cockburn and the Church,' in *Lord Cockburn*, ed. Aian Bell, Edinburgh, 1979, 91.

15. *Selections*, xi.

16. William Hazlitt, *Complete Works*, ed. P. P. Howe, 1930–4, xi, 126.

17. T. B. Macaulay, *Letters*, ed. T. Pinney, iv, 1977, 167.

18. Karl Miller observes a similar pastoralism in Jeffrey's friend Henry Cockburn, 'Cockburn, Nature and Romance,' in *Lord Cockburn*, ed. Bell, 124–65.

19. Henry Cockburn, *Life of Lord Jeffrey*, i, Edinburgh, 1852, 97, 100.

20. The same, i, 176, 175, 179.

21. The same, i, 272.

22. The same, ii, 219.

23. The same, i, 317.

24. The same, i, 350, 400.

25. Francis Horner, *Memoirs and Correspondence*, ed. L. Horner, i, 1853, 296. David A. Wilson, *Carlyle to 'The French Revolution,'* 1924, 128.

26. Cockburn, *Lord Jeffrey*, ii, 415, 465.

27. I discuss Jeffrey's theory in full in 'Principles and Perspectives in Jeffrey's Criticism,' *Studies in Scottish Literature*, iv, 1967, 179–93.

28. In this section I summarize my article 'Wordsworth and Jeffrey,' *Humanities Association Bulletin*, XIX, fall 1968, 17–28.
29. William Wordsworth, *Prose Works*, ed. W. J. B. Owen and J. W. Smyser, III, Oxford, 1974, 82.
30. The same, 84.
31. Here I make use of my article 'Carlyle, Jeffrey and the Edinburgh Review,' *Neophilologus*, LIV, 1970, 297–310.
32. Thomas Carlyle, *Collected Letters*, ed. C. R. Sanders, I, Durham, N.C., 1970, 16.
33. Carlyle, *Reminiscences*, ed. C. E. Norton, II, 1887, 273.
34. Macvey Napier, *Selection from the Correspondence*, ed. his son, 1879, 126.
35. Carlyle, *Reminiscences*, II, 272.
36. The same, II, 273; I, 163.
37. *Quarterly Review*, XCI, June 1852, 151.
38. Cockburn, *Lord Jeffrey*, II, 425–6.
39. By Arthur Pollard, *Crabbe the Critical Heritage*, 1972, 9.
40. *Contributions*, III, 83.
41. 'Telling it makes me shudder,' Virgil, *Aeneid*, Book II, 204.
42. Wordsworth, *Prose Works*, ed. Owen and Smyser, I, 1974, 152.
43. *Biographia Literaria*, ed. J. Shawcross, II, Oxford, 1907, 92.
44. *The Excursion*, New Haven, 1950, 3.
45. *Contributions*, III, 468.
46. September 1818, 275–77.
47. Walter Jackson Bate, *The English Poet and the Burden of the Past*, 1970.
48. Rosemary Ashton, *The German Idea*, 1980, 10, 17.
49. *Edinburgh Review*, VIII, April 1806.
50. *Philosophical Quarterly*, XXVII, 1948, 322.